SOJOURNERS OF THE CARIBBEAN

SOJOURNERS
OF THE
CARIBBEAN

Ethnogenesis and Ethnohistory
of the Garifuna

NANCIE L. GONZALEZ

University of Illinois Press
Urbana and Chicago

© 1988 by the Board of Trustees of the University of Illinois
Manufactured in the United States of America
C 5 4 3 2 1

This book is printed on acid-free paper.

Library of Congress Cataloging-in-Publication Data

Gonzalez, Nancie L. Solien, 1929–
  Sojourners of the Caribbean.

  Bibliography: p.
  Includes index.
  1. Black Carib Indians—History. 2. Black Carib
Indians—Ethnic identity. 3. Indians of Central
America—History. 4. Indians of Central America—
Ethnic identity. 5. Blacks—Central America—History.
6. Blacks—Central America—Race identity.
7. Ethnicity—Case studies. I. Title.
F1505.2.C3G63 1988   972.8′00497   87-6044
ISBN 0-252-01453-7 (alk. paper)

To the Memory of Rebecca
(Livingston, 1920–1972)

A woman of beauty, dignity, courage, and strength. Never a
mother; forever a grandmother. May her spirit live on in the hearts
of all Garifuna.

Contents

Maps and Tables

Map

Tables

Abbreviations

AA	*American Anthropologist*
ADM	Admiralty Office (Great Britain)
AGCA	Archivo General de Centro América
AE	*American Ethnologist*
BS	*Belizean Studies*
CO	Colonial Office (Great Britain)
FO	Foreign Office (Great Britain)
ICA	International Congress of Americanists
ICAES	International Congress of Anthropological and Ethnological Sciences
MMS	Methodist Missionary Society
PLA	*Proceedings of the International Congress for the Study of Pre-Columbian Cultures in the Lesser Antilles*
PRO	Public Record Office (Great Britain)
RG	Record Group (U.S. Archives)
SWJA	*Southwestern Journal of Anthropology*
WO	War Office (Great Britain)

Preface

This book has had a long gestation. I originally went to Guatemala in 1955 to work with highland Indians but became enamored of the easygoing Caribs, of whom no one seemed to know much except that they were supposedly cannibals. In that same year I began fieldwork among them that has continued at intervals ever since. Altogether I have spent more than five years in their midst, including two extended stays, in 1956–57 and 1984–85.

Most of my earlier work was done in the Guatemalan town of Livingston and the outlying hamlets of Quehueche and Río Salado. In 1957 I paid brief visits to all the Belizean (then British Honduran) villages, as well as several villages in Honduras. In 1975, and again in 1976, I invited Dr. Michael Crawford and several of his students to join me in the field for what I anticipated would be a long-term, joint biocultural project. Although we gathered some interesting data, the collaboration did not work out as planned and was abandoned by mutual consent. However, several publications did result in which the "mystery" of the degree of African versus Amerindian ancestry among the Caribs was finally clarified, confirming my earlier opinion that close examination would belie what was, at the time, the "official" and "traditional" version of their history (see Crawford 1983), which essentially emphasized their Amerindian origins and vehemently denied any slave (or, by implication, African) ancestry.

I determined to explore further the documentary sources in an effort to understand and perhaps correct what seemed to me to be a peculiar antihistorical bias. My travels had already taken me to St. Vincent, the Antillean island from which the Caribs' ancestors were deported in 1797. I made the journey primarily because so many Caribs spoke of St. Vincent as though it were Mecca. There I found some interesting and startling descriptions of the war that had preceded their banishment; but, as is so often the case with the historical record, these accounts served to pose as many questions as they answered.

In 1982 I had an opportunity to spend four months in England searching for documents in the School of African and Oriental Studies of the University of London, the British Museum and Library, the Public Record Office at Kew, the Bodleian Library and the Rhodes Institute at Oxford, the Wellington Library for the History of Medicine, and the National Maritime Library at Greenwich. I spent January 1983 and the following summer in Guatemala, doing intensive work at the Archivo General de Centro América (AGCA). The Library of Congress and the Archives of the United States are, happily, in my hometown, so I put as much of my spare time as possible into searching for pertinent references and records in these institutions over several academic years.

On shorter visits I explored the holdings of the Latin American Library at Tulane University, the Philadelphia Historical Society, the archives of the Museum of the University of Pennsylvania, the New York Public Library, the Boston Public Library, the National Maritime Union and the Grace Company in New York City, and the Beineke Caribbean Collection at Hamilton College. Finally, while in Honduras during 1984–85, I had the opportunity to search the national archives and public library there, as well as the libraries at the Universidad Nacional, the Banco Central, and the Instituto Hondureño de Antropología e Historia.

In December 1983, Charles D. Cheek accompanied me to Livingston and the north coast of Honduras on an ethnoarchaeological survey. This was followed in 1985 by a joint project centered in Trujillo and extending to the Patuca River to the east, which we had reason to believe, from historical sources, had been the effective extent of the early Garifuna habitation on the Central American coastline. (Their later move to several sites in Nicaragua is fairly well documented. Furthermore, research in Nicaragua seemed more difficult to arrange than its scientific importance warranted at the time.)

Today, my Carib/Garifuna friends often ask me, "Why are you doing this?" They find it strange that an American white woman of English descent should devote so much of her life to studying an obscure, relatively small, foreign black population with an unwritten language (at least until the 1960s) and an esoteric religious system. I was fortunate in that my personal life kept me in Guatemala for several years, and many of my friends in Livingston were able to visit me in my home in the capital city. Then, my later employment with the Institute of Nutrition of Central America and Panama directed my interest back again toward highland Indians, as well as toward Ladinos. What made me continually return to the coast and the Caribs?

Most important, I believe, was my sense that anthropologists should try to view cultures over time to get a better understanding of the process of culture change and development. Yet I must admit that sometimes I, too, wondered why I felt driven to continue the search for the roots of these people, who by the 1970s were insisting upon their more proper name of Garifuna—a modification of the name Kalinago, by which some of their ancestors were known to Columbus. In part I must have had an urge to solve the intellectual puzzles posed by the inconsistencies among the ethnographic facts I and others had collected and the rudimentary historical record then available. No scientist likes to leave questions unanswered.

Anthropology is not just a science, however, and its practitioners are not merely scientists. Because the subjects of our research are living human beings, and because it is necessary to gain rapport with them in order to collect reliable data, we often become "hooked"—more so, perhaps, on the culture we study first. Although I later studied the cultures of Spanish Americans in New Mexico and of peasants and urbanites in the Dominican Republic, and have more briefly observed agricultural change in China and other parts of Asia, I have never felt about any of these others that they were "my" people. When, during the first week of my 1984 stay in Livingston, I was called forth at a ritual by the spirit of a deceased close friend and informant, I knew that I had "come home," and I understood the power of these rituals to bring their own back into the fold. I also came to a new realization of how it was that participation in the religious ceremonies enabled the Garifuna to include foreigners, even those of another color, within their circle—thereby helping me solve one of the mysteries relating to their mixed ancestry.

For this reason I am dedicating this book to Rebecca—the woman who first befriended me, ridiculed my attempts to paddle a canoe and make cassava bread, taught me to dance *punta,* to love and to fear the *gubida,* and later to manage my own "matrifocal" household. She and her parents (all now deceased) and her surviving siblings—Sara, Popo, and Baldidi—still watch over me—in Livingston, in New York, or wherever I happen to be.

This book owes much to all the Garifuna who have helped me over the years. It is not possible to name each one of them, but I am especially indebted to the Leiva-Mena, López, and Mejía families of Livingston and New York City. Marco Palacio, a young man who dared to question some of his own elders' view of their history, was invaluable to me and Charles Cheek in 1984 in searching by canoe for abandoned habitation sites. Ing. Augusto Mejía and Dr. Claudina Elington, young and idealistic professionals, stimulated my thoughts on the future of the Garifuna in Livingston and elsewhere. The late (American) Father Antonio and the current (Irish) Father Jerry of the Catholic mission in Livingston were helpful in many ways—providing access to church records, allowing us to use church facilities for interviewing and testing during the biocultural study, and sharing their personal observations of Garifuna culture over the years.

In Belize I am especially indebted to the Mena and Apolonio families of Dangriga and Punta Gorda. It has been a joy to watch the scholarly development of Dr. Joseph O. Palacio, who is now resident tutor at the University of the West Indies in Belize. He and his wife, Myrtle Cacho, have been a constant source of friendship and assistance over the years, even before he finished his Ph.D. in anthropology and joined me as a professional colleague.

In Trujillo, I could not have managed without the assistance of Victor Blanco and his entire extended family. To mention all the other Honduran Garifuna who shared their knowledge and thoughts with me and my students would be an impossible task. They know who they are. Let the record show that I am grateful. Father Javier of the Jesuit mission in Trujillo helped with church records, information, transportation, and general moral support, as did the entire Jesuit mission of Sangrelaya. Their interest in and concern for the future of the Garifuna is deep and genuine.

More formal thanks are due the various bodies that funded my work over the years. The Henry L. and Grace Doherty Foundation gave me my first two grants, which were followed by assistance at various times in later years from the Boston University Graduate School, the British Council, the University of Maryland Graduate School, and the National Science Foundation. The most recent work was funded by the University of Maryland, the Fulbright-Hays Commission, and the Wenner-Gren Foundation for Anthropological Research. A small grant-in-aid was provided by the Roger Thayer Stone Center for Latin American Studies to help with my research at Tulane University. While in London, Dr. Adrian Mayer loaned me his lovely house, which provided much-needed peace and quiet. Grateful acknowledgment is made to all, for the work has been cumulative and the present book owes much to the earlier efforts.

The directors and personnel of all the institutions mentioned provided invaluable assistance and moral support. Many of them took a personal interest in my work, proving to me that librarians, as scholars and friends, are indispensable to researchers—especially those operating without benefit of formal training in history. Mention of all of them by name is impossible, but I must single out the Centro de Investigaciones Regionales de Mesoamérica in Antigua, Guatemala, whose director, William Swezey, facilitated my stay in that city and provided me office space and free use of the library, copy machine, and computer facilities. Similarly, I am indebted to Edwin and Virginia Shook of Antigua, who allowed me unlimited use of their massive personal library. In Honduras, I enjoyed the official sponsorship of the Instituto Hondureño de Antropología e Historia through a written contract that specifically set forth our mutual rights and obligations. I hope they feel that I have fulfilled my part of the bargain, as they certainly did theirs.

Finally, I must mention those who have rendered a different kind of service —the literary and intellectual criticism that has made this book more readable and my arguments more cogent. To the extent that it has achieved those goals, I must thank my son, Ian González, who knows the Garifuna almost as well as I do and who writes far better than I. Zoraida Díaz, my research assistant during the Trujillo fieldwork in 1985, took many of the photographs. Virginia Kerns, Carolyn McCommon, Pamela Wright, Joseph Palacio, and Vivian Garrison read all or parts of the manuscript and offered valuable corrections, additions, and criticisms.

In addition, I owe a good deal to discussions or correspondence with Douglas Armstrong, Karen Bruhns, Charles Cheek, Frank Dawson, Betty Meggers, Anna Roosevelt, and Irving Rouse on Caribbean, Central American, and lowland South American archaeology; with Alfonso Arrivillaga, Charles and Mary Gullick, Mary Helms, John Holm and Lillian Howland on Garifuna culture and ethnohistory; with Roger Buckley, Edward Cox, Michael Craton, Victor Cruz, David Miller, and R. Lee Woodward on Central American and Caribbean history; with Richard Howard and Harry Stover on botanical and agricultural matters; and with Abner Cohen, Bill and Scarlett Epstein, Silvia de Groot, Richard and Sally Price, William Stuart, and Eric Wolf on various theoretical points. The chapter on development owes much to my colleagues in "Linkages: World Council for Research on Development." It is always difficult to pin down the exact sources of ideas and insights, but I know that my thinking has benefited from my interactions with all these scholars, and I am grateful to them. This hardly makes them party to any omissions, oversights, or errors of fact or logic, and I trust the reader who finds these will understand that I alone am responsible for them.

As we go to press, I hope the *gubida* approve.

SOJOURNERS OF THE CARIBBEAN

Introduction

The Meaning of Ethnicity

This book is about the Garifuna, more commonly known in the anthropological literature as Black Caribs, a people who presently inhabit the Atlantic littoral of Central America from Belize to Nicaragua; there are also clusters of Garifuna in several Central American cities and in the United States. Many travelers and missionaries, and several ethnologists, have visited and written about the Caribs over the 250 or so years during which they have existed as a distinct people. Their culture and society have been the subject of fifteen or more doctoral dissertations since the 1950s, most of which have purposely dealt with the more "traditional" aspects of Carib culture, in part because that is what anthropologists *do,* and in part because it was recognized that time would soon erode the old ways, leaving only a diminishing memory of them among the elders.

The latter process, known as acculturation, or, sometimes, modernization, has been of concern to many anthropologists, including me (see Gonzalez 1969). The baseline in such studies is always the recent past or even the present, when the aim is to warn development-minded people or agencies what the future portends if this or that policy is or is not followed. To the extent that the earlier history of a people is considered at all, it has been largely reconstructed through oral tradition or myth. In 1976 a geographer, Linda Newson, pointed out that there had been no acculturation studies thus far based on archival materials. Consequently, she undertook to describe the history of the island of Trinidad using archaeological, documentary, and secondary ethnological evidence. The *island* was her sociogeographical unit of analysis, not a particular social segment or cultural component. Her pioneer effort yielded interesting results but told us little of the human and cultural dimensions of special concern to anthropologists. The Trinidadian people themselves, and their culture, remained inscrutable.

Since Newson's study, anthropologists have increasingly turned to the historical record to try to understand better how the cultures with which they work have come to be. We are also expanding our horizons to include the broader world on the margins of which most of our subjects live and have lived. In traditional anthropological style, we continue to define our analytic boundaries less rigidly than in some other disciplines, for fear of missing what may turn out to be the most important clues to a greater understanding of a people. The concept of holism applies to both time and space when dealing with analytic, no less than with concrete, structures.

The use of archaeology to help reconstruct the past of a particular society is, surprisingly, still in its infancy among anthropologists, (e.g., Gonzalez and Cheek 1986). Some new voices claim that the archaeologist's methods can discern and illuminate ethnic differences in both prehistoric and historic populations (Cheek and Friedlander 1986; Hodder 1977; McGuire 1982), but others believe that ethnicity is a cognitive structure and thus beyond the scope of the archaeologist (Allaire 1980:243). I will try to show that archaeology can help us to answer certain questions about populations for which the written and oral historical accounts are inadequate.

During the course of a fairly narrowly focused social anthropological study in 1956–57 (Gonzalez 1969), I became fascinated with how the Black Caribs seemed to be changing almost before my eyes. At the time I was more interested in their future than in their past and assumed we could never really determine the latter; and, in any case, I thought their past was not really very important in understanding their future. I called the Caribs a "neoteric" society—one that seemed to have only shallow roots and that allowed, even encouraged, rapid change as a survival technique—and I suggested that such societies might even be thought of as having been *created* by the circumstances to which they had adapted (Gonzalez 1970a). To defend these ideas against vociferous and competent critics (see especially Helms 1981), I began, about 1975, to turn to the historical records with the intent of identifying and examining Black Carib roots in order to understand who these people were and how much of what they said about their past and their traditions could be verified. They had no written records of their own, so in addition to seeking archival sources, I returned to the field to gather more oral traditions, songs, and stories.

I was immediately faced with the analytic problem of how to define the time and space boundaries of the sociocultural group with which I was dealing. When had they, in fact, become a distinct people? It was known that their ancestors had lived on the island of St. Vincent in the Lesser Antilles and that their language was closely related to those still spoken among Amerindians in

Amazonia. But the blackness of their skin belied the notion that they had no roots in Africa, even though neither their own folklore nor scientific analysis (before 1975) had provided any concrete evidence of that. Should the possibility of an African past be ignored or downplayed, as they themselves preferred in the 1950s? Most anthropologists chose to do that until very recently, even though the empirical evidence caused us to hedge some of the time. Douglas Taylor (1951:143), for example, has described the Black Carib culture as a "Negro cake composed of Amerindian ingredients" and stated it was only in the "imponderable" aspects that their culture differed from that of their Indian forebears. I emphasized the similarities to West Indian societies, suggesting it was not so much African as Afroamerican culture that had penetrated the Amazonian culture the earliest explorers called "Carib" (Gonzalez 1959a). Beauçage (1970:47), working in Honduras about a decade after me, also has referred to the "racial shift" in St. Vincent and suggested that the "Negro" element possessed a greater "dynamism" that enabled the newly formed culture to thrive in ways that its immediate predecessor had not. But he did not further dwell on the Caribs' African past.

Once I started working along these new lines, it seemed there was no end to new material on the Garifuna and their ancestors. And the more I learned, the more salient I considered the African background, even as it became clear that the story was complex and the influences subtle. African roots are fashionable now, even in Central America (although it took twenty years for that notion to diffuse from the United States and other parts of the Caribbean).

The more I read and talked with elders in the field, the more I became convinced of my early view (Gonzalez 1970a) that the Caribs' ability to adapt individual behavior—as well as sociocultural rules and expectations—to rapid change has been one of their most important characteristics for hundreds of years, even though at any given moment they will solemnly declare that what they do is what they have *always* done. I became increasingly uncomfortable with the idea that their modern sociocultural system was a direct descendant, with much of the outlines and detail intact, of that of the Island Caribs, descriptions of which we have only from the beginning of the seventeenth century onward. For that matter, there is considerable question as to how cohesive and distinct an ethnic category the "Island Caribs" were themselves (Allaire 1980; Drummond 1977).

Over the past few years a number of scholars have begun to rethink the concept of tradition, and all of us have been surprised, I think, to find that many or most cultures fool themselves into thinking that the old ways are best, when what they really mean is that people are more likely to accept the present as "best" if they think it is old (Bloch 1977; Hobsbawm 1983; Handler and Linnekin 1984; Shils 1981; M. E. Smith 1982). Everywhere the notion of tradition seems to be linked with the concept of ethnicity—"ways" must be attached to a particular people, and what makes people "particular" is their cultural heritage. So it follows that heritages must be preserved, or invented, when need be, if ethnicity is to be a useful social tool or facilitator.

Studies of the contemporary Garifuna show without a doubt that ethnicity has become important to them, both as a conscious value for its own sake and (often unrealized by them) as a means of improving their position within the modern complex societies in which they live (W. Davidson 1983; Gonzalez 1976; C. Gullick 1976a; Owen 1975; Palacio 1974; Sanford 1974). Inevitably, then, I began to think about the origins of the Garifuna sense of ethnicity and how it may have helped or hindered their efforts to survive. This book is an attempt to make sense of the various historical, archaeological, and ethnographic materials available that relate to the Garifuna and their ancestors. It is not intended to provide a systematic or exhaustive ethnography; rather, it uses that methodology and perspective to explore certain sociocultural problems. At the same time, it is my hope to do more than merely document the Garifuna. I believe their story sheds light on how even a preliterate society may use the symbols of ethnicity to further its members' own interests and survive the onslaught of a stronger, technologically superior civilization. Ethnicity, then, becomes a structural principle; and as such, it may be important long before the society can be said to have become an "ethnic group." Drummond (1977:82), in an article on Guyanese Caribs, correctly points out that stereotypes of ethnic identity "must be considered part of the social fabric of everyday life and treated as an aspect of the objectifiable world."

The ethnogenesis of the modern Garifuna occurred on the Central American coastline in the twentieth century. Linguistic, genetic, and ethnographic studies all document the Amerindian roots of these people.[1] But it is quite obvious, too, that there is an African component; in fact, many casual observers have mistakenly assumed that the Garifuna are of pure African descent. Until recently, these people have been known as Black Caribs, a term that, despite its European origin, correctly denoted their Afroamerican heritage. We can only speculate on the nature of the process by which the Amerindian and African became fused, for accounts are few and often contradictory, and there has been virtually no archaeological work specifically directed to the problem. Nevertheless, over the centuries various writers have offered explanations of Black Carib origins, and with time some of these have become generally accepted by both scholars and modern Garifuna. However, we will never know where or how these writers obtained their "facts"; indeed, until recently, most of them were untrained observers and amateur ethnographers, insufficiently critical of what they saw and heard. Not all of their observations and conclusions can be accepted at face value, anymore than we can accept unconditionally the oral traditions of the people themselves. The trick, of course, is to combine all the possible sources in such a way that major contradictions are eliminated or explained; often the archaeological record can turn us in the right direction.

Thus, to understand who the Garifuna are today, I have sought ways to look more closely at their history and to trace the ethnogenesis of the peoples or "cultures" generally conceded to have been their direct ancestors. I refer here to the Island Caribs and their successors, the Black Caribs. The former are commonly believed to have come into being in the Lesser Antilles when Carib-speaking peoples moved out of their Amazonian riverine homes to trade with and then conquer Arawak-speaking groups already living on the islands. Allaire (1980) has pointed out, quite rightly, that this tradition, told to Columbus by the people he first encountered (Sauer 1966:31) and then recorded independently by the French missionary Raymond Breton (1665), has yet to be confirmed by archaeological investigation. In fact, Allaire suggests that the actual events may have been the other way around—that Arawak-speaking people, with the help of the earliest Spaniards, may have been encroaching upon the Caribs in the Lesser Antilles in the decades immediately following the European discovery. We have no clear evidence one way or the other at present, but undoubtedly we will have more in the future as increased attention is paid to the Caribbean area.

The ill-fated Caliban (Kalina, or Galibi—from which "cannibal" derives) encountered by the earliest Europeans exhibited characteristics of each of the groups we have come to think of as Caribs and Arawaks. Their struggles to defend themselves and their islands were generally unsuccessful; the people and their culture nearly passed into oblivion, except for the fact that their name came to designate the American "Mediterranean," or Caribbean Sea.[2] The term "Carib" has also lived on in parts of South and Central America as a name for a language and for several different modern-day ethnic groups (Basso 1977).

It is arguable whether the Island Caribs should be classed as a true ethnic group in the sense in which that term is commonly used today;[3] that is, they were not integrated, even marginally, into any kind of plural society, though they certainly had a consciousness of kind and a set of social and symbolic characteristics by which they differentiated themselves from others. Like so many other isolated, autonomous, preliterate societies, the Island Caribs were in their own eyes simply "the people," who apparently wanted nothing so much as to be left alone to govern themselves, even though they were infamous for their harassment of other peoples. Although they probably made pottery, there is still no agreement among archaeologists as to which, if any, of the several ceramic traditions known in the Caribbean may have belonged to them (R. Bullen 1976; Allaire 1980; Haag 1968; Rouse 1948, 1956, 1983).

Soon after their initial contact with Europeans, the Island Caribs began to absorb individuals (both European and African) captured or adopted from the new settlements, perhaps merely continuing an interactive pattern already established in relation to other groups of Amerindians. On some islands, notably St. Vincent, the amount of African intermixture was great enough to bring about a dramatic change in the phenotype. By 1700, perhaps earlier, a new society had emerged on St. Vincent that was racially and culturally distinct from that of the Island Caribs, though undeniably related to it. This group achieved a self-conscious ethnic and political identity that depended in part upon the establishment of a new complex (colonial) society made up of Island Caribs, French and British colonial, religious, and military bodies, and slaves belonging to all of the latter, as well as some free "coloureds" and a small group of Maroons. Although their rhetoric, as preserved in a few European records of the time, suggested that the Black Caribs, like their predecessors, merely wanted to be left alone, their actions showed them to be adapted to the idea and the reality of living in a world peopled by other distinct groups, some of which they manipulated to improve their own position. These Black Caribs, in turn, gave rise to the Garifuna some 200 years later.

The Garifuna are a transnational,[4] modern ethnic group whose members live under a variety of circumstances in several Central American countries, the United States, Canada, and England. Some are highly educated, sophisticated citizens of the world, while others are illiterate migrant laborers, farmers, and fishermen. Their use of a distinctive and esoteric language and a sense of common origin holds them together; and in Honduras and Belize, at least, they are beginning to attract attention as a potentially important political force.

The book is divided into three parts. In Part 1 (chapters 1–3), the historical situations and events that gave rise to the different phases or societies I refer to as Island Caribs, Black Caribs, and Garifuna are described. In one sense, we are dealing with a single "ethnicity"—or "ethnos," as Bromley (1983) puts it—and its transformations through time. In this process, diverse cultural elements were absorbed, along with many individuals of non-Carib origin. The latter lost their original identity as their descendants coalesced into a single social category, with a distinct language and what they came to think of as a unique and immutable heritage. Thus, of all the Garifuna ancestral lines, only one tends to be remembered, and all innovations are fitted into it. One might say everything becomes "Garifunized" (see Kopytoff 1986 for parallel thinking on modern Africa.)

Part 2, comprised of chapters 4–7, describes the cultural features that are and have been most important as ethnic markers for these people, showing how and when the different "traditions" were adopted and reinterpreted to meet their needs at any given time. Wells (1982b) has found that Garifuna in

Belize identify four important areas of tradition, including language, ancestor ceremonies, dance and drumming, and work patterns. Here, I do not deal with language per se, since I am not a linguist and this subject has been extensively explored by others (e.g., Taylor 1948, 1951, 1958, 1963, 1967; Escure 1978; Hadel 1975; Holm 1978a, 1978b; Wright 1986). There have been significant linguistic changes for this ethnic group over the centuries, most of which have been clearly related to changes in ethnic identification, as between Arawak and Carib, between Island Carib and Central American Carib, and between Garifuna and non-Garifuna speech patterns in the Central American countries today. Thus, although I deal, when it is appropriate, with names for people and things, I do not attempt linguistic analyses.

Similarly, thorough analysis of Garifuna musical styles and motifs requires more skill and knowledge than I can bring to the task. Whipple (1971, 1979) has made a start, and a Guatemalan musicologist, Alfonso Arrivillaga, is now working on the subject. Folklore has been touched upon by nearly every ethnographer who has worked among these people, and it is a crucial area, especially so because it really is fast disappearing. I had difficulty in both Livingston (Guatemala) and Trujillo (Honduras) finding informants who knew any stories at all, and only a few people were able to interpret the meanings of old songs, even though the words have been committed to memory. Hadel's (1972) still unpublished dissertation remains the only full-length study of folklore to date, although Lillian Howland of the Summer Institute of Linguistics has accumulated a great deal of material that she will undoubtedly publish in the future. The folkloric material gathered during this study requires more detailed analysis than I can give it here, but I do cite illustrative materials when relevant.

Part 3, comprised of chapters 8–9, deals with the processes and institutions by which Carib/Garifuna culture has adapted and evolved to its present configuration. I have suggested elsewhere (Gonzalez 1970a) that the ability to adjust rapidly to new circumstances has enhanced long-term survival for the Garifuna, both as individuals and as an ethnic group, even in the face of extraordinary difficulties. In this book I document the toll these adaptive institutions have exacted: reduced individual success and happiness and eroded well-being of the hometowns and villages.

This study ends with a discussion of the meaning of "development" for an ethnic group, as opposed to its meaning for a nation. Does the future of the Garifuna really depend upon the preservation of their ethnic heritage, as many of them now believe (see Wells 1982b)? And if so, *which* aspects of that tradition will serve them best? Is it possible that the old traditions have outlived their usefulness as cushions against a hostile world and must now be reconsidered and perhaps even rejected in favor of new ones? Is this not what has happened repeatedly in the past, not only for the Island Caribs/Black Caribs/

Garifuna, but perhaps for all ethnic groups that have survived for any length of time? Finally, could the current passion to assert their social and cultural identity be merely a reflection of the fact that they are about to lose it? Anthropologists have analyzed many similar movements, calling them "nativistic," or "revivalistic," and Sanford (1974), with the Garifuna as her primary case, has joined others in suggesting that an organized effort to reconstruct and preserve the past may be an indicator of completed acculturation.

In relation to ethnicity, there are in this study both theoretical and practical problems of continuing concern to many social scientists and others. One such problem relates to the structural position of an ethnic group vis-à-vis the larger society and what that or any other configuration may mean for the continued well-being of both. One aspect of this problem is how the individual segments of a transnational ethnic group can sustain a sense of unity. How can they achieve political power or influence when they are fragmented, or even scattered around the globe? This could only happen, we might argue, in the modern world, with its rapid communication and transportation systems. The earliest Amerindian experiences in the Lesser Antilles with the different European colonial powers provide an interesting parallel. Of course, most of those people failed to preserve themselves or their culture.

Today the modern Garifuna form "part societies" within several countries. Their position in Honduras is very different from that in Guatemala, and both are different from the situation in either Belize or Nicaragua. In a sense, they may be thought of as having been preadapted to a world in which international migration has begun to break down the rigidities of nationalism. Many Garifuna today have become U.S. citizens, yet they think of themselves as members of two (or more) societies. They travel back and forth frequently, and upon retirement many return to their native villages, much as their fathers and grandfathers did.

The development of Garifuna enclaves in the United States poses still other intellectual and practical problems, for there they are perforce associated with local black populations, which offer neither structural nor psychological shelter to the newcomers. In this regard, we may raise the question of how race interrelates with ethnicity. Is it better to suffer race prejudice masquerading as cultural bias, or vice versa, as has been described for Panama (Biesanz 1953)? Is it worth it to cast off one's ethnic identity so as to blend in with a larger minority whose problems, though far from solved, are at least being discussed? And how does the larger and generally successful West Indian black minority in the United States relate to the Garifuna subgroup? Is it possible for individuals consciously to change their ethnic allegiance and group membership? Can the American black example teach anything to the Garifuna that will be of use to them in Central America, or in New York? Can the Garifuna experience contribute anything to the solution of the so-called race problem in the United States?

All these concerns derive from what Drummond (1977) calls the "myth of ethnicity," or the "ideological idiom of ethnicity." I agree that this has increasingly become a structural principle and a driving behavioral determinant in today's multiracial and multiethnic modern societies. Ethnic pride sometimes is a force for improving the condition of an individual or group, but it may also be used as a means of—or have the effect of—discouraging or barring some groups from fullest participation in the larger society, with the attendant pleasures and miseries (or rights and obligations, to use more objective terms) that participation implies. I believe the issue is one that will continue to be debated in the United States and, increasingly, in the countries from which present-day Garifuna come—especially Honduras, Guatemala, and Belize. Ethnicity is such a popular concept today that to appear to speak against it is to incur amazement, if not contempt. Nevertheless, I intend to raise these and other uncomfortable issues.

NOTES

1. Douglas Taylor was the prime exponent of both the Island Carib and the Central American Carib languages, and the interested reader is directed to his many publications listed in the bibliography. Crawford (1984) has brought together the most important work on the genetics and physical anthropology of this group. Ethnographic descriptions abound, starting with Conzemius (1928), Taylor (1951), and Coehlo (1955) and continuing through the work of C. Gullick (1976) and Gonzalez (1969) to that of Kerns and others. As Kerns pointed out in 1977, we are now in the "third generation" of research on the so-called Black Caribs.

2. In 1974 Harold Conklin brought to my attention a map of the Philippines that was published in Spain from data compiled between 1815 and 1820. Astonishingly, it shows an area on the coast of northeastern Luzon clearly labeled "Negros Caribes Bravos." He also cited a reference in Blair and Robertson (1903, 48:119) as follows: ". . . [one padre] made his way into the most secluded places in which there are many apostates and Carib blacks, of which sort are all those who are in the mountains of these islands." This was in reference to missionary activities beginning in 1728 on the island of Panay.

In Central America, the term "Caribe" was used by Spaniards to refer to the "wild" Indians of the interior, such as the Rama, Towka, Woolwarks, and Paya. Floyd (1967:123–24) erred when he failed to differentiate these from the Black Caribs, who only arrived on the coast at the end of the eighteenth century. (The documents in the Spanish archives are filled with such references, so the unwary reader can easily become confused.) Dick (1977:17) has stated that as early as 1503 "Caribe" had entered the Spanish vocabulary as a term for "primitive," "wild," "untamed" ethnic groups whose members were considered "fair game" for capture and sale.

3. The term and concept "ethnic group" has become so fashionable in recent years that several encyclopedic compilations have resulted (e.g., Riggs 1985). The latter is reminiscent of the Kroeber and Kluckhohn (1952) attempt to create some order out of the proliferation of definitions of the culture concept. As in all such exercises, perfect order and precision are unattainable. Scholars must simply define and use terms as they see fit, hoping readers will agree that the usage is sensible. Eventually a semblance of agreement on commonly used terms in the social sciences may be achieved. In the present case, sociologists, political scientists, and anthropologists have taken to using the term "ethnic group" in somewhat different manners. I trust my usage here is not so far removed from that of other theorists in my own discipline as to cause difficulties in communication. Although the self-conscious recognition of cultural differences is probably found in all societies, I believe some degree of social and cultural pluralism (Furnivall 1977; M. G. Smith 1965) is necessary before it is useful to speak of ethnic *groups.*

4. I am indebted to COCTA (Riggs 1985) for the term "transnational," which I find extremely useful to designate a single ethnic group whose members reside in more than one country.

PART ONE

Ethnohistory

The term "ethnohistory" refers to attempts to trace the past of peoples with no formal, written histories. Such a state may come about because the people themselves have not yet developed or adopted literacy as a major value and are too isolated from or considered too unimportant by the literate segments of the society to which they belong to have had their culture documented. If they speak an esoteric language, as is most often the case, this contributes to their historical isolation, for even after some of their members become literate in what will be for them a foreign language, they may neglect to write the story of their own people.

Anthropology has several ways to try to write the story of the people "without history." Sophisticated analyses of known genetic traits can give us a start in ascertaining who the people are and from whence they came. Linguistics also reveals a good deal about the history of a people—not only the roots of their language but the source and time of borrowing foreign words. Archaeology helps us interpret the more distant past, that beyond the ken even of the oldest living people, but it is limited to the more material aspects of the culture, as well as to some of the behavioral patterns that produce and/or derive from these artifacts. Certain aspects of social organization—food production, settlement patterns, division of labor, stratification, and even family organization—can often be deduced from the archaeological record, but for the more philosophical or ideological side of the culture, other sources prove more valuable.

Folklore and oral traditions can reveal much, but we must be cautious about assuming that traditional accounts are necessarily historically accurate—even taking into consideration that most history is biased by the perceptions and sometimes by the intentions of the writer. Finally, we can search the records, reminiscences, and "official" histories for mention of the people in question.

Sometimes there will be only a line or two; often the comments are so pejorative as to seem almost worthless. Yet even a brief comment at least establishes their presence at a certain time and place.

This book is the product of all of these methods, which have been blended together in my interpretations and analyses. Not all of anthropology is historical, but without history we risk serious misunderstandings of the nature of the culture process.

1

The Lesser Antilles

Early European Political History of St. Vincent

The story begins on St. Vincent, a small eastern Caribbean island of extraordinary beauty and fertility. The interior is mountainous, with many plains and well-watered valleys, which before the nineteenth century were covered with forests (Burton 1685:177; W. Young 1764:9–10). The colonization of the island by Europeans was typical of the Lesser Antilles. Spaniards were the first to touch upon its shores, but finding neither pearls nor gold nor silver, they turned their attention to more lucrative conquests. Some trading and a mutual slave-raiding pattern were established between Spaniards and Island Caribs throughout the area, however, and that pattern extended to other Europeans and continued throughout the next two centuries (Andrews 1978:26–27). Civrieux (1976) has presented persuasive reasons for considering the Lesser Antilles and the Orinoco-Amazon basin on the South American mainland as a single "conquest area" between the sixteenth and eighteenth centuries.

Burton (1685:177) described St. Vincent Caribs trading food for iron tools with a handful of English settlers in the late seventeenth century. The island was less intruded upon than many others in the area at this time because a 1659 agreement between the English and French established it as Carib territory (Oliver 1894, (1:xxvii). Nevertheless, by the beginning of the eighteenth century the French were regularly visiting the island from nearby Martinique, Grenada, and St. Lucia, where they had made successful settlements in 1635, 1649, and 1650 respectively, following unsuccessful British attempts on the latter two islands two generations earlier (Crouse 1940, appendix; Andrews 1978:240). On St. Vincent, the French quietly moved in on the leeward side during the first two decades of the eighteenth century, where they cultivated coffee, indigo, cotton, and cacao (Russell 1778:102; Martin 1837, 2:212). They also raised livestock and cultivated provisions for trade to neighboring French islands where sugarcane predominated and food supplies were scarce (Miller 1979:64). Living for the most part on small holdings, the French settlers seem to have gotten along well with the local inhabitants, though there were some initial problems when the Indians believed the French intended to enslave them. After the Peace of Utrecht in 1713, the English escalated their visits to and explorations of the island, though they did not succeed in establishing a colony. Uring (1726) found when he visited in 1722 that some of the Indians already spoke French and that considerable intermixture with Africans had occurred. In fact, at that time there appear to have been two politically separate groups: the Black Caribs, led by a "chief," and the Red (or Yellow) Caribs, led by a "general" (Uring 1726:109).

In 1748 the Treaty of Aix la Chapelle attempted to establish once again an "Indian territory," declaring the islands of St. Vincent, Dominica, St. Lucia, and Tobago to be neutral. This agreement among European nations, obviously made to keep each other at bay, was not formally rescinded until 1763, when the Seven Years War between Great Britain and the French-Spanish coalition was terminated. At that time the Treaty of Paris ceded the islands of St. Vincent, Dominica, Tobago, Grenada, and the Grenadines to England, while Guadeloupe and Martinique reverted to France, along with the formerly neutral St. Lucia. It was at this time that the British became serious about establishing sugar plantations on St. Vincent. In spite of the earlier neutrality agreements, the French had maintained and expanded their clandestine settlements, and by 1763 they had thoroughly ingratiated themselves with the natives, the majority of whom by now were referred to as "black."

Between 1764 and 1770 the British surveyed and mapped the island of St. Vincent and tried by cajolery, intimidation, and force to remove the Caribs from their extensive and fertile lands. French-speaking liaisons arranged dubious "purchases," often for what were admitted by the British to be "trifling sums" (CO 101/16:221). All accounts refer to the natives involved in such purchases as being black; there is no evidence of similar machinations vis-à-vis the Yellow or Red Caribs, and it is likely that by this time they were either allies and brothers of the former or, if independent, so few in number as to pose little competition or threat to the British.

In the events that followed, it is not clear whether the Caribs or the British were more duplicitous. Certainly, each side was highly motivated, and both were experienced and skilled negotiators; but their systems of diplomacy and warfare differed, and there were ups and downs for both sides before the British finally prevailed. By 1772 there was open warfare due to the escalating tensions caused by insistent British encroachment upon Carib territory in defiance of the latters' remonstrances and threats of violence. After "calming" the

Caribs by bringing in troops from Boston, the British signed a treaty with them in which the Caribs lost all but about 4,000 acres[1] in the northeastern (i.e., windward) part of the island (W. Young 1971; Authentic Papers 1773; see Map 1).

The British land survey in 1763 found nearly 700 French settlers with some 3,400 slaves occupying about 7,000 acres of land on St. Vincent, mostly on the southwestern part of the island (Miller 1979:60–61.) Many of these people elected to stay where they were, believing the new government would build roads and provide greater trading opportunities, thus improving their lot (Stein 1979:30). They were permitted to retain their lands by lease if they declared allegiance to Britain. Yet they chafed, finding their new English neighbors and government demanding and difficult (CO 101/16, f.153). So in 1779, when France again declared war on Britain, the unhappy French and Caribs seized St. Vincent with help from French troops sent over from Martinique. In spite of a devastating hurricane in 1780 and a smallpox epidemic that killed many Caribs shortly thereafter (Morris 1787:181), the French/Carib domination on St. Vincent lasted for four years. At that time there were said to be, in addition to several thousand Caribs, 500 whites and 7,000–8,000 slaves living on the island (Raynal 1783, 6:384). Most of the increase in the number of slaves was probably due to British demand for workers, for sugar cultivation was far more labor-intensive than coffee and cacao production. Although most of the British settlers remained and even prospered during this period of French/Carib domination, they were generally harassed by the Caribs, no doubt with the full approval of the French (Coke 1808, 1:195).

By 1783, when the island was again formally returned to Great Britain, it was said to include sixty-one English sugar estates and an unspecified number of smaller farms (Martin 1837, 2:220). Dependent upon the St. Vincent government were several smaller islands, where produce and cotton were grown for export; these included Bequia, Union, Canouane, Mustique, Petit Martinique, Petit St. Vincent, Maillerau, and Baliceaux.[2] By 1790, the inhabitants of these islands numbered 1,450 whites and 11,853 slaves, 1,600 of the latter living on the dependent islands (Winterbotham 1796, 4:279). Thus, the European population had nearly tripled between 1775 and 1790, in spite of their problems with the Caribs. Estimates of the Carib population vary widely, but 7,000–8,000 seems not unreasonable, given known figures for captives of the 1795–96 so-called Carib War and estimates of battle mortality.[3]

Accounts of the Carib War are numerous; not unexpectedly, most reveal the bias of the writer.[4] Although some accounts are more sympathetic to the plight of the indigenous people than others, all assumed that the Europeans had as much or more right as the Caribs to live on the islands. As happened in so many parts of the world, the British assumed the Caribs had far more land than they needed or could use. Thus, as in North America, the British felt

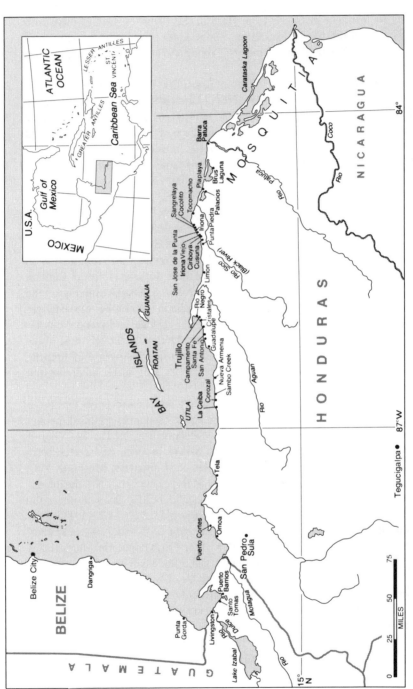

Map 1. The Bay of Honduras and Relevant Portions of the Caribbean and Central America, showing Garifuna Settlements.

perfectly justified in requesting, demanding, and finally seizing Carib lands in the name of the British king (Washburn 1959:24). It did not occur to them that the Caribs might themselves aspire to production for export, even though at least two (and probably more) chiefs were said to have plantations of their own, worked by slaves (Anderson 1983:66; W. Young 1971:300). Miller (1979:69), after the most complete search of the documentary evidence for St. Vincent yet made, has asserted that by 1763 the Carib economy was far above subsistence level.

The British also assumed that all societies had a maximal authority vested in a single individual, and they persisted in making "treaties" with the person they thought was in charge, or the one they appointed to be in charge, holding the entire group responsible when others refused to adhere to these "agreements." Actually, the preconquest Island Caribs did conduct internecine raids against each other, led by their war chiefs, and their successors among the Black Caribs may have wielded more authority in the last quarter of the eighteenth century than has been supposed. In part this may have been a sociocultural development in response to the almost constant skirmishing with the British after 1763.

The fact that the British guile was recognized as such by some authorities even at that time is shown in the account of Valentine Morris, captain general and governor-in-chief of St. Vincent in the fateful year of 1779, when the French/Carib alliance retook the island. He noted that when the 1772 treaty with the Caribs had been signed, there had been no English official present who spoke either the Carib language or French, and that the Caribs spoke no English. Only one purchaser, Lieutenant Colonel Etherington (one of the commanders of the troops from Boston), operating on his own behalf, was able to communicate with them at all. Chatoyer, a name that was repeatedly mentioned as the "Carib King" or "principal chief" at that time, alleged later that he and the other chiefs had never meant to do more than lease a few acres of their land; certainly, they had not meant to sell it, as they were later told the papers upon which each had placed his "X" indicated. In spite of his doubts, however, Morris concluded that the Caribs were lying and only wanted their lands back after having spent the money paid them (Morris 1787:175–76; Townsend 1772:5).[5]

Papers preserved in British archives show that the idea of removing the Caribs from St. Vincent entirely had been seriously considered as early as 1772, even before any treaty had been signed and in spite of the fact that numerous military reports stated that the Caribs were quiet and had made no efforts to prepare themselves for their own defense (Authentic Papers 1773). In a letter dated April 18, 1772, the Earl of Hillsborough told the governor of St. Vincent, ". . . if necessity demand the removal of the charibbs, you do take up such vessels as can be procured, to serve as transports for the conveyance of them to some unfrequented part of the coast of Africa, or to some desert island adjacent thereto, care being taken that they be treated on the voyage with every degree of humanity their situation will admit of; and what-soever may be judged necessary to subsist them for a reasonable time, and with such tools and implements as may enable them to provide for their future subsistence."

Twenty-five years later, almost to the day, similar instructions landed the Caribs on the island of Roatan, off the coast of Honduras. Thus, we see that the deportation of 1797 had been seriously considered for some time and was not merely in revenge for Carib acts committed in desperation during the Carib War of 1795–96, as was frequently suggested by apologists at the time. It must also be remembered that the Caribs had an alliance during that war with the French mulatto revolutionary Victor Hugue, a serious and formidable enemy of the British and of the entire slave-buttressed colonial system. Hugue and his men reinforced the Caribs from their stronghold on St. Lucia (Ellis 1885:72), and after that island was taken by the British in September 1795, he sent supplies and men to St. Vincent from the main center of French military operations at Guadeloupe (Buckley 1979:83). Even though the primary concern of the St. Vincent planters was to obtain the Carib lands, they and the British government were also frightened by the repercussions in the West Indies of the French Revolution, including the rebellions and eventual revolution in Haiti. It was feared that British slaves throughout the area would be influenced to revolt, and by 1795 there were enough of them on St. Vincent to have created real havoc had that happened. But the latter spoke no French and had neither islandwide leaders nor a centralized social organization; thus, without knowing or understanding the broader situation, most of the slaves remained faithful to their British masters. Also, as Turnbull (1795:5) and Edwards (1819, 4:15–16) noted, competition between Caribs and slaves to sell their produce in the local markets increased the animosity between the groups.

Details of the final stages of the war have been described elsewhere (Shepherd 1831; Southey 1827; Kirby and Martin 1972; C. Gullick 1976b); I will simply note that the Caribs, with arms, ammunition, and other supplies furnished by the French, fought fiercely alongside white, black, and mulatto Frenchmen, usually collectively termed "Brigands," or sometimes *Carmagnoles* (Howard 1796–98, 1:27), after a song that was popular at the time of the French Revolution. The stakes for the French were clearly more than the small island of St. Vincent, and the Caribs undoubtedly were ignorant of what was happening in Europe, where France was undergoing massive internal change and was threatening the British Isles as well. The end of 1796 was said to have been the low point of the war from the British perspective (Lloyd 1954:163).

The British had a superior military position on St. Vincent because they

Table 1.1 Black Carib Survivors at Different Points in the Deportation, 1796–97

	Men	Women	Children	Total
Captured and taken to Baliceaux, July 1796–February 1797	1,004	1,779	1,555	4,338
Embarked, March 11, 1797	722	806	720	2,248
Landed, Roatan, April 12, 1797	664	1,362	[a]	2,026
Landed, Trujillo, September 23, 1797	496	547	422	1,465
Still at Roatan, October 17, 1797	83	70	53	206

[a] Women and children were not counted separately.
Source: WO 1/82:645; AGCA A3.16/2025/194.

controlled the only good harbor and port facilities at Kingstown, and they finally overwhelmed their enemy by sheer numbers, nearly 4,000 troops having been sent to the island to bolster British forces (Coke 1808, 1:240). But the story of what happened after the formal French/Carib surrender on June 10, 1796, is less well known, and information recently discovered in the War Office records in England (see Table 1.1) suggests some new interpretations.[6]

Upon surrender, the French were accorded the standard treatment for prisoners of war and deported to Guadeloupe and thence to Europe.[7] Some of those who were resident on the island were permitted to stay after they declared allegiance to the British. The Caribs, however, were required to surrender unconditionally, which for them meant loss of their entire homeland, their culture, perhaps their lives. In fact, as early as 1772 the Caribs had insisted that they would never submit, never give up their lands, preferring to die first (CO 101/16, f.164). Thus, when they refused to surrender, they were hunted down without mercy, over 1,000 of their houses and 200 canoes were burned, their crops were destroyed, and their stores of food were confiscated (Shepherd 1831:168; Ellis 1885:72). Starvation and disease took their toll as the summer wore on. By October 1796, 4,195 Black Caribs, plus 44 slaves said to belong to them and 102 so-called Yellow Caribs, had been captured and sent to Baliceaux;[8] all of those in the last two categories were later returned to St. Vincent.

Between October 1796 and March 1797, some 2,400 interned Caribs died of a mysterious "malignant fever," most probably either typhus or yellow fever. The impact was aggravated, without doubt, by malnutrition: the Carib death rate was 85 percent, compared to a reported rate of only 5 percent for the British slaves and Negro troops, who also suffered from the disease (Gonzalez 1986a). Actually, the death rate for yellow fever among military troops and civilians in the Caribbean at that time was really much higher; and it is possible that the lower rate recorded for non-Caribs on Baliceaux was due to the fact that most of the troops stationed there, like the slaves, had been recruited directly from Africa, where they would have acquired immunity after having been exposed to the disease as children (Buckley 1979).

The symptoms, causes, and treatment of yellow fever, or Bulam's Fever as it was sometimes called, were extremely controversial, even among the leading medical authorities of the time (Clark 1797; Chisholm 1801, 1809; Pinckard 1806; Lloyd 1965). Between 1793 and 1796 about 80,000 cases of yellow fever were reported in the area, of which about one-half resulted in death (Lloyd 1965:194). Slaveowners on St. Vincent, as part of the damages they claimed from the British government after the "reduction" of the Caribs, included a large sum for slaves lost through "epidemical disease" (CO 123/14). Lewis (1960:406) has noted that the primary killer of British naval personnel between 1793 and 1815 was fever, especially yellow fever and typhus, and the description of the disease that struck St. Vincent and Baliceaux in 1796 seems to match the symptoms of typhus. Even though typhus is generally thought not to occur in the tropics, there was an epidemic reported in Barbados in 1795 (Lloyd and Coulter 1961:172). Some medical historians, however, believe the diagnosis was mistaken and that it was likely yellow fever (Geggus 1982:365).[9] We shall probably never know for sure.

Whatever the microorganism responsible, it is interesting that Garifuna oral tradition has not preserved the horrors of this epidemic, other than to assert that the British poisoned many of their people by mixing "lime" with their flour (Beauçage 1970:52). No doubt the awful symptoms of the disease, so often followed in just a few days by death, must have seemed like poison in the absence of other experience. Even the attending British physician was unable to account for what he saw (Dickinson 1797).

What was the maximum number of Caribs who ever lived on St. Vincent? The accounts vary. As Miller (1979) has shown, the European observers were never very clear as to which groups they were discussing, and figures were always mere guesses. However, given the number of Caribs who surrendered, and judging by accounts of battle casualties as well as allowing for deaths before they surrendered, I believe that the 7,000–8,000 estimate given earlier is reasonable. Contrary to what has been suggested by Taylor (1951:30) and C. Gullick (1978), the Black Caribs seem not to have reached the limits of their resource base, although they certainly had begun to perceive of their surroundings as being somewhat crowded (see chapter 5). And the constant pressure to give up more and more of their land would have placed them in a defensive and aggressive position. Ethnological and psychological theories lead us to expect that internal political disputes—whatever their motivation— would have been exacerbated under such crowding. Furthermore, the need to cooperate in the face of the European threat might have countered centrifugal tendencies.

On March 3, 1797, under the supervision of Maj. John Wilson of the

Seventh West India Regiment, the Caribs were boarded, and on March 11 they sailed from the Lesser Antilles in a convoy made up of eight or nine ships, commanded by Capt. John Barrett in the flagship *Experiment*. [10] Some of those on board were still sick, and others apparently were left behind if they seemed too weak to withstand the trip; even so, many more died on the passage itself (Gonzalez 1986a). The British considered several different sites before they decided upon the Bay Islands; among others, these included Africa, the Bahamas, and the peninsula of Samana on the island of Hispaniola (WO 1/82, f.583; WO 1/640).

It is important to note that, upon their surrender, the Caribs were classified according to color, the British sending the "yellow" (lighter-skinned) people back to St. Vincent, thus perhaps separating members of families. It was assumed that the lighter Caribs were of a different political and ethnic group than the blacks, and basically benign. I have found no definitive answer to whether there were one or two political groups by that time, but I have seen no evidence of negotiations with any organized or informal separate group identified as Yellow Caribs. It may be that the two were ethnically separate but united temporarily against a common oppressor. Alexander Anderson, a resident botanist who visited the Carib territory on the island just before the final war, believed there were no more than two or three families of pure-blooded (Yellow) Caribs left (1983:44). After the deportation, arms and ammunition were found in the huts of some of these so-called Yellow Caribs, leading the British to alter their former view of them (WO 1/767:367). Such evidence is hardly decisive, but it does suggest they were ready to defend themselves against whatever enemy came along.

The die had been cast, however, and the lighter-skinned people were returned to St. Vincent, even though many Vincentian planters urged that they too be sent to Honduras. In spite of subsequent speculation, there is no evidence that further deportations to Roatan or Central America occurred.[11] Within a few years all Caribs remaining on St. Vincent were "pardoned" and granted lands, although they were explicitly denied the right to participate in political affairs (Report of the Committee 1831:22). It is not known how many Caribs remained after the original deportation, but judging by later clues, their number was not trivial and must have included many Black Caribs as well as those labeled "yellow" or "red." Many died in the eruption of Mt. Soufrière in 1812, and others fled to Trinidad following that incident (Shepherd 1831:179). Yet by 1833 there were said to be about 1,000 Caribs on the island (Alexander 1833, 1:279). Although Ober (1895:300) said there were only about 600 Caribs on both St. Vincent and Dominica at the time of his visit in the 1880s, some 2,000 were reported to have died at the time of the next major eruption of Soufrière in 1902 (Whitney 1902). Part of the problem in counting them was that their culture and whatever ethnic identity they may have had at the time of the deportation were soon largely destroyed or submerged as this small group gradually became assimilated into the general postemancipation black population (Ober 1895:300). Today, although there is a sense of being somewhat different from the rest, and their self-identification as Caribs is explicit, little survives of their language, religion, music, or crafts. Thus, it has been difficult to distinguish them from their neighbors, in spite of contemporary attempts to revive some of the old ways[12] (Bernárdez 1984; C. Gullick 1979; Layng 1983). In 1985 a film about the Caribs of Dominica was released, entitled *Last of the Karaphuna*. It featured an interview with the young "chief" of the group, who had been educated in the United States, where by his own admission he was deeply influenced by the Native American rights movement (Teuscher 1985).

Carib Culture History on St. Vincent

Several archaeologists have done surveys on St. Vincent over the past seventy or so years, but their publications cast very little light on the way of life of the so-called Island Caribs (Bullen and Bullen 1972; Joyce 1916; Fewkes 1922; Loven 1935; Rouse 1948).[13] Fewkes reported evidence of a sedentary culture on St. Vincent before the arrival of the Caribs; presumably these were the Igneri, or "true Arawak-speakers" (Taylor and Rouse 1955). Those people lived for the most part on the leeward (western) side of the island, especially wherever there were convenient landing places or where valleys opening to the sea presented available land, although Fewkes (1922:10) also found several middens on the windward side. Considerable pottery of distinctive design was found, some with animal heads as handles or legs.

Joyce (1916) and Loven (1935) used travelers' accounts as well as archaeological material to depict the preconquest culture of St. Vincent. Both mentioned fishhooks, and Loven described three-pronged arrows for shooting fish or crustaceans, as well as harpoons with detachable points for hunting sea turtles (1935:423). Fewkes recovered a harpoon and several fishhooks; he also found shallow burials, including pottery and other items of daily use, at Baliceaux and speculated that he had discovered the site of the 1796–97 Black Carib internment (1922:12). Bullen and Bullen (1972), because there was inadequate historical information available to them, cast doubt on this interpretation. They assumed that only a small percentage of the Black Caribs captured had been quartered on Baliceaux (1972:40). We now know there were massive deaths among both Caribs and black and white soldiers during their stay on the island, so it would be strange if there were not some evidence of that ordeal (see chapter 2).

The Bullens never excavated on St. Vincent, but their work on what they believed to be a Carib site on St. Lucia, as well as information from numerous surveys on other islands, suggests that Caribs, in contrast to Arawaks, preferred high, windswept promontories overlooking the sea. The Bullens (1970:76) inferred that the Carib culture was better able to exploit the marine resources of the windward coasts than was that of their predecessors, perhaps because their canoes and knowledge of the sea were superior. Most scholars have tended to agree with this interpretation, even though they may disagree with the Bullens' (1972:166) assertion that the Suazey ceramic complex correlates with the historic Island Carib culture. Haag (1968:121), following Rouse (1948:547), is adamant that until historic Carib and/or Arawak sites can be identified through archival work, followed by archaeological excavation, we should refrain from labeling materials by one or another term. Allaire (1980), also a student of Rouse, agrees.

Nevertheless, because Suazey is the latest pre-European pottery found in the Lesser Antilles, it is reasonable to suppose it was made by the people encountered by Columbus and the other early explorers and missionaries—whatever they were called and wherever they may have come from. While archaeological evidence for early Black Carib living patterns is nonexistent, the Bullens did find a distinctive pottery on St. Vincent they termed "peasant ware," which they associated with Black Caribs for reasons they failed to outline (1972:62).[14] The question of who made the pottery throughout the entire period is crucial, given the assumption that men were the primary newcomers in both the transition from Arawak to Carib and from Island Carib to Black Carib. Allaire (1977:62) suggests it may have been men, but most scholars assume it was women, in which case we should not expect such major stylistic changes, since mythology suggests a continuity of females throughout the various conquests. Questions concerning the associations between known complexes in time and space are rife but unresolved. In any case, the people may have begun to use some imported European ware by 1750. Further archaeological work must include a historical component, and comparisons with slave-quarter remains may also be instructive (Armstrong 1985; Posnansky 1983).

The earliest useful descriptions we have of life among the "Caribbeans" on St. Vincent come from the pens of seventeenth-century French and English explorers and Jesuit priests (Breton 1665; Burton 1685; Du Tertre 1667–71; Labat 1970; La Borde 1674; Rochefort 1666). It is important to note, however, that only Breton and perhaps La Borde spent any significant amount of time living in close relations with the Indians (Taylor 1949:381). Unfortunately, by the time these Europeans came to document the customs of the islanders, the latter had already been in contact with Europeans, and especially Africans, for several generations. As we shall see, this requires us to examine more carefully the apparent parallels between Carib/Arawak and African customary practices and beliefs. Some or many of them may turn out to be syncretisms, in Melville Herskovits's original sense of that term, rather than independent invention, products of similar adaptive processes, or of psychic "unity." For a comparative analysis, then, it is important to draw also upon ethnographic accounts of Carib- and Arawak-speaking peoples still living in Amazonia (Basso 1977; Carneiro 1961; Dole 1978; Dreyfus 1982; Farabee 1967a, 1967b; Gillin 1936; Kloos 1971).

It is generally thought that the first Africans reached St. Vincent in 1635, when two Spanish slave boats were wrecked in the vicinity (Great Britain 1880). Yet Dominican Caribs frequently raided European settlements between 1558 and 1580, taking both whites and blacks as slaves (Boromé 1966:35, 41). It is likely that St. Vincent Caribs were similarly engaged and had at least some contact with Africans several generations before the 1635 shipwreck (Crouse 1940:216). A young Spanish black woman kept captive on Dominica before 1574 reported later that the Island Caribs there had more than thirty Spaniards and some forty black slaves in captivity (quoted by Dreyfus 1982:14). Du Tertre (1667–71:574) reported a complaint by Martiniquan planters that more than 500 of their slaves had been kidnapped by Caribs from nearby islands. Some of these may have been ritually killed and eaten as war captives, but most were probably absorbed into Carib society, perhaps as slaves.[15] The male captives were encouraged to cohabit with Carib women, and their progeny were accepted as full-fledged Caribs, with all the rights that implied (Beauçage 1982:184). It is possible that the Europeans reporting on this matter mistook a kind of bride service for chattel slavery of the sort they themselves practiced. Africans would probably have found life more familiar and tolerable among the Caribs than among the Europeans, even under the yoke of slavery. Distances, currents, and winds are such in the area that escaping slaves could easily have reached St. Vincent in small craft from other islands, as their descendants were known to do in later times.

Breton, Rochefort, and Labat described in varying detail the language, physical appearance, dress and adornment, housing, diet, diversions, life-crisis rites, and religious practices of the Island Caribs in this early period. The most salient characteristic, considered astounding by most observers, was that the men and women spoke different languages, the first being of Carib origin, the latter Arawak. Supposedly, Carib conquerors, coming out of the Orinoco about a century before Columbus, had taken Arawak wives (Taylor and Rouse 1955), who had perpetuated their own language among their children. In later years, as the boys spent more time with their fathers, they also became fluent in Carib, while the girls suffered along speaking only Arawak. While remnants of this male-female linguistic distinction survive, it is clearly Arawak that has won out, forming the basis of the language today known as Island Carib, which in turn underlies Central American Carib. The latter has incorporated a large number of loanwords from French, Spanish, English, and Miskito (Holm 1978a). Recently, Taylor and Hoff (1980), following Gomberville (1682), have suggested that the men's language of the seventeenth century was actually a Carib pidgin, spoken widely in the islands and on the mainland. This provides a more satisfying explanation for its persistence among the men, who traveled widely then, even as now (Morales and Arévalo-Jiménez 1981; Da Prato-Perelli 1981; Dreyfus 1982:13).

For our purposes, it is interesting to note that, like Amazonian Central Arawaks (Farabee 1967a), the earliest Island Caribs lived in round houses, rather than the rectangular ones known during later colonial and modern times, and that they had separate "public houses" where the menfolk congregated and slept and which were used for feasts. Neither the historical nor the archaeological record is clear as to when rectangular houses with squared corners became the norm. Since men traditionally have been the housebuilders nearly everywhere, it is tempting to speculate that this was an early African modification. Archaeologists place a good deal of emphasis on house shape and style as being diagnostic of ethnic status. Thus, one wonders how and under what circumstances such a major stylistic change might have occurred. The point is especially intriguing because much of the other Carib domestic material culture is, even today, almost identical to that found among Carib and Arawak speakers in Amazonia.[16]

Although the Island Caribs had canoes, "some as large as schooners," and were accomplished in long-distance travel (Anderson 1983:59), it is important to note that slaves coming from the Gold Coast were also accomplished fishermen and extremely adept at making large canoes (Long 1774:403). Among the items destroyed by the British after the Carib War were "many large canoes, some said to hold fifty persons, and of dimensions never heard of before" (Coke 1808, 1:245; Ellis 1885:72). Like their ancestors, the Garifuna today are known for their skill in making canoes (Craig 1966), constructing some as large as five feet across and thirty feet long (Dudek 1985). McKusick (1960:5) dates the use of sails to 1608, when a Spanish friar claimed to have saved his own life by teaching the islanders how to manufacture and use spritsails, a type of "fore and aft" arrangement (Bowker and Budd 1944). In spite of the somewhat apocryphal nature of this story, I have found nothing among the scanty data on sails to contradict it. Nicholson (1976:102) accepts the story but emphasizes that the speeds and distances reported for early Carib seafarers were made possible not by the use of sails but by their technique of using as many as twenty-four men paddling at one time, thus freeing them from dependency upon the elements and allowing them to proceed for long distances without rest or sleep.

According to the chroniclers, pottery was manufactured by Island Carib women on St. Vincent, although there is no mention of it for Black Caribs during the final period before or just after the deportation. Clay griddles, so common in archaeological sites, had been replaced by iron ones at least by

1787 (Davidson 1787:12). Indeed, Burton (1685:177) said the Caribs were already trading for iron tools and equipment shortly after the mid-seventeenth century. Other ceramic items may have continued to be made, even in Central America, though perhaps with a sharp decline in quality and quantity when English glass and stoneware became more generally available. To date we have not been able to distinguish any "foreign" types among the redwares available in Honduras in the early nineteenth century. Both Island and Black Carib men made basketry items, including the special equipment needed to extract the poisonous juice (hydrocyanic acid) from bitter manioc and to process it for consumption. Baskets of Carib style and design were adopted by the slave populations and continued to be made and used in St. Vincent and Dominica until recently (Alexander 1833, 1:279; Taylor 1935:267). These baskets, as well as some other items manufactured by men, such as silkgrass *(Aechmea magdalenensis)* fishlines and hammocks, and wooden kitchen dishes, were also in demand among Europeans (Anderson 1983:66).

Both men and women had important roles in agriculture. The men cleared and burned the gardens for which women were then largely responsible. Women were active in local marketing, while men traded to nearby islands. Hunting, fishing, and warfare were the main occupations of the Island Carib men. It is noteworthy, since it is not usually mentioned, that the Black Caribs, at least, did not live exclusively on the seacoast, as the Garifuna do today, but also inland along the rivers, which provided them with their major fish supply. All English accounts of St. Vincent between 1763 and 1797 describe Carib villages and hamlets as being scattered inland, as well as on the windward coast. The records are not so clear for the Red (or Yellow) Caribs—we only know they were concentrated on the western, or leeward, side of the island before 1763.

Rochefort (1666) described in some detail the activities of shamans, who could invoke the spirits of the dead to give advice to or cure the living. He reported that frequent feasts were held at which cassava or pineapple wine was drunk in large quantities. Although Loven (1935) stated that dancing was done to the accompaniment of drums and maracas, we have no really good descriptions of it—for example, we do not know whether the dancers were men or women, or if they wore special dress or ornaments. Most early chroniclers failed to mention dancing at all, even when they described feasts. Yet, like Loven, we can piece together a few things. Burton (1685:177) spoke of island Indians dancing all night, "making a noise with gourds, wherein are many pebble stones . . ." to ward off evil spirits. Women are mentioned as wearing shell bands on their legs that shook as they moved—a custom reserved for male dancers among modern Garifuna (quoted in Baxter 1970:26). Dancing to the rhythms of drums is described for Arawaks but not for the Caribs of the Lesser Antilles. We might conclude that drums could not have been as prominent a feature of Carib ceremonial life as they are today without having stimulated greater comment. Loven (1935:495) claimed that in the seventeenth century the drum was known only in the form of the "European skin-drum," by which he apparently meant a log with skin over one end. Presumably he got this description from Rochefort (1666:307). Unfortunately, no sketches of the drum were made, so it is impossible to tell whether it was similar to those used today by Garifuna. South American Carib/Arawak peoples apparently do not use the same drum form, so it is likely that the modern type was copied very early either from Europeans or from Africans. Farabee (1967a:84) described the Central Arawaks of British Guiana in 1918 as using both rattles and bone or bamboo flutes to accompany their dancing and singing, which involved a solo voice plus a chorus. The same can be said for Garifuna music today, though the comment is so general as to be not very meaningful.

As for the South American Central Arawaks, oil and red paint *(Bixa orellana* or *roucou)* were more important than clothing as body adornment and protection for the Island Caribs, though loincloths were reported in use by both sexes. In addition, women's calves were bound for beauty's sake, as were the heads of both sexes. Several sources claim that the Black Caribs started molding their children's heads only after the French had brought in slaves in the early eighteenth century, the better to distinguish themselves from these other blacks (Russell 1778, 2:99; Martin 1836–37, 2:236; Coke 1808–11, 2:182). However, since head-molding was mentioned for the Island Caribs from the beginning, it seems probable that the blacks merely continued what some of their ancestors had done. There were certainly other characteristics that separated them from the slaves, and head-molding seems an extreme measure if they had not already been convinced of its aesthetic value. Anderson (1983:63) said that St. Vincent Black Caribs gave it up shortly before the Carib War because they had been ridiculed by other blacks. Head-shaping was commented upon in Central America several generations later (Douglas 1868–69:29; Pim and Seeman 1869:308), though it is not clear how common it was at that time. Garifuna today have no memory of it.[17]

The Methodist missionaries Mr. and Mrs. Baxter had the following to say about the Black Caribs of St. Vincent in 1788: "As a people they are much handsomer than the negroes. They appear more muscular and alert, and almost constantly assume a martial air. Even their women put on a warlike appearance, and seem familiarized with the weapons of destruction. Cutlasses, and other accoutrements, are frequently in their hands; and knives are suspended by their naked sides. Even in times of peace they exhibit an armed neutrality; and both sexes display a state of preparation, either for offensive or defensive war" (quoted in Coke 1793:265). Of course, by 1788 the Black Caribs had been pressured by the British for more than a generation, and it is not surprising that they should have been constantly on guard. Although some of them attended the Baxters' school for a while to learn English, they were not swayed by the new religion that was being taught to them, and the Baxters soon gave up in disgust. Only a very few of the Black Caribs who arrived in Central America seem to have been English-speakers, so it is probable that these combined English and religion lessons reached only a few people and/or were too short-lived to have been successful.[18]

The domestic organization of the Island Caribs can be, and has been, interpreted in a number of different ways. Some of the early accounts state that residence for a couple after marriage was uxorilocal, although there is a hint of bride service, which suggests that this may have been a temporary measure during the first years. Uxorilocality would accord both with recent South American Carib ethnography and with Farabee's 1918 observations for the Arawaks (1967a). The fact that the term for "wife" was the same as that for "mother's brother's daughter" (Gonzalez 1960) further supports this interpretation, since preferential matrilateral cross-cousin marriage often coincides with uxorilocality (Murdock 1949). The practice perpetuates a residential core of related men, in spite of the fact that it is the bride who remains "at home" after marriage (Taylor 1951:83–84).

As in some, but not all, mainland Carib groups (Schwerin 1982), the Island Carib men spent much of their time in a village men's house, leaving their wives and children to occupy their individual huts. As Taylor (1951:28) noted, "Such a socio-economic unit was divided, by its very nature, into an in-group consisting of the women together with their unmarried sons, and an out-group containing all the husbands. . . ." Helms (1976) has argued, on the basis of the early accounts, that Island Carib domestic organization was basically consanguineal, with the men as husband-fathers being somewhat peripheral, similar to the matrifocal or consanguineal households described for the Garifuna (Gonzalez 1969; see also chapter 7). My reading of the data, as well as my understanding of the structure of matrifocality and consanguineal households, has led me to reject Helms's idea entirely. There is simply no evidence for the Island Carib women having anything like the status and authority we see today among the Garifuna.

There are many contrary data that make Helms's argument difficult to accept. Not only was divorce said to be frequent and easy for the men (but not for the women), but polygamy was also permitted for chiefs. In the latter case, a chief established a separate village, containing his several wives and their children, each apparently in a separate house. Presumably, then, when his daughters married, their husbands would join their father-in-law for some unspecified period of time; and if the sons-in-law did not become chiefs themselves, perhaps they stayed in the wife's village permanently. If these in-marrying husbands were also the sons of the chief's sisters, this would have been a means of perpetuating a newly localized matrilineage — but only if the polygamy were also sororal polygyny, so that all of the chief's daughters belonged to the same lineage. Taylor (1951:84) found linguistic forms he thought suggested that such a marriage form was prevalent. Also, divorce under normal circumstances would put the man, not the woman, at a disadvantage, for he would be the one who had to leave the settlement. Finally, it would have given the chiefs authority over their sisters' sons, rather than over their own. However, it is important to note that all of this is hypothetical, since we have no direct evidence of the existence of a unilineal descent system among either the Island or the Black Caribs.

In fact, Island Carib leadership, at least in the late eighteenth century, was at least partially hereditary from father to son. It is possible that we are dealing here with a form of domestic organization that became highly altered as a result of the nearly constant warfare described above. Dreyfus (1977, 1982, 1985) provides a thoughtful and detailed analysis of the early Island Carib domestic and political organization, based upon available documentary records. She notes that raiding forays and trading networks were important means for the chiefs to build up their spheres of influence, and she likens the resulting definitions of status to that of the Big Man in Melanesia. It may be that there was, in fact, an incipient hierarchical organization by the end of the eighteenth century, in which success in actual warfare (as opposed to raiding for captives), as well as success in related diplomatic activity, were skills taught by fathers to their sons. By that time there is no evidence whatever of bonds between a Carib man and his sister's son, but the Europeans may have failed to discern what they would have seen as an "unnatural" tie. When Chief Chatoyer was killed in 1795, his son, said to be only twelve years old, was recognized as the new leader by both the British and Black Caribs (but see p. 47 for another interpretation of the basis of Chatoyer's power). Furthermore, two brothers shared the leadership of one faction among those deported in 1797 (Anonymous 1797). It is also significant that only the chiefs were reported as owning slaves and engaging in significant trade. Their "dependent males" were apparently not merely their sons, nephews, and sons-in-law but captured or even purchased blacks, some of whom eventually achieved son-in-law status as well (Beauçage 1982).

The importance of diplomatic skills for the Caribs during the centuries of contact with Europeans cannot be overemphasized. The ability to speak a European language placed a man in a position to obtain information about trading and employment opportunities, as well as about possible enemy maneuvers. At some point before leaving St. Vincent, oratory skills were learned, for at least two accounts of impassioned Carib speeches are on record (Coke 1808, 1:243; Anonymous 1797; and see chapter 2). Obviously, the ability of the Black Caribs to get the French to assist them in their attempts to retain their homelands also required some negotiation. There is circumstantial evidence that some segments of the St. Vincent Black Carib population had established "friendly" relations with the British, notwithstanding the difficulties and apparent misunderstandings that had occurred over their lands. Indeed, we cannot simply assume that the French and/or the British always used the Black Caribs as they pleased for their own purposes.

I have tried to demonstrate that by the 1770s Island Carib social structure had been replaced by a new pattern that was, nonetheless, unlike what we observe today among the Garifuna. I believe new social and cultural forms were in the process of evolving at the time they were cut off, never to be revived, with the deportation in 1797. Throughout the final months between the formal French surrender and the rounding up of the defeated Black Caribs, there are references to particular chiefs who either were killed or surrendered along with "their people." Many were mentioned by name in ways that show they were well known to their enemies.

The names of those mentioned in 1796 can be compared with the names of twenty-eight Black Carib chiefs who signed the infamous 1772 treaty with the British (see Table 1.2). The only two names on both lists are Chatoyer and Du Vallet/Duvalle. These two, and someone named Manuel, are also on the list of "captains" taken by the Spaniards from Roatan to Trujillo in May 1797, although "Chatoyer" had become "Satulle," referring to the son of the chief killed in the Carib War, and Du Vallet/Duvalle had become Dubale. The 1772 list shows both a "Lalime, junior" and a "Lalime, senior," presumably father and son; Duvalle's son (also called a chief) was named Regis. While it is not possible to trace genealogies from these lists, we can probably assume that there were more than these four father-son pairs.

It is clear that the Black Carib population on St. Vincent had grown considerably by the end of the eighteenth century. Although many of the details mentioned by the earliest priests and travelers are still recognizable in the later accounts, it is my judgment that Carib society had by 1763 entered a new phase with different basic characteristics from its predecessor. Island Carib had become Black Carib, and contrary to what has previously been believed, the Afroeuropean overlay was probably structurally significant. The ecological setting had also changed, of course, for both Island Carib and Black Carib territory had been severely diminished, and the former raiding and trading networks with other Carib-speaking peoples had been largely replaced by war and trade with Europeans.

Clearly, by this time the Black Caribs had an efficient food production and storage system and the beginnings of what we might call a foreign policy. The adoption of new crops and the domestication of fowl, pigs, and cattle both improved their own diet and opened markets for them, leading to the development of a money economy. Larger canoes were valuable in transporting goods and people from St. Vincent to the other islands, both in times of peace and in

Table 1.2 Names of Black Carib Chiefs as Recorded by British and Spanish Authorities on St. Vincent and Roatan

1772 St. Vincent	1796 St. Vincent	1797 Roatan
Chatoyer	Chatoyer	Satulle
Du Vallet	Duvalle	Dubale
Bayordell	Delaprade	Sambula
Dirang	Hippolite	Duran
Doucre Baramont	Emanuel	Manuel
Lalime (junior)	Thunder	Athelet
Lalime (senior)	Toussaint	Bruno
Broca	Jean Toulie	Jean Pierre
Saioe	Letraille	Palangure
Francois Laron	Dimmey	Luisson
Saint Laron	Cuffy Wilson	Huayba
Anisette		Pascal
Clement		Babiar
Bigott		Nicolas
Simon		Jean Joseph
Bauamont		Petan
Justin Bauamont		Jack
Matthieu		David
Jean Louis Pacquin		Regis
Gadel Goibau		Michel
John Baptiste		Juan Baptiste
Lonen		Jacque
Boyudon		Pierre
Boucharie		Fiolin
Deruba Babilliard		Charles
Canaia		Etienne
		Joseph
		Nicolas
		Pierre Jacque
		Juan Baptiste
		Juan Baptiste

Source: The 1772 list is from CO 260/9; the 1796 list is from Shepherd (1831); and the 1797 list is from AGCA A3.16/2025/194.

war. There were, perhaps, incipient chiefdoms, although there is too little information to be sure. Leaders were not only fluent in French (and perhaps in English), but they were sophisticated in dealing with Europeans in general. Anderson (1983:61) stated, "They were not an ignorant people. From their long communication with Europeans they were far more intelligent than any other race of savages." A lady in St. Vincent wrote in June 1789, "I saw several of them, among whom some are greatly civilized, and a few can read. There is something very noble in the spirit and manners of those that are improved, far surpassing the Negroes in general" (MMS, box 111, item 12).

By 1797, nearly all the Caribs had adopted French names.[19] Some had converted to Roman Catholicism, probably in part as a diplomatic move. Their success in warfare cannot be attributed to French leadership, for their tactics were notoriously different, much to the distress of the English, who were not accustomed to adversaries who hid in the cane fields, shot from the branches of trees, and preferred to attack at night (Narrative 1795; Stewart 1978:436). Carib guerrilla attacks and raids succeeded in destroying an estimated one-third of the British properties on St. Vincent before the war was over (Martin 1836–37, 2:213).

The conquest and subsequent exile of the Black Caribs from St. Vincent destroyed a more developed society than scholars and modern Garifuna have previously thought. Even though their numbers were diminished by perhaps as much as 75 percent, the surviving deportees managed to retain their sense of sociocultural identity, dramatically expanding both their population size and their territory over the ensuing 200 years. They incorporated other blacks and eventually emerged as a unique people, dominating the labor market on the coast of Central America for more than 100 years. How they managed to do this in spite of so many obstacles placed before them relates to the concepts of ethnicity and ethnogenesis, which are the subject of the rest of this book.

NOTES

1. Judging by the number of people who died or were captured a generation later, the Black Caribs would have been quite crowded on just 4,000 acres of land, given their hunting and fishing economy with shifting cultivation. All the evidence suggests, however, that they had no difficulty providing for both their own subsistence and for a considerable surplus. In part this must have been because they enjoyed abundant fishing, combined with the high caloric yields per land unit typical of bitter manioc (see chapter 5).

2. Baliceaux is spelled in the early accounts as Baliseu, Balliseaux, Ballisou, and so on. I have followed *Rand McNally's New International Atlas*.

3. A recent master's thesis by Miller (1979) reviews the historical literature concerning Black Caribs and other groups on St. Vincent at that time and concludes that the figures given and the ethnic identifications made are so fraught with error that it is difficult to use them in any effort to quantify population. Still, these data are all we have, and some judicious consideration of what the different views meant seems warranted.

4. For analyses of the larger economic and political background of the Carib War, see Ragatz (1928), Lloyd (1954), and Niddrie (1966).

5. Valentine Morris is often pictured as having been incompetent; in fact, he was recalled to Britain in disgrace after St. Vincent was conquered by the French in 1779. However, his self-defense during his court martial shows that he had a more accurate view of what was happening than did many others (Morris 1787; Waters 1964).

6. During the summer of 1982 I searched through various archives in London, Greenwich, Kew, and Oxford, England. While at Kew I literally stumbled upon some documents that had been misfiled—who knows how long ago?—and I am grateful to Beverly Gartrell, an anthropological colleague, who reported to me a chance remark made at lunch by still another researcher, which eventually led me to the important data that follow. The War Office files in question are WO 1/82 and WO 1/769, which contain the "Return of the Charaibs landed at Balliceaux from July 25, 1796, to February 2, 1797," and an account of the "malignant pestilential disease" by Dr. Dickinson, an assistant surgeon in the British Navy.

7. The articles of surrender laid down by Lt. Gen. Ralph Abercromby stated:

a. Slaves were to be returned to their proprietors.

b. The rest of the garrison became prisoners of war. Officers might retain their swords and keep personal effects.

c. Those guilty of murder or of burning houses or estates, must be subject to judgement of the laws of the island.

d. All posts in possession of the French to be given up and troops to be made prisoners.

e. All are pardoned for having departed from their allegiance to his majesty except those guilty under section c. (Annual Register 1796:80).

All Caribs were assumed to come under Article 3 (section c). Seven hundred twenty-five "Brigands" were said to have surrendered, and in a letter to the transport board in London on August 19, 1796, it was reported that some 1,300 prisoners of war from St. Lucia, Grenada, and St. Vincent were being sent to England. Instructions were to keep blacks separate from others "as much as circumstances permit," so it clearly was a mixed group (ADM/MT/416). There was great concern in England that yellow fever and other "infectious diseases" might be introduced there by the prisoners. Therefore, most of the latter were returned to France (ADM/F/27).

8. Shepherd (1831:171) stated that by October 26, 1796, 5,080 Caribs had surrendered in all, yet by that date the number sent to Baliceaux was only 4,044, and the total number ever sent was apparently only 4,195. It is likely that Shepherd's figure included the "Brigands" mentioned earlier, as well as sundry slaves and Yellow Caribs. Furthermore, the death rate immediately after surrender must have been high—a fact that would have contributed to the discrepancy in the numbers.

9. The symptoms noted included fever, petechial ulcers, emaciation, and weakness. Death occurred within a week, apparently preceded by considerable pain, as indicated by the patients' "pitiful complaints" (Dickinson 1797). Vomiting and jaundice, so frequently characteristic of yellow fever, were not mentioned.

10. Curiously, the accounts of the deportation are confused, not to say inaccurate. The log of the *Experiment*'s captain does not agree with that of its master, and letters from Wilson to his superiors sometimes contradict both. No wonder historians have

written such diverse accounts! Even the dates of certain events, as well as the names and number of ships involved, are recorded differently by different persons (ADM 1/1518/74; WO 1/82/535, 639; WO 52/2976.) Fortunately, there is also at least one Spanish account (Saenz 1797), and by putting all of these together I have come up with the following list of ships:

Experiment—5th rate, 44 guns

Sovereign (or *Severn*)—a transport, 5th rate, 44 guns

Boyton (or *Boyston* or *Boston*)—5th rate, 32 guns

Topaze (captured from the French in 1793)—5th rate, 38 guns; said to have "gotten lost" (WO 1/690)

Ganges—"Indiaman" (i.e., leased from the East India Co.), 74 guns

Fortitude—a transport, late a prison ship, 3rd rate, 74 guns; "went aground" on the trip (WO 1/690)

Prince William Henry—a transport, also a prison ship; captured by the Spaniards on the trip

John and Mary—a transport; sprung a leak and may have been abandoned at Jamaica

Sea Nymph—a transport

Britannia—a transport

an American brig *(Sally?)*—impressed out of Jamaica and used in bombardment of Trujillo

Specifications were determined by research on ships of the period in the library of the National Maritime Museum at Greenwich, England. I am indebted to the director and the staff there for their interest and advice in identifying the ships (see especially Colledge 1969).

To understand the magnitude of this operation the reader should know that, according to Steele's list of British ships for 1796, there were only fifty British naval ships of all types in the West Indies and Jamaica at the time. In addition, Captain Barrett noted that during the passage they captured a Danish and a Spanish ship but lost the *Prince William Henry* to the Spaniards near the island of Guanaja; they retrieved it later, only to abandon it with Black Caribs aboard as they left for Nova Scotia. The captain also spoke of "seven transports" and repeatedly mentioned that "seven sails" accompanied him. The *Experiment*'s log states that on May 2, after leaving Trujillo and enroute to Roatan, still another ship ("a strange sail") was boarded, the crew and passengers removed, and Black Caribs left on board. If this was the *Prince William Henry*, it is odd that the captain did not say so; the clear implication is that it was not. There is no further record of what might have happened to this ship or to what nation she belonged (ADM 51/1266).

11. The only reference I have found suggesting that a later deportation occurred is Shepherd (1831:177). He noted that by 1799 other Caribs had been captured, including one "Cuffy Wilson," and that orders had been received to send them to the Spanish Main. It is possible that a few Black Caribs had taken refuge with Maroon and former slave allies. But Shepherd may have been referring to a letter from England to Governor Seton on St. Vincent, dated January 19, 1798, telling him that if he insisted, he might send the Yellow Caribs to Honduras, but only with the assurance of a friendly

reception by the Black Caribs there (WO 1/767, f.367). I have found no evidence that they were actually sent, or that they ever arrived in Central America. The historian Edward Cox has noted in a personal communication (1985) that it was common for the British to send captive blacks to any of the Spanish mainland territories, presumably not only to rid themselves of their presence but to inflict problems upon the Spanish.

12. Alexander (1833:279) said there were 1,000 Caribs on St. Vincent. When Mt. Soufrière erupted again in 1902, it was said that 2,000 people, mostly Carib Indians, died (Whitney 1902). Thus, either there were more Caribs left than was first assumed, or their fertility was as high as that of their exiled brethren in Central America, who have achieved considerable notoriety in this regard (McCommon 1982; Crawford 1984). For further discussion of the awakening of ethnic consciousness among the St. Vincent segment, see chapter 9.

13. In a recent publication, Myers (1984:173) quotes a 1979 letter from Rouse in which the latter admitted that neither he nor his students had yet been able to distinguish Carib from other sites in the Lesser Antilles. The Bullens, however, believed the Suazey style in St. Vincent and elsewhere to be Carib. This makes it awkward for the nonarchaeologist to speculate on what the various ceramic types may mean, but the fact that they do differ measurably over time suggests the successive presence of different mental sets or fashions. Whether these were evolutionary local modifications of tradition, or transformations stimulated by immigration and/or diffusion, cannot be answered at present.

This writer, with Charles Cheek, surveyed the Central American coast from Livingston, Guatemala, to the Río Patuca in Honduras between January 1984 and April 1985. We believe the flint microflakes, as used in cassava graters, to be the only recoverable distinguishing marker of Central American Black Carib/Garifuna culture, since pottery making was apparently abandoned upon arrival in Central America, if not before. Analysis of complete assemblages from Trujillo, Honduras, may allow more definite identifications, but that work has not been completed.

St. Vincent should be fertile ground for demonstrating the value of archaeological exploration in ethnic identification and analysis, providing there has been reasonable preservation. Not only should it be possible to distinguish Island Carib from Black Carib settlements on the basis of pottery, house forms, fishhooks, and so on, but differences should also be apparent among both of these and slave living patterns.

14. This pottery was described as being thick (0.8–1.2 cm), tempered with coarse sand and occasional small whitish particles (soft to the fingernail), black to brown in color and well burnished. Folded, incurving lips, straight vertical necks, and globular bodies were most common. It was said to be similar to Suazey but harder, well fired, and made of a well-mixed paste (Bullen and Bullen 1972:62).

15. Myers (1984:173) presents a compelling argument against Carib cannibalism that parallels the thinking of Arens (1979). However, the early accounts are so similar to those of Amazonian cannibalism, for which many modern ethnographers have respect, that I believe the case cannot yet be closed. Myers and Arens both take the ethnocentric view that cannibalism is inherently horrible, ignoring the possibility that it may have been a ritual and symbolic act with considerable positive emotional content (see Brown and Tuzin 1983; Sanday 1986).

16. Farabee's (1967a, 1967b) pictures of Carib and Arawak societies in the Ama-

zonian tropical forest are especially informative on this point. They were originally published in 1924, having been taken in the field between 1911 and 1918.

17. Interestingly, head scarves, tied in various decorative fashions and ubiquitous today among black women throughout the Caribbean, are worn by men in some of Brunius's paintings, of which four originals are in the collection of the Peabody Museum, Harvard University; see also Craton (1982, plate 16).

18. Farabee (1967a:82) mentioned that the Central Arawaks had magical formulas for learning a new language in a month. Although Amazonian peoples' abilities in language learning are well documented (Sorenson 1971), apparently the Island Caribs did not have access to this same magic! Anderson (1983:64), however, claimed that many of the Black Carib men understood English but refused to speak it out of hatred for the British.

19. Fashion was probably as much or more of a determinant than politics in the adoption of other names by the Caribs. The list of those arriving in Trujillo included men and women with English names like Jack and Nancy. Of course, it can be argued that fashion is itself responsive to political events and pressures, but it is difficult to imagine that the average Carib at that time would have consciously named his/her children to woo the favor of foreign oppressors. It is likely that many or most people had both a Carib and a European name, the latter to be used only in interethnic situations.

2

The Deportation, 1797

It is clear that the forced departure of Black Caribs from St. Vincent and Baliceaux brought about a major change in their way of living, as well as in the symbols by which Carib ethnicity was manifested and perceived, both among themselves and by outsiders. This chapter describes the impact of the deportation upon the Caribs' sense of "peoplehood" and continues the exploration of the extent to which they might have constituted a political entity both before and after their capture and banishment.

After leaving Baliceaux the convoy stopped at Bequia and Grenada to load supplies, troops, and perhaps more prisoners.[1] It then headed directly for Jamaica, where there was a layover of eighteen days while more supplies were loaded and repairs made on the *Experiment,* as well as on the *John and Mary,* which had sprung a leak. It is not clear if the latter ship continued on to Roatan, or if its cargo and prisoners were redistributed among the other ships.[2] There are frequent references to sickness among the passengers and troops.

The Landing at Roatan and the Seige of Trujillo

On April 11, 1797, the convoy arrived at Roatan, where they found a small Spanish fort and garrison, whose commandant quickly accepted the English terms of surrender. Obviously, the appearance of such a large fleet (eight to ten ships) suggested surrender as the most prudent course of action. The next day, Captain Barrett recorded in his log that the Caribs were landed at Port Royal, on the southeastern coast of Roatan, along with various supplies (see Table 2.1). That same day they learned that the *Prince William Henry,* carrying some 300 Caribs, had been captured by the Spanish near the island of Guanaja, another of the Bay Islands, east of Roatan. Even though many of the

Table 2.1 Supplies Provided by the British for the Use of the Black Caribs on Roatan, 1797

Item	Amount Shipped	Amount Landed
Flour	169,344 lb.	150,864 lb.
Farine	14,175 lb.	11,000 lb.
Biscuits	42,640 lb.	43 casks
Beef	12,200 lb.	800 lb.
Tasso[a] (jerked beef)	45,410 lb.	17,000 lb.
Salt fish	106,940 lb.	41,749 lb.
Indian corn	7 bbl. (for planting)	7 bbl.
Guinea corn	4 bbl. (for planting)	4 bbl.
Pidgeon pease	3 bbl. (for planting)	3 bbl.
Sweet potatoes	8 bbl.	8 bbl.
Yam plants	9 bbl.	9 bbl.
Ocre [okra] seeds	2 bbl.	1 bbl.
Pepper seeds	1 bag	1 bag
Cassada plants	21 bundles	21 bundles
Sugar	?	1,820 lb.
Cocoa	?	916 lb.
Oatmeal	?	105 bu.
Rum	?	26 gal.
Osnaburghs (cloth)	8000 yd.	6000 yd.
Fishing tackle	16,700 hooks, 225 lines	2 cases
Griddles	21	21
Graters	53	53
Assorted tools	?	1,591
Muskets	?	300
Ammunition	?	5 boxes
Gunpowder	?	10 bbl.
Balls	?	6 cases

[a] From Spanish *tasajo*.
Source: WO 1/82.

sailors and troops were still sick, Captain Barrett ordered three of his ships, including an American brig that had been impressed on the high seas, to Trujillo. He was determined to exchange his new prisoners for the Caribs.

The modern military man or woman would be astonished to read the accounts of the action that followed. The official reports by eye witnesses differ in such details as the date, time of attack, number of casualties, and even the outcome. Both the English and the Spanish claimed victory, the latter offering a thanksgiving mass a few days later. Most Spanish accounts fail to mention the capture of the Caribs as an issue in the attack, attributing it merely to English "piracy," even though Spain and England were officially at war at the time. The English, however, though formidable on the seas, could not match the tactics of the Spanish on the mainland. Upon heavy bombardment from the three English ships, the Spanish simply withdrew from Trujillo, leaving behind a small hidden intelligence force. When the English, assuming victory, swooped in to sack the houses, the Spanish, lying in wait a short distance away, fell upon them. The English attributed their subsequent inability to take the town to the Spanish having brought reinforcements from some interior post. According to the Spanish, however, the town was nearly lost, and indeed might have been had the English not been so intent upon seizing booty and had the Spanish not freed prisoners in the local jail and called upon those hospitalized to help defend the plaza. No other reinforcements seem to have been available. At least one source attributed the victory to the fighting skills of a company of "French Negroes" recently arrived from Santo Domingo, whence they had been exiled (AGCA A2.4/02268/120).

In any case, the English finally succeeded in retrieving the *Prince William Henry,* along with its Carib passengers, and started back to Roatan on April 29. On the way, they sighted several enemy ships and, to avoid an unwanted encounter, Captain Barrett instructed the entire convoy to set sail immediately for Nova Scotia. The *Prince William Henry,* with the Caribs aboard, was simply abandoned; shortly thereafter it crashed on the reefs and sank. Squier (1855:113), quoting a British naval captain familiar with the Bay Islands, said, "Generally speaking, these harbors are surrounded by reefs of coral. Their channels are narrow and ought never to be attempted by strangers." Several accounts given to me by Garifuna elders suggest that many persons drowned in this mishap.

What fate, then, befell these Black Caribs, exiled from the only homeland they had ever known? A visitor to the area in 1802 predicted, "Their total extinction is . . . near at hand . . ." (McKinnen 1804:51). As we know, this was far from accurate, but the future must have seemed perilous for the survivors at that point. Many were ill, most had lost close relatives and loved ones, they were far from familiar territory, and the supplies left for them were inadequate and in poor condition. The British clearly expected the Caribs to recreate a life-style similar to the one they had left behind, to be based on agriculture, fishing, and mercenary soldiering, plus odd bits of trading and wage labor. An intriguing reference in the British Honduran archives shows that the Belizeans intended to turn the famed military prowess of the Caribs to their own advantage against the Spanish. Not only did the British leave muskets and ammunition behind on Roatan, but military uniforms awaited the Caribs' anticipated arrival in Belize City. Once it was learned that the Caribs had defected to the Spanish, the uniforms were issued instead to slaves commandeered to defend the settlement at Belize (Burdon 1933:248). All the British plans went awry, however, because the Caribs did not colonize Roatan and their military skills were quickly recognized and utilized by Spaniards in Trujillo. How, when, and why did they leave Roatan? This question has been pondered by modern Garifuna as well as by historians and anthropologists.

The Trouble with Roatan

Beauçage (1970:53) has recorded oral traditions from Honduras which assert that the Caribs left Roatan because there were no cohune *(Attalea cohune Mart.)* palm trees there, whose fronds were needed to roof their houses. Here we have an example of oral tradition that is of little help, and it seems a bit odd that the story should have been believed by a serious student of culture. Lack of cohunes seems an unlikely reason for leaving the island on several grounds. First, palm trees of various sorts suitable for roofing undoubtedly grew on the island, since these were mentioned as being common only a few years earlier (Long 1774:333). On Dominica, Hodge (1942) reported that modern Caribs were using thatching of *yatahu (Rhyticocas amara),* which suggests that alternative thatching was either known or easily adopted. Second, housing was not the Caribs' most immediate need. Both English and Spanish accounts mention that those who stayed on the southern shore of Roatan found shelter in the military barracks or other structures already there.[3] Finally, it seems that only a week or two after arrival, three Carib men found their way to Trujillo to petition the Spanish to liberate them from the island (Pérez Brito 1797). Obviously, at least some of the new arrivals were eager to leave at once. Perhaps they thought they might be able to find a way to return to St. Vincent, although they surely understood enough about navigation to know how far away that was. More likely, the political acumen they had achieved over the past few generations suggested that negotiation with these new Europeans might improve their chances of survival. Those captured aboard the *Prince William Henry,* having spent several days in the harbor at Trujillo, may have suggested this move. Indeed, some of them may have landed and observed the presence of other French-speaking blacks in that port. At least two Caribs had accompanied the British ships sent to Trujillo to negotiate an exchange of prisoners (ADM 51/1226, Apr. 14, 1797). In fact, they may have been the "emissaries" to whom Pérez Brito referred.

There is no evidence that the Caribs arrived on the mainland in large numbers until October 1797, when a census was made of them in Trujillo (Dambrine 1797). Oral traditions recorded by me and other ethnographers say that the people arrived on the mainland on rafts. A few may have done so, but the available historical evidence does not confirm the point. In fact, Major Wilson reported that they were busily "clearing land" when the convoy left (WO 1/82, f.719). This could well have been primarily, and was certainly incidentally, intended to secure trees for rafts and/or dugout canoes. The transport of many hundreds of persons, however, would have required more canoes and/or rafts than they could have found or quickly manufactured.[4] Thus, help was sought from the Europeans, with their larger schooners and brigantines. Don José Rossi y Rubí, to whom the Caribs formally surrendered on May 19, 1797, was beseiged by men and women, all of whom wanted to go immediately to the mainland with him. He apparently accommodated some and promised to return soon for the others, although there is no direct evidence that he or anyone else did so until October.

We now know when and how, but why did the Caribs desert an island that literally had been handed to them as their own? Why did they not settle in, planting the seeds and cuttings left for them, fishing, and gradually exploring the possibilities on the mainland for trade and/or work? The answer seems to lie in the nature of the island itself, in the dearth of foodstuffs available to them, and in the international and local political situation in which the Caribs were only a pawn.

There is little agreement, even today, as to the fertility of Roatan's soils, some extolling their virtues, others decrying their sterility. But the southeastern portion of the island, where the Caribs were landed, is today pine-covered, with red, sandy, rather uninviting soil, and it was probably not much different in the later eighteenth century (Squier 1870). The northern side of the island is somewhat better, and it is significant that Rossi y Rubí first landed there, at a place then called the Huerta del Rey (The King's Garden), a name that suggests some planting had already been done there by others. Indeed, there is evidence that a few blacks, former slaves of the British on the mainland, may have settled there in 1786 (Rúbio Sánchez 1975, 3:618–23). A 105-year-old Garifuna woman on Roatan told me in 1984 that her grandmother always said the first Caribs had gone to what is now called Camp Bay (Garifuna: Gombé), although only non-Carib blacks live there now. Today this place can be reached on foot from Port Royal in less than two hours, and it seems possible that some of the first Caribs, in exploring the island, thought this to be a more favorable spot for settlement. They may also have found other black people there.

Water was and is a problem on the southern side of the island, since the few small streams from the hilly interior flow north. In April it is likely that even these streams would have been mere trickles until the rains began again sometime around the middle of September. As I have suggested elsewhere (Gonzalez 1986a), clearing and planting fields sufficient to feed some 1,800 people would have been difficult, even if the people had otherwise been in good health and had viable seeds and cuttings. With insufficient rainfall, a harvest would have been impossible. Major Wilson, in a desperate plea to his superiors, requested that another boatload of supplies be sent from England to sustain the Caribs until they might achieve a harvest (see Table 2.2; see also chapter

Table 2.2 Request for Extra Supplies to be Sent to the Caribs at Roatan, August 21, 1797

Item	Amount	
Flour (¾ lb./person/day)	246,950	lb.
Salt fish (¼ lb./person/day)	91,500	lb.
Salt beef	90	bbl.
Indian corn	40	bbl.
Cassada	80	bundles
Pidgeon pease	20	bundles
Yams	40	bundles
Tobacco	10	bundles
Tobacco	?	
Okra seed	10	bags
Taniers (*Xanthosoma*)	10	bbl.
Plantains	?	
Hooks of different sizes	100,000	
Lines	2,000	
(?) for planting to make lines	30	bundles
Cutlasses	600	
Large saws	10	
Small saws	40	
Adzes	60	
Grindstones	10	
Hatchets	50	
Bill hooks	100	
Muskets	300	
Small iron pots	300	
Ammunition	40,000	rounds
Flints	2	bbl.
Powder	4	bbl.
Coarse linen for women	3,000	yd.
Thin canvas for hammocks	8,000	yd.
Rope and twine	?	
Coarse salt	40	bbl.
Hats	700	
Jackets & trousers	700	
Shirts	700	
Blankets	2,000	

Source: WO 1/799, f.759.

5). He mentioned that many of the "cassada" [*sic*] cuttings had been water-soaked and probably would not germinate (WO 1/799, f.759).

Let us assume, however, that some agriculture would have been possible, especially on the northern side of the island, where today we find the Garifuna town of Punta Gorda, as well as other villages composed of non-Garifuna. Could they have survived until their first harvest? Table 2.1 shows the amounts of foods, tools, and other supplies said to have been shipped and landed by the British for the use of the Caribs. The flour was most likely wheat, but it might have been mixed with barley and rye, since the 1795–96 harvests in England had been unusually poor and near-famine conditions prevailed there. (The price of wheat doubled that year in England, and there were attempts at home to get people to substitute barley, rye, potatoes, and rice for the very scarce wheat, without much success at first [Chambers and Mingay 1984:116–17].) In any case, the amount of flour provided, along with the biscuit, also presumably of wheat, was actually quite generous for the time.

The "farine" was probably cassava meal, an indigenous Carib food, but there were only about six pounds per person. There were nearly ten pounds per person of *tasso* (from Spanish *tasajo*), or dried, jerked meat, in addition to a small amount of fresh beef, and about twenty-three pounds per person of salt fish. To calculate just what these supplies might have meant for the maintenance of the people left on the island, we can compare the quantities with those allowed as seamen's rations at the time. Fresh beef was the primary protein mainstay of the navy, it being customary to carry live animals on board to be butchered as needed. The allowance was from four to seven pounds per man per week, depending on whether salt pork and/or salt fish were also available. Salt fish was of lower status and more generally the food for slaves, although sometimes it was fed to sailors; one-half pound per person per day was considered sufficient. Dundas (1796) mentioned one pound of beef, two pounds of wheat flour, and two pounds of potatoes per man per day as a normal ration. Lewis (1960:404) has stated that naval men in 1808 received the following per week: six pounds of beef and/or pork, seven pounds of biscuit, two pints of pease, one and one-half pints of oatmeal, six ounces of sugar, six ounces of butter, and twelve ounces of cheese.

The supplies landed for the Caribs show the biggest discrepancies between beef loaded and landed, for additional supplies of dressed meat and live bullocks had been boarded at Jamaica. Large quantities of beef were used during the journey to feed the company—especially the sick, since beef was considered highly nourishing; the captain repeatedly noted that he had sent beef to the hospital ships for this purpose. During the journey the original amount of salt fish was reduced by more than half, though a goodly amount remained, perhaps because this was less palatable to the British than beef. Apparently the convoy went off to Nova Scotia with much of what remained of the other supplies, putting the needs of the sick troops ahead of those of the Caribs. In further considering the discrepancies between the amounts of other foods boarded and landed, we must also remember that much food had been used on the journey, which was prolonged beyond expectations by the lengthy stopover in Jamaica and by the seige of Trujillo. Furthermore, on March 20, Captain Barrett had condemned nearly 10,000 pounds of bread, 736 pounds of flour, and 567 pounds of sugar, presumably because they had been waterdamaged (ADM 51/1226, captain's log, H.M.S. *Experiment*), and it is entirely reasonable to assume that other supplies suffered the same fate. Finally, of course, one or both lists may have been in error, either by accident or design.

Using these rough guidelines we can calculate how long the supplies landed would last if there had been 1,800 Caribs (not adjusting for sex or age). The flour would have been enough for about forty days, the beef and salt fish together about twelve to fifteen days, and the biscuits about twenty-four days. The sugar amounted to about a pound per person and the cocoa about one-half pound per person, total. If only the men drank the rum, there would have been about one cup each, hardly enough to help them forget their troubles, much less get drunk.[5]

Although the foods provided were not exactly what the Caribs were accustomed to, they were not faced with immediate starvation, as has sometimes been suggested in the oral traditions (Beauçage 1970; C. Gullick 1976b; Kirby and Martin 1972). Undoubtedly they were able to do some fishing, since hooks and lines were provided and since it appears that they either made or found a few canoes in a fairly short time. It is also clear, however, that they would have been unable to survive until they could obtain a harvest. Probably, they even ate their "seed corn," which might not have germinated anyway. As experienced cultivators, they must have realized, too, that the soils of Roatan, even at the Huerta del Rey, were not comparable to those of St. Vincent. Rúbio Sánchez (1975, 3:622) mentions that the Spanish colonists on Roatan in 1791 found agriculture difficult because of arid conditions and depredations by wild animals. Finally, having arrived on the island during the driest season of the year, they may have suffered from lack of water, and without knowing the time of the onset of rains in this part of the world, they may have despaired and rejected planting altogether.[6]

The Politics of Survival

A still more satisfactory explanation for the Black Caribs' abandonment of Roatan requires consideration of sociopolitical factors, including those at the international or state level as well as those deriving from the recent St. Vincent events. As we have seen in chapter 1, there appears to have been a rudimentary chiefdom type of organization on St. Vincent; and in spite of massive losses through warfare, disease, malnourishment before and after leaving the island, and drowning, the system seems to have survived the deportation. The censuses taken by the Spanish upon the Caribs' arrival in Trujillo list every person by name, sex, age, religious preference, and what we may call "political affiliation" (i.e., membership in a "company" headed by what the Spanish called "captains"). As suggested in the previous chapter, these were apparently the same leaders called "chiefs" by the British on St. Vincent. The Spanish lists name each leader, along with the number of his followers.

Leadership at that time seems to have involved a certain amount of authority to make decisions, although it is also apparent that this authority was not absolute, since several references suggest that the people sometimes rebelled — "murmuring," or more likely shouting down decisions they did not approve (Rossi y Rubí, *Gaceta de Guatemala,* June 26, 1797). Anderson (1983:27) noted that the older Chatoyer's authority derived from his advanced age, which gave him more information than many other members of his group. This reasonable and anthropologically satisfying comment fits better with what we know of such societies than does the notion of a twelve-year-old heir wielding authority merely because of his dead father's position. Still, some respect clearly attached to the kinship unit itself, and filiation, in a society that emphasizes the continuity of life after death and control of the affairs of the living from the afterworld, might have given the son some degree of access to his father's power.

Contrary to what was assumed at the time by the British, and sometimes since then by both Garifuna and Garifuna scholars, there was no single, overall political organization among Caribs on St. Vincent. Hadel (1972:6) has recorded an oral tradition from Belize that there had been two endogamous factions and that they had persisted for 100 years after arriving in Central America; one was supposedly called Asiragena and the other Uriana. Each had its own chief, and they made frequent night raids on each other, taking captives, robbing, and destroying each other's crops. This sounds suspiciously like Yellow versus Black Caribs, each with a paramount chief. The story also coincides with early descriptions of dual organization on other islands inhabited by Island Caribs (Boromé 1966:31).

Even if there had been such a political organization, it seems not to have persisted in Central America. The only hint of a binary division there is in reference to the partisans of the French versus those of the British. It is clear from Spanish accounts that some of the blacks they encountered on Roatan spoke some English and considered themselves to be friendly to the British rather than the French.[7] But even if the people disagreed on "foreign policy," there is no evidence that there were two groups that went so far as to damage each other's lives and livelihood, or that such a division underlay any of the settlement decisions in Central America.

None of my informants in Guatemala or Honduras can explain Hadel's informants' comments, nor do such comments accord with the documentary evidence I have seen. Rather, there seem to have been numerous residentially separate groups headed by hereditary leaders on St. Vincent. In 1796 these chiefs, or "captains," surrendered or were captured, along with their people, at different times and in different places. This organization into smaller groups survived Baliceaux and the deportation and may have been crucial in determining the Black Caribs' eventual Central American mainland settlement patterns. By the time they reached Roatan, however, whatever disagreements or differing loyalties the various groups may have had on St. Vincent seem to have been submerged in favor of a more pan-Carib perspective. The following entry from Rossi y Rubí's diary, made shortly after his encounter with one of the leaders, who was said to have spoken in English, illustrates this point: "I do not command in the name of anyone. I am not English, nor French, nor Spanish, nor do I care to be any of these. I am a Carib, a Carib subordinate to no one. I do not care to be more or to have more than I have" (*Gaceta de Guatemala,* June 26, 1797).[8]

Had the Black Caribs stayed on Roatan, they would have been limited to desultory subsistence agriculture in an inhospitable environment. Breaking into smaller traditional residential groups would not have improved their lot much, for they would have had little to live on, no houses, and no jobs. Other than the strategic location of the island, which made it a valuable prize for any seafaring nation, Roatan was not inherently rich. Yet the British clearly intended that the Caribs defend the island against the Spanish, if necessary. What the Caribs saw of the two European powers on April 25–26, 1797, may have convinced them to throw in their lot (at least momentarily) with the Spanish. When they arrived in Trujillo the *commandante* of that military post noted with surprise and pleasure that most of the men and many of the boys were capable of bearing arms and had some familiarity with their use (Dambrine 1797). They were immediately absorbed into the local militia, thus assuring their peoples' survival over the short run, at least.

As we shall see in the next chapter, the Black Carib alliance with these new Euroamericans, who called themselves "Spaniards," did not prevent them from seeking employment and trading partners with all the various populations on the Caribbean coast of Central America, from Cape Gracias a Díos to Belize City. In fact, within a generation they had made this largely "their" territory, driving the Miskito (Sambos) to the east and eventually threatening the latter's hold in what is now Nicaragua.

The time on Roatan was a temporary and unhappy lull in the Carib journey.

Although some may have stayed behind to found the northern village of Punta Gorda, neither oral tradition, nor documentary history, nor archaeological evidence support that view; rather, it appears that all those who had survived so far ventured to the mainland to seek their fortunes. Oral tradition sometimes suggests that the winds blew their small craft here and there on the crossing to the Central American mainland. Chapter 3 presents alternate explanations for their scattered settlement pattern.

NOTES

1. One of the unsolved mysteries of this saga is whether any non-Carib blacks were deported at the same time. Some of the Spanish accounts of their first encounter with the refugees on Roatan suggest the possibility that a few of the deportees were actually former French slaves. Rossi y Rubí (1797:165) noted that "a good part of the Blacks of Roatan are Frenchmen from St. Vincent and Martinique, made prisoner and taken to Jamaica. The rest are also natives of these islands, but independent—known as Caribs. Among them, then, are true French, others aligned with the British, and some (the majority) who recognize no party or nation. Those who command, in the name of Great Britain, are two Black Carib brothers named 'Jack'." This would be consistent with the occasional reference to the capture and deportation of "Republican Negroes," who were much feared by British authorities and colonists.

2. In this account I have relied on the following documentary sources: for England, see ADM 51/1226 (log of the *Experiment*'s captain); WO 52/2976 (log of the *Experiment*'s master); WO 1/82, ff.654–55; see also the letter from J. Wilson to H. Dundas, July 9, 1797, from Halifax, WO 1/82, f.631. The Spanish records perused include: AGCA A1.6/45366/5365 and AGCA A1.6/45363/5365; see also *Gaceta de Guatemala*, no. 16, May 22, 1797, pp. 117–18; Saenz (1797).

3. Rúbio Sánchez (1975, 3:618–23) has translated documents detailing the presence on Roatan in 1791 of Gallegan and Asturian colonists from Spain who had built barracks and storehouses, as well as houses for themselves.

4. Discussion with Garifuna canoe makers has made it clear that a skilled craftsman, under pressure and with tools and sufficient helpers, can manufacture a seaworthy canoe of perhaps eighteen to twenty feet, sufficient to carry three men, in one week. Naturally, this assumes the availability of suitable trees. Roatan was, at that time, rather heavily forested, so this should not have been a problem. The osnaburgh cloth left by the English (see Table 2.1) would have been perfect for making sails, assuming the Caribs could cut and bind it to masts and booms; however, no scissors, knives, needles, or thread are specifically mentioned among the tools and materials provided. There were a number of hoes, bills, felling axes, cutlases, saws, and adzes, which would have served all their agricultural and house-building purposes. The inclusion of adzes is especially significant, for these are necessary in shaping the interior of a dugout canoe. It is also interesting to note that the modern Garifuna sometimes lash together two or three canoes—dubbed "rafts"—in order to carry larger loads and gain stability. These may have been the same kind of "rafts" some claim were used to transport their ancestors to the mainland.

5. I assume that the twenty-six gallons reported were English gallons, or about twenty-two U.S. gallons, which I have divided by 650, approximately the number of men. Rossi y Rubí's (1797) account intimated that the men who met him were drunk, which suggests that those with greater authority may have reserved the rum for themselves. It is also possible that the Caribs were still suffering from fever and hunger, thus giving them the "wild appearance" he related.

6. Although certainly a possibility, I consider this rather remote. Increasingly, there is evidence of the Caribs having been in contact with other local folk, at least some of whom would have told them about the seasons and what might be expected (Rúbio Sánchez 1975, 3:618). Also, the climatic and vegetative cycles in the western Caribbean are similar to those with which they were familiar, and they probably would have realized what lay ahead.

7. These accounts are somewhat confusing and open to alternative interpretations. Given the fact that some English-speaking blacks had been left on Roatan in 1786, they may have been the ones with whom Rossi y Rubí first spoke on the northern shore; or perhaps these were the people of Gombe (Camp Bay). While it is plain that the British had appointed two brothers, both named Jack, to be in charge on Roatan, most of the Caribs rejected these men as supreme leaders, preferring to follow the captains of their indigenous groupings. The fact that some people had English given names (sometimes combined with French surnames) is also suggestive of an "English faction" among them. When the chips were down, however, it seems that the British did not differentiate between their "friends" and their enemies.

8. This was reported in Spanish, though said to have been delivered in English. I have translated it from the Spanish.

3

Central American Settlement, 1800–1900

Anglo-Hispanic Competition for Hegemony

Upon arrival in Trujillo, the nearly 1,700 Black Caribs were quickly settled. Local opinions vary as to where their first houses were built, but most people believe they were divided between what is now the barrio Rio Negro on the east and the barrio Cristales, near the river of the same name on the western edge of the town. The Garifuna name for the former—Garibalu (Spanish: Caribal; "place where Caribs live")—suggests its primacy. They also were said to have lived on the slopes and crests of the hills behind Trujillo in 1804 (Vallejo 1889:124), so some Caribs must have settled inland, perhaps replicating the patterns described for them on St. Vincent. Settling such a large group must have posed logistical difficulties, since Trujillo had not been so heavily populated in some time. The town was one of the earliest Spanish settlements in Central America, having been founded in 1502, and had been repeatedly sacked by pirates; in fact, the port was officially abandoned after the Dutch demolished it in 1643. Some sort of settlement apparently remained, however, to be mercilessly ravaged again and again—by the English in 1645 and 1688, and by the English and French in 1772. The fort was rebuilt in 1780, but Trujillo remained vulnerable to attack well into the twentieth century.[1]

One source states that the British made their initial appearance in Central America during the time of Henry VIII, trading logwood from Belize in the early sixteenth century (CO 123/1). If so, it took them more than 100 years to regularize their presence, a concession from Spain finally having been granted in 1667 by the Treaty of Utrecht. Meanwhile, Cape Gracias a Dios was settled in 1634 by colonists from Providence Island, and from these two places the British gradually spread to some sixteen other locations in what are now

Nicaragua and Honduras, including a settlement in 1742 at Roatan. Probably the best known and certainly the largest of these settlements was at Black River, or La Criba, as it is sometimes known even today, although its official Spanish name has always been Río Tinto.

Using both slave and free labor, the British planted sugarcane and raised cattle; they also cut wood and collected sarsaparilla, tiger (ocelot [*Felis pardalis*] or jaguar [*Felis onca*]) and deer skins, gums, and other forest products for export to Europe. In the earliest days they initiated a slave trade with the Miskito Indians, who enriched themselves by raiding interior groups and selling the captives to the British. This commerce established a long-standing relationship that benefited both the Miskitos and the British in many ways, though in the long run it proved a dead end for both (Helms 1982; Olien 1983). One of the most important advantages for the British in the seventeenth and eighteenth centuries was in providing a loyal local militia (Long 1774:320). The Miskitos sold forest products to the British, provided them with fish and game, and facilitated their considerable contraband trade with the Spanish creoles in the highlands (Long 1774:319; Newson 1984:74).

As part of their system of indirect rule, the British supplied the Miskitos with arms and ammunition and created a Miskito monarchy patterned somewhat after their own, in which each succeeding hereditary "king" was ceremoniously crowned by the British king's representative, either in Jamaica or in Belize. Subordinate leaders assumed titles such as "governor," "admiral," "general," and, at the local level, "captain." Remnants of this kingship remained until the twentieth century (Olien 1983), and to this day the Miskitos express a nostalgia for "the good old days" of British domination, claiming to prefer English speakers to the Spanish among whom they now live.

With the help of the Miskito, the coastal area of Central America remained in British control for about 150 years, although there was continual harassment by the Spanish. Routed from the Mosquito Shore in 1730 and again in 1754, the British were forced to flee to Roatan in 1763 when the Treaty of Paris was signed in Europe. They returned soon after, however, only to be ignominiously forced out again in 1779 and sent as prisoners to Merida and Havana. The Treaty of Versailles in 1783 was the final blow for them, especially its 1786 sequel, the Convention of London, in which the British Crown sacrificed the Mosquito Shore and the Bay Islands for expanded concessions in Belize and on Gibraltar (Humphreys 1961:6). At that time the Shore settlers were instructed to relocate to Belize, where they were given land for themselves and their slaves. Many refused to leave, however, until the Spanish used force against them in 1787 (CO 123/14). Some then fled to Roatan but were pursued and expelled by Spanish forces, only a small number of their former slaves being allowed to remain (see chapter 1).

When the Caribs arrived in Trujillo in 1797, there were already in the vicinity about 300 French Negroes from Santo Domingo (Houdaille 1954); an unspecified number of "free coloreds," perhaps from Grenada, with some women and children (Cox 1984:80); about 40 "English" blacks (former slaves of the British colonists); and perhaps as many as 700 mestizos and whites (Vallejo 1889). Anguiano referred to 300 English blacks at nearby Campamento, in addition to the French blacks at Trujillo (in Vallejo 1893:127). According to Burdon (1933:217), a group of French had established themselves near Trujillo in 1796, but it is not clear if these were the same blacks described by Houdaille (1954). Some may have been white refugees from San Domingue (now Haiti) or other French colonies who would have brought some slaves with them. Lands were granted to several of these individuals, including at least one marquise, who settled at Punta Quemar, or Quemada (today, Punta Betulia), near Trujillo (Vallejo 1884). Some of the earliest Black Caribs settled there too, possibly to help work his lands (Cáceres 1958:9). Other whites included nearly 500 Spanish colonists from the Canaries, Galicia, and Asturias, brought over in 1787–88 and settled at Roatan, Cape Gracias a Dios, Black River, and Trujillo. A total of 1,298 settlers arrived, although there was heavy mortality among them during the first years and they were not successful in their agricultural endeavors (AGCA A1/17517/2335). Starving and harassed by hostile Miskitos, most of the settlers soon abandoned the area, the survivors flocking to Trujillo, with only a handful remaining at Roatan (Peralta 1898:416).

The influx of Caribs was a godsend in terms of their labor potential, but they soon began to be perceived as a threat to the security of Trujillo and the Shore. They were not only black and foreign but were thought by the Spanish, with some good reason, to be likely to align themselves with the Miskito and the English. In 1804 Ramón Anguiano, the governor of Comayagua, reflected the near panic of some officials when he advised the immediate removal of *all* blacks from the coast of Honduras, before their numbers increased to the point where that would become impossible (Vallejo 1889:124). The Caribs at Trujillo reportedly numbered 4,000, which seems impossible even if we concede a high initial fertility; the figure probably included some or all of the various other blacks in the area. The Spanish were apparently unable to distinguish among these people as individuals, even though they recognized that there were different sociocultural groups present. Their confusion is evidenced not only in the 1804 report but in other ways over the years, even to the present time (see chapter 6).

Governor Anguiano's concern is evidence that the British strategy of dumping rebellious and republican blacks in Spanish territories had, in fact, some of the effect intended. In the long run, however, the black immigration seems to have benefited, rather than endangered, the Spanish position. The governor's recommendation was to return all blacks to the French colonies whence they supposedly had come, or else to the French Republic itself! By 1813, however, Anguiano had modified his stance, clearly revealing his ambivalence toward the newcomers, suggesting that a few be retained at Trujillo but the majority be encouraged to settle in the interior of Honduras or along the various rivers of Mosquitia (Anguiano 1813; Rúbio Sánchez 1975, 2:474–75; Vallejo 1889:124).

Almost from the beginning the Caribs began to make themselves known, building a reputation for intelligence, independence, fierceness, and hard work (see chapter 6). On May 14, 1799, some 100 Caribs, proclaiming their hatred of the British, helped defend Trujillo against two ships of that nation (*Gaceta de Guatemala,* June 18, 1799). By 1802, though perhaps as early as 1799, some Caribs were journeying to Belize to seek work in the British woodworks and to bring back contraband goods for sale in Honduras (Burdon 1933:57, 60). In 1804 some Caribs encountered off Trujillo by officers of the British sloop *Snake Downs* declared their hatred of the Spanish; at about the same time they were complaining to the Spanish that they disliked being sent against the British, who seemed friendly to them (CO 123/17). Instructions were sent from Jamaica to the superintendent at Belize to do all he could to further friendly relations between the Caribs and the Miskitos and to encourage the latter to attack Trujillo to "liberate the Charibs from their present situation" there (Burdon 1933:84).

We do not know exactly what happened next, but in 1807 the Caribs of Trujillo fled that town, joining the Miskitos at Patuca (FO 15/19, no. 33; Clarendon Papers 246(14): 38). In spite of this apparent fulfillment of Governor Anguiano's desire, local Spaniards pursued and brought the Caribs back, though the evidence is that at least some stayed behind or soon returned to settle at various spots along what they today call the Costa Arriba.[2] Clearly, some Caribs had been there earlier, for in 1804 Henderson (1809:134) encountered Caribs between Black River and Caratasca, in the territory of General Robinson, a prominent Miskito leader then living at Black River (Floyd 1967:184).

What was the context within which these events occurred? First of all, the Spanish were extremely fearful, with good reason, that the British would capture permanently the entire coastline and adjoining lowlands of Belize, Guatemala, Honduras, and Nicaragua. The British presence in the Bay and on the Shore,[3] compounded by the large number of slaves and free blacks associated with them, plus their alliance with the Miskitos, was formidable. Even after their settlements were abandoned, British naval superiority allowed them to harass the Spanish coastal settlements and conduct an enormously profitable contraband trade throughout the 1790s.

Concomitantly, the Spanish colonists on the Shore were not prospering. Sorsby (1972) describes the various problems they faced, including inept administration, their lack of preparedness for living in an isolated, difficult environment, and failure to win over the Miskitos. Food shortages were severe; little was produced locally and supplies from Havana were unreliable, insufficient, and expensive (Peralta 1898:239). Finally, disease was a continual and serious threat for Europeans as well as for Indians and mestizos from the highland areas.[4]

The Baymen of Belize, by contrast, lived in constant fear of invasion by Spanish forces from Yucatan and/or Trujillo. Since the wood supply in the northern part of Belize was poor due to overcutting, new stands were sought and often illegally cut farther south in the neighborhood of the Río Dulce and Lake Izabal, well beyond the River Sheboon, which limit had been only recently conceded by the Treaty of Versailles (CO 123/15). The British were aware that these transgressions increased the justification for and thus the risk of Spanish attack, but the woodcutters ignored their government's admonitions. George Arthur, superintendent of the settlement in 1821, wrote to the Earl of Bath: "It is very difficult to convince the Magistrates [all merchants] and the Public of Honduras that they are amenable to any superior authority whatever" (CO 123/30). Certainly, the recent independence of their near neighbors influenced their attitudes, but they had been growing more irascible for years.

After 1807, when England abolished the slave trade, the woodcutters faced a new dilemma. Slaves from the Caribbean area were suspected of being "infected" with revolutionary fervor; "new" ones from Africa were impossible to obtain legally and were therefore very expensive. Belizean slave women were more fertile than those elsewhere, but conditions were still so unfavorable that the slave population could not be sustained through natural means.[5] The Miskitos and other lowland indigenous groups could not be persuaded to work, and highland Indians did not survive long on the coast.[6] The labor shortage was further aggravated by the continual flight of slaves to Spanish territory, where the law permitted them to remain if they came seeking Christian (i.e., Catholic) baptism. Although this had been going on since the sixteenth century, in the late eighteenth and early nineteenth centuries the Spanish used deliberate enticement of slaves to undermine the British presence in Central America.[7] As a result, the Caribs were quickly but clandestinely hired and soon became skilled woodcutters and incomparable smugglers (see chapter 6). Deep River and Stann Creek (now Dangriga) were occupied in 1799 or 1800, probably with their help (CO 123/15, 123/18).

Although the Spanish and British states were repeatedly and nearly continuously at war at the turn of the century, there were brief periods during which they allied themselves in their even greater mutual fear of the French. Between 1806 and 1808 the Spanish Crown aligned itself with Napoleon, a situation that changed again with the latter's invasion of Spain in 1808. This led to a nationalistic opposition to both the foreign invader and to their own monarchy. A new, more democratic constitution was adopted, which dismayed the Royalists, while inspiring those creoles in America who already yearned for independence. In the same year a treaty again united Spain and England, and England renounced her intention of liberating or conquering Spanish America (Rúbio Sánchez 1975, 2:438–39; see also Samayoa Guevara 1965:24).

During the intensely anti-French years between 1803 and 1812, a series of measures was taken in Belize to prevent any blacks thought to have French connections from entering the settlement (Burdon 1933:46, 55, 68, 139, 169; Crowe 1850:204). This included the Black Caribs, who were sometimes specifically cited as being "dangerous." Even though their labor was greatly valued, most of them had French names, spoke that language, and were known to have sided with France during the struggles on St. Vincent. Furthermore, both the Spanish and the English had reason to suspect that the Caribs might not be completely loyal to either of them. Thus, on July 6, 1812, a fine of fifty pounds sterling was set for anyone who hired or employed in Belize any Carib or French or free Spanish blacks (*Honduras Gazette* 2(84), October 17, 1827). Still, in spite of both fears and injunctions, the Spanish Royalists and the Belizean woodcutters apparently went right on hiring Caribs.[8]

After Napoleon's downfall in 1815, the Spanish fear of the French was replaced by their fear of colonial revolts, themselves inspired in part by the French Revolution and assisted by idealistic French adventurers. As the Spanish nation trembled and buckled under Fernando VII, who in 1820 reestablished the old repressive constitution, revolutionary activities in the various Central American provinces increased, and Caribs, along with escaped Belizean slaves, became the mainstay of the Royalist armies.[9] In 1812 Caribs made up the Battalion of Olancho and fought under General Pedro Gutierres in a campaign against insurgents located between Tegucigalpa and Masaya in Honduras. It was noted that the presence of the Caribs struck fear into the hearts of all, including other soldiers fighting for the Royalist cause (Gutierres 1905). In 1819 an all-Carib company, headed by Carib Col. Pedro Gregorio, manned the fort at San Felipe on the Rio Dulce in Guatemala (AGCA B1.14/8526/496). In 1820, when the French mercenary revolutionist Aury attacked Trujillo, it was largely Caribs who defended the town, two of them dying in the effort (Mejia 1983:441–45). Caribs also formed part of the permanent Spanish garrison in Tegucigalpa (S. Gutiérrez 1822) and in Guatemala (García Granados 1952, 1:103).

Having declared their independence from Spain on September 15, 1821, the Central American provinces were annexed to Mexico on January 5, 1822. They soon realized this was probably not to their best advantage, and by 1823 most of them were again in revolt. After many internal power struggles, Manuel José Arce became the first president of the Federation of Central American States in 1825. He was overthrown in 1829 by Francisco Morazán, who shortly afterward was elected president. The latter began a massive program of radical economic and social development, which included banishment of most of the Catholic monastic orders, encouragement of religious freedom and foreign colonization, exploration of an interoceanic canal, fiscal modernization, and sweeping legal reforms.[10]

Throughout Morazán's presidency, which lasted until 1840, Arce and his followers, representing the elite creole classes and the Catholic church, attempted many counterrevolutions, in many of which the Caribs figured prominently as soldiers (García Granados 1952, 1:101-3). Unsophisticated in political philosophy, and like other of the undereducated and less affluent segments of the population, the Caribs were likely to be swayed by factors having little to do with the real or imagined future well-being of the state; in other words, they fought for those who paid them well and regularly. Haefkens (1969:286), who traveled in 1826 noted, "More than once they have proved dangerous for the Republican government." There is, however, another possible reason for their involvement in the counterrevolutions. In spite of the fact that many of the Black Caribs were at least nominally Catholic upon arrival in Trujillo, the church paid little attention to them until 1813, when special missionaries were sent to Trujillo to tend to their souls.[11] Because the church was, for the most part, a conservative force in the Honduran provincial world (Montufar 1970:77), the Caribs may have been moved by ideological as well as monetary values in resisting moves toward independence. Unfortunately, the records are silent on this issue.

In early 1832 a series of incidents occurred that continue to be recounted both in history books and in Garifuna oral tradition, though in somewhat different detail. Three allied revolutionary armies simultaneously attacked the government forces of Francisco Morazán. One army was led by former president Arce in the interior, another by Colonel Vicente Domínguez at Trujillo, and the third by Ramón Guzmán at Omoa. Caribs fought with all three forces,[12] although in Trujillo they were also employed by Morazán, having been recruited by a government agent under false pretenses at Omoa and then transported to the more eastern port. When the Caribs found themselves off Trujillo, facing their fellows, who had helped Domínguez take that town without a shot, they refused to fight, and the government effort to retake the port was momentarily thwarted (FO 15/11). At San Felipe, in the Guatemalan Gulf of Dulce, where Caribs had been in charge of the fort, the revolutionary force quickly took over, leaving the Carib commander and troops as they were. Two hundred *morenos,* at least some of whom must have been Caribs, participated in the capture of Omoa, above which the victors unfurled the Spanish flag, much to the ire of many patriotic creoles, including those opposed to Morazán's government (Montufar 1970:152).

Although much of the populace, and even the British superintendent at

Belize, believed Arce and his sympathizers would win (FO 15/11), Morazán's forces were eventually victorious in all locations, and the rebels were accused of high treason. Fearful for their lives, most of the Caribs residing in Central American territory, especially those in Trujillo, Omoa, Livingston, and San Felipe, fled to Belize, the merchants there having also quietly supported Arce's cause (FO 15/11).[13] In 1834 García Granados (1952, 2:388) found only two or three Carib families in Livingston. Some Caribs remained abroad permanently, joining others already well ensconced at so-called Carib Town (Stann Creek, now Dangriga) and at Punta Gorda. A few also seem to have fled from Trujillo to Mosquitia, a relatively isolated place, where they were safe from irate private citizens as well as government authorities.

Another possible contributing factor to the flight from Trujillo can be found in the work of Victor Cruz Reyes (1986), who notes that cholera was rampant in Honduras in the 1830s. The disease was thought to have entered that territory via Belize in December 1833 and again in 1836 and 1837. *Morenos* were specifically noted as having brought it back to the woodcutting establishments after visiting relatives in Belize during the Christmas holidays. Since the Black Caribs and others who had joined them were the primary labor force in both of those areas, I think it likely that the *morenos* in this case were indeed Caribs. The general populace in the interior was terrorized by the threat of this dreaded malady, and the coastal area was ordered closed by the authorities. Records of the Methodist missionaries in Punta Gorda and Stann Creek confirm both the presence of cholera in those towns and the fact that the Caribs were beset by fear and uncertainty (MMS, box 225). It may be that many fled to Mosquitia simply to avoid the disease. Of course, if they were perceived to have introduced it into Honduras, that would have further contributed to their social isolation.

The Central American government recognized and valued the labor potential of the Caribs, so in spite of the general fear of cholera, several efforts were made in 1836 to get them to return to both Guatemala and Honduras.[14] At that time there were many schemes to encourage European immigration into Central America, and the Caribs were represented as being a ready, willing, and hard-working labor force (British Museum 40510/274; AGCA 8113.2/ 50004/240). They had cleared fields and constructed dwellings for a group of Englishmen known as the Poyais colony, who, after suffering near extinction in Honduras, were moved to the Stann Creek area in 1823 (Douglas 1868–69:39; Hasbrouck 1927). At about the same time, eight Carib families were persuaded to move to San Felipe and Izabal, in the Gulf of Dulce and Lake Izabal areas. Their presence was intended to improve the defense of the historic route to the interior, thus encouraging both commerce and agricultural development (AGCA B10.8/Leg. 79641, Ex. 3483). Following that advice, both the Belgian colony at St. Tomas and the English colony at Abbotsville, on the Polochic River near Lake Izabal, had employed Caribs as servants, carriers, and fieldworkers (Griffith 1965:222; Blondeel Van Cuelebrouk 1846; La Compagnie Belge de Colonisation 1844:158). In 1834 a group of Caribs was sent to settle at the Pacific port of La Union, but they soon fled (Durón 1965:89).

Beauçage (1970:61) has stated that the Black Caribs pretty much established their present settlement area and living pattern by about 1820 or 1830, and William Davidson's (1976, 1979, 1983, 1984) work seems to echo that view (see also Table 3.1). The data accumulated for this study necessitate another conclusion. Not only was the area between Omoa and Trujillo settled after 1850, but many sites elsewhere were occupied in the early days and subsequently abandoned. The Caribs' earlier settlement was more extensive than today but excluded the area between Puerto Cortes and Balfate. Oral tradition, ethnohistorical works, and archaeological surveys all indicate that after arriving at Trujillo the Caribs began almost immediately to seek more attractive settlement sites. Within a year or two they had investigated the possibilities in Belize, and by 1804 they were familiar with the Miskito territory near Black River. But from the very beginning in Trujillo I suspect they rather quickly, perhaps in "companies" headed by different captains/chiefs, dispersed to such nearby places as the Trujillo hills, Río Negro, Cristales, Campamento, Punta Betulia (then Punta de Quemar), and the present villages of Santa Fé, San Antonio, and Guadalupe (see Map 1). These groups probably retained their indigenous social organization and small size, in line with the kind of life to which they had previously been accustomed. Town living, especially in the company of foreigners, would probably have been difficult, or at least uncomfortable, given the nature of Carib religious ceremonies (see chapter 3). Besides, the early emphasis on agricultural pursuits for the women would have made it more expedient to spread themselves out so as to spend less time getting to the fields.

In 1807 there was a significant movement to Mosquitia, followed by the 1832 diaspora described earlier. Before the middle of the nineteenth century the Caribs had established small settlements in many places along the (Honduran) Mosquito Coast. In 1840 they were reported to be living along the coast east of Patuca (Herrera 1911:177). Squier (1855:316) stated, "The Caribs have had a large association with whites. They now occupy the coast from Trujillo to Carataska Lagoon, whence they have gradually expelled the Sambos or Mosquitos. Their towns are all along the coast near the mouths of various rivers." He went on to note that they not only exported considerable quantities of their vegetable and animal produce but that the able-bodied Carib men were principally employed in mahogany works, then extant not only in Belize and around Livingston (Guatemala) but also at Trujillo, the Limas (or Lamas; today, Limon) River and the Roman (today, Aguan) River in Hon-

Table 3.1 Garifuna Settlements in Three Central American Countries

Honduras (present-day)	Honduras (nineteenth century)
Masca[a]	Punta Castilla[b]
Tulián[a]	Punta Quemar
Cieneguita[a]	Barra de Chapagua
Travesía[a]	Barra de Aguán[b]
Baja Mar[a]	Salado Lis-Lis
Saragüina	Balfate
Río Tinto	Campamento[b]
Tornabé[a]	Punta Betulia[b]
San Juán[a]	Dereza[b]
La Enseñada	
Triunfo de la Cruz[a]	**Belize (present-day)**
Nuevo Go (Nevagó?)	
Cayo Venado	
Rosita	Dangriga[a]
Monte Pobre	Silkgrass
Punta Gorda[a]	Hopkins[a]
Corozal[a]	Seine Bight[a]
Sambo Creek[a]	Punta Gorda[a]
Nueva Armenia[a]	Barranco[a]
Río Esteban[a]	Georgetown
Guadalupe[a]	
San Antonio[a]	**Belize (nineteenth century)**
Sante Fé[a]	
Cristales[a]	
Río Negro[a]	Middle River
Barranco Blanco[a]	Commerce Bight
Santa Rosa de Aguán[a]	Redcliff (Barranco)
Limón[a]	
Punta de Piedra[a]	**Guatemala (present-day)**
Cusuna[a]	
Ciriboya[a]	
Iriona Viejo[a]	Quehueche[a]
San José de la Punta[a]	Livingston[a]
Sangrelaya[a]	Río Salado[b]
Cocalito[a]	
Tocomacho[a]	**Guatemala (nineteenth century)**
San Pedro[a]	
Batalla[a]	
Buena Vista[a]	San Gil[b]
Pueblo Nuevo[a]	Baltimore[b]
La Fé[a]	Punta Palma[b]
Plaplaya[a]	Máquina[b]

[a] Denotes sites visited by the author.
[b] Denotes archaeological or historical sites visited by author.

duras (1855:316; see also Squier 1858:238). Methodist missionaries found them well settled at both Stann Creek and Punta Gorda by 1830.

Although William Davidson's analyses (1976, 1979, 1984) of the types of sites they preferred are interesting and useful, they tell us little about the reasons the Caribs had for settling in specific places at certain times. I found oral traditions to be inexact, most informants assuming founding dates much earlier than actual historical or archaeological evidence could confirm. I was also frustrated by the fact that, with one exception, no one could name an ancestor who had been born on St. Vincent. Regardless of the ages of my informants, all lines led back to the first generation born in Central America. One man, aged 107, said that one of his great-grandmothers had come to Central America as a baby. In fact, there were only six nursing infants who arrived with the original group, and they were all males (Pérez Brito 1797).

It is clear that Trujillo was the original Central American dispersal point, which confirms folk attitudes about its importance in Carib history. Once the original "companies" had located themselves, individuals and, according to tradition, sets of brothers, some with their wives, ventured out to Belize and down the Mosquito Coast. Each time there was a flare-up, such as in 1807, larger numbers would join those who had already established a beachhead. One observer noted that whenever the Caribs were annoyed or dissatisfied with something, they would simply pack up their belongings and move (Fowler 1879:52). Some of the refugees would stay on in the new locations, while others returned to the original sites, thus gradually expanding the boundaries of their effective settlement area. I believe the present towns between Trujillo and Plaplaya began as small farming settlements that grew when mahogany cutting and then banana cultivation became important in the area. Several of these sites, such as at Black River and Ciriboya, were once inhabited by the British.

It is clear that Caribs once lived at many places where they are no longer to be found. This is true for the Patuca River area and for Carataska, Brus, and Ibans lagoons, for example, which were frequently mentioned as having Carib settlements by travelers of the mid-nineteenth century. According to local informants, the Lagoon of Guaimoreto near Trujillo was also once dotted with small settlements, only one of which (Barranco Blanco) is still extant. Punta Betulia and Campamento are now deserted. At one time Caribs lived along the outer shore near Punta Castilla, and in the Río Dulce (Livingston) area there were settlements at Punta Palma, Baltimore, Río Salado, Punta Manabique, and San Gil de Buenavista, as well as along the River Quehueche, at Cocoli, and all along the coast up to the present town of Barranco in Belize (see Map 1). These places live on today primarily in folklore, although some locations where rites are performed are sacred to the memory of the ancestors.

A complicating factor is just who should be counted as ancestors of the

Garifuna. At the time of the Black Carib arrival on the Central American coastline, there were numerous black people already there. The Caribs were immediately recognized as being somewhat different from the others, primarily because of their language and their non-Western, "wild" appearance. They were clearly distinguished from the Sambos/Miskitos, even though both were of Amerindian-African stock. Neither were they ever confused with mulattos, or those of African/Spanish/Indian ancestry. A general term, *morenos,* came into use for blacks, usually those whose skin was very dark and showed little or no evidence of mixture. Later *moreno* came to be synonymous with Garifuna, but I believe it was used with far more abandon in the early nineteenth century. Thus, the baptismal records of the Catholic church variously list people as "Morenos," "Caribes," "Caribes Morenos," "Morenos Franceses," and so on; less often one finds "Negros Caribes" or "Caribes Pardos" (but never "Caribes Mulattos"). Of course, since many of these dark-skinned people had only recently been brought to the Shore from the Caribbean, there may have been a tendency to use the term "Caribes" in a more generic sense.

In the majority of baptismal and birth records only the name of the mother is given, and often there is no surname at all; thus the reconstruction of genealogies from these sources is impossible. What is clear, however, is that there was considerable intermixture among all the black peoples at the time, in spite of claims to the contrary both then and now (Kerns 1984). I conclude that the other, less numerous groups with a different ethnic heritage gradually faded into oblivion as their members mated with and became absorbed by the Black Caribs. This hypothesis helps make sense of a number of otherwise inexplicable bits of information. For example, 300 English Blacks were said to be at the site of Campamento, one league from Trujillo, in 1797 (Rúbio Sánchez 1975, 2:412); yet in 1799 the name of one of the black residents there was given as Babiar—a St. Vincent chief (*Gaceta de Guatemala* 3:109). Some Trujillanos today name Campamento as one of the original settlements of the St. Vincent immigrants; yet surely, as its name implies, it was a military encampment—probably the very one from which the black forces retook Trujillo in April 1797.

Church records in Trujillo give the name of the people who lived there in the 1850s as "Morenos" and sometimes "Morenos Caribes." The same is true for the village at the mouth of the Chapagua River near Trujillo, which official records say was first established by "French blacks" but was listed as a Carib settlement by Alvarado (1905:99) and by William Davidson (1984). At the present time the Garifuna of Trujillo say only non-Garifuna blacks live there.

Livingston is commonly said to have been settled by a "Haitian," and in 1860 a French traveler found there an elderly local leader called "Tata Marco" who was apparently conversant in French (Valois 1861:162–76). Other French blacks from Trujillo tried to colonize Roatan in 1829–30 but were repulsed by the British superintendent at Belize. In that encounter, an armed Carib from Trujillo claimed to be the Spanish officer in charge (FO 15/10, f.229). Haefkens (1969:286), in describing the people he called Caribes, said in 1826, "Most are from St. Vincent, with a few refugees from Santo Domingo."

On the island of Roatan there is a non-Garifuna black community known as Camp Bay, yet several older Garifuna told me that Camp Bay was one of the first sites settled by their ancestors—perhaps before Punta Gorda, which some informants say, and archaeological evidence confirms, was founded late in the nineteenth century by people from the mainland. José Rossi y Rubí's original meeting with indigenous people at about that place suggests they were from St. Vincent but perhaps were not Caribs (see chapter 2). Even in the town of Punta Gorda itself there is a dividing line beyond which live those black people who claim not to be Garifuna or descended from Garifuna but who some informants claim "really" are.

Many informants have suggested spontaneously that the people along the coast are completely "scrambled," and when genealogies are sought, numerous non-Garifuna ancestors turn up. Some of these are said to have been Miskito Indians (usually termed Sambos or Waiknas), but others were French, English, and, increasingly, American blacks.[15] There were also whites of English, Spanish, French, and American ancestry, some of whom can be traced by their surnames—although the majority of surnames today seem to have been conferred by godparents or adopted from given names, which in some cases appear to have been passed on for generations.

Analysis of Names

When one is attempting to trace the past of peoples who have no written history of their own, it is necessary to depend upon references to them, often cursory or casual, made by others. The use of names and titles has long been important in denoting status by Westerners, and this practice has now diffused to much of the rest of the world. Throughout history, when Westerners met others with different languages and different ways, they often insisted upon labeling them with names and titles from their own culture, in part because they could not pronounce the indigenous terms and in part because they disvalued or misunderstood the naming system of the people in question. In the records relating to the Caribs, names are sprinkled here and there—letters, censuses, church records, tombstones, and governmental papers of all sorts. I have collected and studied these names to see what they reveal about Carib history. Lasker (1985) utilizes the clustering of names in British locales over time to demonstrate some interesting and important truths concerning population genetics in England, and it was my hope that I could provide similar data of use to geneticists trying to study founder effects upon the current frequencies of inherited characters among the Garifuna (see Crawford 1984). Unfortunately, data of sufficient precision were not available, nor is it likely they ever will be. Still, the presentation of my findings may inspire others to discover meaning where I have not.

For the Island Caribs we have only a very few personal names, and because these appear in myths and songs they may refer only to mythical beings. Among the thousands of Black Caribs on St. Vincent over the half-century during which they were visited and observed by Europeans, only about 35 individuals' names were entered in English records for one reason or another before the deportation. All of these were said to have been chiefs, especially war chiefs, and some of these names appear over and over again in different types of documents. Because the Spaniards took censuses upon the Black Caribs' arrival in Trujillo, we have the given names of more than 200 persons of that time, including men, women, and children.

During the nineteenth and early twentieth centuries, travelers in Central America frequently mentioned names of persons with whom they had come in contact, particularly when the latter served them especially well or when they showed outstanding leadership qualities among their own people. In addition, I have collected surnames up and down the coast for thirty years in the course of my own ethnographic research, something I began doing because the people of Livingston told me that not only could one identify Caribs by their surnames but that certain names "belonged" to specific towns. I was curious as to whether I could ascertain any objective support for their assertion. In fact, as will be shown, I discovered that some names are found in every town and village today, and a few names are so rare as to be found in only one. Most names do show distinct clustering, although these do not always match up with the names of people said to have founded different places. Furthermore, due to the widespread wandering of the men, there may have been more than one center for a given name.[16] Still, I thought it useful to consider names as one means of analyzing settlement patterns during the nineteenth and twentieth centuries.

On the basis of my analysis, a number of generalizations are possible. Before about 1830 the distinction between given names and surnames was meaningless, and most people had only one, which in most cases was not passed on to offspring; however, in the case of the son of a famous chief or captain, he sometimes did take the name of his father. The names of famous historical figures, such as the so-called paramount chief on St. Vincent, Chatoyer, also have been preserved as surnames, although some famous ancestors—often shamans—are remembered only by their nicknames.

The use of nicknames is common, yet it is not clear to what extent this is a continuation of an old practice, for the official censuses list only Christian names (with one or two exceptions). It is likely that those names recited to the census takers were in most cases "formal" names, the people being known to one another by other appellations. Nineteenth-century travelers' records seem to have included more of the latter. For example, one famous individual in the 1860s was known and is still remembered as "Captain Bul"; his formal name is variously recorded as Francisco Beneri (Lamorthe 1958:267), Juan Franco Benedi (Garrido 1964:72), and Bull (Mazier 1869:129). It is likely that the "Bul" so frequently recorded as a surname today originated with this man and that it was indeed his nickname.

After contact with Europeans, formal names tended to be adopted from the politically dominant culture at any given time. Thus, at the time of the deportation, 90 percent of the names were French (see Table 3.2). At the present time, given names are heavily dominated by Spanish in Guatemala and Honduras and by English in Belize. A good sprinkling of English names is to be found in all countries, however, which is perhaps due to recent migration to the United States. The fact that no French names have filtered down to the present is probably due to the extreme reaction against French blacks and French people generally in the early 1800s.[17] The overwhelming majority of all surnames today are Spanish, even in Belize, and most of these were probably adopted early in the nineteenth century, some from godparents and others perhaps from famous Spaniards or Spanish creoles.

Many given names eventually appear as surnames (compare Tables 3.2, 3.3 and 3.4), and I presume these were adopted very early in place of French names and then passed on when it became customary to use two names rather than one. The Caribs of Dominica were reported to use only given names as late as the 1930s, each individual also adopting the given name of his father or her mother as a kind of further marking system (Taylor 1945:521). Such a naming system, of course, was also used by various Europeans, including the early Spanish. Just when and how such systems break down, with a single name being passed down consistently through the generations, is not clear. In the case of the Caribs, very few of the Vincentian chiefs or captains survived the deportation. Some references to them appear in records of the nineteenth century, but their names have disappeared today; these include Babiar, Athelet (Atili), Pascal, Jack, Regis, and Bruno.

One name on the 1797 census, Coisy, is also found among the French blacks who sought land near the Chapagua River early in the nineteenth century (Vallejo 1884). Since this seems to have been a fairly common French given name for blacks at the time, it is not possible to tell whether this was the original Carib immigrant of that name or one of the French Republican exiles already there when the Caribs arrived. In either case, as I suggested earlier, I believe the two groups joined forces and often intermarried.

A few of the chiefs' names survive today as surnames, including David, Chatoyer, Sambula, Duvale, Michel, Mauricio, and perhaps Lalin (from

Table 3.2 Carib Names Recorded on Arrival in Honduras

Captains	Females	Males
Athelet	Reine	Juan Francois
Babiar	Mariezabete	Louis
Bruno	Marijane	Juan Pierre
Charles[a]	Roziete	Jean
David[a]	Marilouise	Bonome
Duran	Francoise	Justin
Duvale	Marguerite	Jean Louis
Etienne[a]	Beludine	Jean Baptiste
Fiolin[a]	Nanon	Jean Charles
Huayba	Zabete	Manace
Jacque (Jack?)[a]	Mariemadelene	Archambos
Jean Joseph	Mariane	Gerome
Jean Pierre	Justine	Alexey
Joseph[a]	Marie Marta	Gabriele
Juan Baptiste[a]	Rozales	Commandant
Luisson	Victoire	Coisy
Manuel	Janis	Sinete
Michel (Miguel?)[a]	Marie	Nonbadis
Nicolas[a]	Lorine	Valantin
Palangure	Suizane	Leron
Pascal	Salnete	Dominique
Petan	Jacline	Joseph
Pierre[a]	Rozete	Dumarie
Pierre Jacque[a]	Nansy	Castete
Regis	Marelene	Aglece
Sambula	Polone	Vinsan
Satulle	Therese	Lamitour
	Engelique	Enrie
	Ariguas	Migos
	Ane	Ducase
	Binas (Venus?)	German
	Colastique	Mathiu
	Jeannete	Satane
	Marisete	Laline
	Jeanelure	Frouques
	Medis	Jean Taris
	Elene	Fertenant
	Mery	Modeste
	Bagube	Baguidy
	Marian	Calin
	Roze	Cartien
	Eriquas	Carbe

Table 3.2 Carib Names Recorded on Arrival in Honduras *(continued)*

Captains	Females	Males
	Charlote	Lucume
	Jane	Caliste
	Jeunis	Rene
	Pelagis	Marelon
	Seleste	Debison
	Nanete	Joisin
		Benois
		Samon
		Bame
		Saridan
		Janos
		Petronis

[a] Recorded as being Catholic
Source: AGCA A3.16/2025/194 (4) Honduras 16 Octubre 1797.

Table 3.3 Garifuna Surnames in Cristales (Trujillo), Honduras, 1982

Alvarez	Arana	Araus
Arriola	Arzú	Avila
Aviles	Balledares	Ballestero
Baltazar	Barrios	Bátiz
Benedit	Bermúdez	Bernárdez
Blanco	Bonilla	Buelto
Bustillo	Caballero	Cacho
Calderón	Cáliz	Casildo
Castrillo	Castro	Colón
Contreras	Chávez	Chamorro
Chavarria	Cuvas	Chimilio
David [a]	Dolmo	Figueroa
Flores	Franzua	Fuentes
García	Gil	González
Gotay	Guity	Gutiérrez
Guzmán	Herrera	Laboriel
Lacayo	Lambert	Leiva
Lino	López	Loredo
Lucas	Marín	Martínez
Martinel	Meléndez	Mena
Miranda	Molina	Montero
Moreira	Norales	Núñez
Oliva	Pérez	Pery
Quioto	Reyes	Rivas

Table 3.3 Garifuna Surnames in Cristales (Trujillo), Honduras, 1982 *(continued)*

Robledo	Ruíz	Sabio
Sacaza	Saldana	Sambolá [a]
Sánchez	Sandoval	Santos
Solano	Solíz	Suazo
Tifre	Urbano	Velázquez
Zapata	Zuñiga	

[a] Names appearing in 1797 census.
Source: Cristales Catholic Church Census.

Table 3.4 Present-day Garifuna Surnames Not Mentioned in Cristales Censuses, 1832–1985

Abaloy	Apolonio	Aquino
Augustine	Barborena	Batiz
Bengochea	Bonifacio	Bul
Bulnes	Castillo	Cayetano
Centeno	Ciego	Clack
Crisanto	Daniels	Dionicio
Eligio	Elington	Ellis
Enriques	Espinosa	Estero
Felix	Fernández	Francisco
Gamboa	Gómez	Green
Gregorio	Guerrero	Guevara
Jiménez	Julián	Lima
Marcial	Mauricio	Mejía
Michel	Miguel	Monroy
Munguia	Neri	Ocampo
Ogáldez	Palacio	Palacios
Pitillo	Quevedo	Ramírez
Ramos	Reyes	Rivas
Roches	Rojas	Rosa
Rodríguez	Rucino	Rufino
Sandoval	Sheppard	Thomas
Torres	Trigueño	Valenzuela
Vargas	Véliz	Vicente
Villafranco	Williams	Zelaya

Lalime). One informant in Santa Fé claimed descent from someone named Guaymá, which may have been the Guayba on the 1797 list. If so, this is the only example of a non-Western name surviving exclusively in oral tradition. My informant, now 100 years old, was unable to trace his exact descent from this individual. However, since the name is not one I have seen preserved in any written document, I can only conclude that his assertion was based on recollection of old stories.[18]

Some of the earliest recorded surnames, a few surviving today, seem to be descriptive and may have been ascribed as nicknames to a particular ancestor in the early days. These include Guerrero (Warrior), Prieto (Dark One), Trigueño (Brunette), Ciego (Blind One), Sabio (Wise One), Mayordomo (Headman), and Nieto (Grandchild). Others are shared with the Miskitos, who also did not use surnames at all until well into the nineteenth century. Early baptismal records for the Miskitos are even more fragmentary and vague than for the Caribs—some children are referred to almost in passing, for example, "Maria, daughter of a dead Samba" (*Libro de Bautizos,* Trujillo, 1832). Surnames shared by the two ethnic groups include Bul, Green, Tifre, and Clak (Clark).

Some of the Spanish surnames common today were probably conferred by godparents when the individual was baptized. This practice continues today, especially in cases where the child has been given the surname of his or her mother only. Surprisingly, perhaps, I see little distinction between practices for men and women in this regard. Because legal marriage is so unusual, even today, and because in the Spanish-speaking countries both the patronymic and the matronymic are in common usage, many individuals freely switch back and forth between their mother's and father's surnames. This is a perpetual problem in the schools, where a teacher's records may give one surname but the child uses another; the same child may, in fact, use one name on one day and the other on another day. Children appear to forget which surname should come first—perhaps because, as with their ancestors, only their first name is important to them at the time.

Some surnames, particularly in Belize and Livingston, are of English or Scottish origin and were probably adopted relatively late from foreign fathers. Some have been Hispanicized, as in Esmit (from Smith), Roches (from Rogers), Guity (perhaps from White), Elinton (from Ellington), and Gutri (from Guthrie). Finally, some surnames appear here and there that I have been unable to identify, including Antimuelos, Bulnes, Maradiaya, Granizao, and Abaloy.

What can we tell of early settlement decisions by an analysis of surnames? I diffidently suggest that Captain David may have taken his company to what is now Santa Fé, because not only is the frequency of that surname very high there and in neighboring communities (including Trujillo) but the river separating that village from its neighbor, San Antonio, is called the David River. Babiar was reported to have lived at Campamento in 1799, but perhaps he was only stationed there as a soldier. Sambolá, whose name is very common today in Honduras and Nicaragua, seems to have journeyed to Mosquitia at an early date; an oral tradition recorded in the 1880s attributes to him the founding of the village of Sangrelaya in 1814 (Cáceres 1958:8). During a trip to the area, Governor Cáceres was told that El Limón (Limón) had been founded by Juán de Diós, followed later by three more Caribs named Juán Bautista, Marcelino Calderón, and Manuel Antonio Barberena; they were said to have settled there by permission of the Miskito king, which suggests the early nineteenth century. Juán de Diós was said to have gone there after "a war in Trujillo with pirates"; and as we have seen, this might refer to any one of a number of occasions, although there was an attack on Trujillo by the English in 1799. Duvalé may have taken his people to the Roman River, founding the settlement there which today is known as Santa Rosa de Aguán. Church records of 1858 show the surname Divalé in that area, but it seems to have disappeared since.[19] Another Sambolá was said to have founded the village of Orinoco in Nicaragua late in the nineteenth century (Carr 1953; Nietschmann 1979).

In conclusion, settlement patterns during the nineteenth century were bound up with a changing ethnic configuration that has today culminated in the establishment of the Garifuna as a distinct ethnic group. As the early immigrants moved from place to place seeking peace and a better way of life, they freely absorbed other people and their culture traits. I see the nineteenth century as a formative period, and when I refer to the Garifuna as a "neoteric" society with shallow roots (Gonzalez 1970a), this is what I have in mind. Naturally, the resulting culture contains elements that can be traced back to the Island Caribs—it would be very strange if it did not. By the same token, it exhibits other traits and patterns that appear to link the Garifuna with West Indian or Miskito or Ladino patterns in Guatemala and Honduras. The Garifuna are what they are—a brand-new (since about 1960) sociocultural entity that is trying to find its place within the complex society of the modern world. They are known as an ethnic group not only in Central America but in New York City, New Orleans, Los Angeles, and London. In the chapters that follow, I will describe, discuss, and analyze the cultural configurations that seem most conspicuous and that the Garifuna themselves believe to be most important in defining their ethnicity.

NOTES

1. Trujillo was occupied by revolutionary forces invading from Nicaragua in 1907, in 1911, and again in 1932 (Vallejo 1975:66–68).

2. Roberts (1827:274) said they first went to the Patuca under the "Mosquito King" and then retreated under General Robinson. He may have been referring to Stephen, sometimes called "King," but actually only regent after the death of his brother George II. There were constant power struggles during this period among three Miskito group-

ings, which were based on ethnic as well as political differences. As early as 1757 Hodgson, an early British settler on the Shore, reported, (CO 123/1), "To all extents and purposes these are one people, yet they are more like three states united, each nearly independent of the others." He characterized one group as being "original Indians," headed by a "Governor"; the middle group as "Sambos," whose leader was "King"; and the most westward as being made up of Indians and Sambos mixed, with a headman called "General."

3. "Bay" was the usual designation for Belize, and "Shore" referred to the settlements in Mosquitia. The settlers themselves were known as "Baymen" and "Shoremen," terms that are still occasionally used in the area, although the former now refers to inhabitants of the Bay Islands.

4. The fort at Omoa, built between 1759 and 1775, had been known as the "cemetery of the Caribbean" (García Peláez 1852 1:121) because of the large number of workers who had died there over the years. African slaves were finally imported by the Spanish king to finish the work, even though he had himself forbidden the bringing of new slaves to America (AGCA A3.29/28130/1749, f.215), and they remained afterward to swell the local population. In fact, black people generally thrived on the coast, probably due to their greater resistance to malaria and yellow fever. The former is related to the presence of the sickle-cell trait and the absence of the Duffy antigen, but there is no known genetic reason to account for the fact that yellow fever tends to be less virulent among blacks (Boles 1983:98).

5. All the evidence shows that the slave population simply did not reproduce itself. Among other factors, there were too few women, and pregnancy was inhibited or terminated early by poor nutrition, too much heavy physical labor, poor prenatal and birthing assistance, and self-induced abortion to avoid bringing a child into the harsh world of slavery. Slave women impregnated by white men, if especially favored, may have had less difficulty, but their offspring were seldom included in the slave category, even though they were legally slaves. Mulattos were considered to have less value as laborers, so their fathers often educated them to the trades—partly out of affection, perhaps, but also to avoid financial loss (Chandler 1972; Clyde 1980).

6. The Spanish would not have knowingly allowed these groups to leave their territory anyway. In 1807 tribute from Indians was the single largest item of income in the Spanish American provinces, constituting 18.8 percent of the total (FO 15/4, "Memoir on Central America," Apr. 1825).

7. Before about 1795, slaves from Belize caught in Spanish territory were sometimes arrested and later released to their masters, providing the latter paid all costs and promised not to punish them with death, mutilation, or perpetual imprisonment (National Archives, dispatch no. 40, from J. O'Reilly, dated Nov. 10, 1827, quoting "Memo Relative to the Desertion of Slaves from Honduras to the Province of Guatemala"). However, a perusal of the archival materials shows that as early as 1700 the British complained to the Spanish authorities that their slaves were being seduced by promises of freedom in the nearby territory. As time went on, the British became more frantic about the continual loss and even accused the United States of encouraging the Spanish in the practice, especially during the hostilities of 1812-13 (FO 15/5, f.343).

8. A reading of documents relating to local governmental affairs of the settlement

during this period shows that the more affluent, and thus influential, merchants and woodcutters generally ignored and sometimes actively opposed the British superintendent appointed by the king and sent from London. In theory the magistrates' council could be overruled by the latter, but the local group was usually able to act with impunity, even in breaking the laws of England. Although not yet officially a colony, but merely a settlement, they were already testing their independence. A thorough reading of Burdon (1933–35) and of the *Honduras Gazette,* of which only six volumes remain (1826–30, 1839), is revealing.

9. AGCA B1.14/8526/496.

10. Morazán's political views and actions still appear to be the single most fascinating subject for Honduran historians. He has been eulogized as a true revolutionary by Marxists (Becerra 1983), though some berate him because they believe he turned traitor to the cause in later years (Díaz Chávez 1965). Even moderates have looked back with respect and admiration on what he tried to do (Montufar 1970; Martínez López 1931). The literature concerning his life and times is immense and often confusing. In English, see Chamberlain (1950) and Griffith (1972, 1977).

11. According to Mariñas (1983:45), Juán Belgines was the first priest assigned to them, but Padre Dominico Frai Juán Vilaginet was the name specified as their first *cura* by the Bishop of Comayagua on January 28, 1813 (AGCA A1.12.1/525/51). The next year three missionaries of the order of San Francisco El Colegio de Cristo Misioneros Apostólicos were sent from Madrid (AGCA B1.14/8492/496). Since the Franciscans were among those expelled from the country by Morazán in 1829, the Caribs may have been influenced against him by their allegiance to these missionaries. However, there had been very little time for the Franciscans to have made such an impression on these people, said to be so difficult to convert. I am inclined to think the Caribs fought against Morazán because they had misjudged the power politics, perhaps because of their experiences in Belize and because of their earlier service under the Spanish Crown. Juán Galindo, writing contemporaneously (1833), commented only that the Caribs had been "seduced" to fight for a lost cause—he does not say by whom.

12. Garifuna oral tradition, at least as recounted to me in Livingston and Trujillo, says they fought for Morazán and had to flee when he was deposed.

13. The Belizean merchants were worried about the disruption of trade and believed Arce's elitist Restoring party would help return things to their normal state. Of course, the Caribs, themselves an integral part of this trading system, would also have been hurt. Ironically, the British consul, recently appointed and himself a merchant in Guatemala, favored Morazán, apparently believing the latter's proforeign sentiments to be more in line with his own and his country's long-range interests. This difference in their views becomes apparent when reading the various dispatches to the British Foreign Office from the two officials during the crucial weeks and months of 1831–32 (FO 15/11).

14. The authorities were so desperate to populate the coast that they freed prisoners from the interior to settle at Livingston (AGCA B119.2/56884/2520/ f.2, 12). They also sent Marcos Monteros, "Jefe Político Comandante de Armas del Distrito de Livingston," to Belize to persuade the Caribs to come back. Some did, arriving on September 13, 1836, following Marcos Sánchez (AGCA B119.2/56992/2521, f.1).

15. Several of my Carib friends who have traveled to the United States have married or lived with American blacks, who have introduced a new sense of black consciousness and pride among them. One man, now close to seventy years old, told me that as a teenager he met a young Alabama woman in a bar in New York who told him he was good-looking and stroked his cheek. He said he had never been spoken to that way before nor thought of himself as anything but ugly. He did not marry her, but he did contract a legal marriage with another black American, which later ended because she was infertile.

16. Genealogical investigation has been frustrating in the extreme. Many people never knew their fathers personally, so information on paternal ancestors was skimpy. In the early part of the nineteenth century birth records often gave only the first name of the mother; this was not merely a function of formal illegitimacy, for fathers' names were sometimes included even when it was clear that the parents were not married. Time depth was shallow, and no informants could tell me about relatives more than four generations removed from them; and most of these people did not know the names of more than one of their great-grandparents (usually their mother's mother's mother). Yet there was a distinct sense of "family," which, as shown in chapter 4, is strongly supported by the religious system.

17. There are two apparent exceptions to this—one is Franzua and the other Laboriel. The first of these probably derives from François, a given name frequently found in the early census lists. Laboriel may have been conferred by a more recent Frenchman on the coast. I have found no reference to this surname in any records, however.

18. This individual also gave me other stories, which he has apparently shared frequently with the many anthropologists and curiosity seekers who have visited his village. Many of his "recollections," like those of some other informants who have achieved something of a reputation for having "historical" knowledge, seem to be based on secondary published materials, usually those of a somewhat popular nature. Others must be classified as pure individual fantasy, sometimes merely to please the listener. The danger of such materials becoming sanctified, as it were, by being incorporated into ethnographies is great. Professionals should know how to sort through such data and interpret them in the larger context. Unfortunately, as interest in surviving traditional peoples is awakened in many countries, there are an increasing number of amateur anthropologists and beginning students venturing into the villages to seek the "truth." They are invariably sent to the same people, who repeat their stories gleefully, embellishing them a bit more each time. It is not clear to me if these individuals consciously mislead their listeners or if they are merely inventing stories because they love having an audience.

19. There is, today, a small store in Santa Fé called Duvalier, but its owners say that the name was chosen in honor of the Haitian leader and they disclaim knowledge of the name as being Garifuna. Those with whom I spoke were unable to elaborate on the reasons for their admiration of the Haitian dictator. It occurs to me that their generation may have forgotten this name existed in their past and that the prominence of the Haitian name in the contemporary news took precedence in their minds. Unfortunately, I was unable to interview older members of the family.

Group of "Yellow Caribs" on St. Vincent, late nineteenth century (Ober 1895).

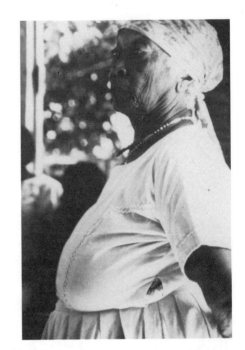

Right: Old Black Carib woman, 1985 (Z. Diaz). *Bottom:* Socialization often depends on the retirees in the absence of parents, 1985.

Top: Miskito women husking rice with mortars and pestles, 1985. *Bottom:* Miskito men drying fish for sale, 1985.

Left: Honduran *buwiye* "blessing" a *cugu* (Z. Diaz). *Bottom:* Preparing food for the *gubida* and guests (Z. Diaz).

Right: Table laden with food for the *gubida* (Z. Diaz). *Bottom:* Drummer holding cock before its sacrifice (Z. Diaz).

Right: Woman dancing in trance.
Bottom: Woman and child in a
hammock after the ceremonial meal.

Top: Dancing the *punta. Left:* "Moorish" queen and her escorts, Trujillo Tira, 1985.

Top: Walagante Dance Group, Los Angeles, California, 1986. *Bottom: Wanaragua,* or John Canoe, Livingston, New Years Day, 1986.

PART TWO

The Cultural Bases of Ethnicity

Social scientists who deal with ethnicity have used various criteria in establishing the boundaries between ethnic groups and in determining just who should be assigned to which group (or groups). Both cultural and social factors may be important, especially when multiple ethnicities are found in a single society or polity. But certain cultural markers seem more important than others —if not universally, at least along the Caribbean coast of Central America. Therefore, I have used religious beliefs, foods, and what I call "work identity" to define the ethnicity of the Island Caribs/Black Caribs/Garifuna. These elements may be seen as having been both cause and effect of the process transforming the culture from one phase to another, but they have also been important in distinguishing all Caribs (of whatever period) from other ethnic groups with whom they claim no affiliation.

4

The Ancestors: Heart of Garifuna Religious Expression

All observers, starting with the French priests Rochefort (1666), Du Tertre (1667–71), and Labat (1970), have been fascinated by the rituals and ceremonies conducted at irregular intervals by Island Caribs, Black Caribs, and Garifuna. The best, or most detailed, of the earliest observations were made by missionaries, and all of them associated the rituals with beliefs concerning death, the afterlife, and the nature of the spirit world. Although the understandable bias of these Christian men is apparent in their writings, and their descriptions are inadequate as ethnographic data, many of their comments do give us clues as to the origins of present-day funeral customs and to understanding the continuing interaction between the living and the dead, which at least today is the most outstanding feature of Garifuna religious life.

Illness, a condition somewhere between life and death, is interpreted by the Garifuna as an affliction that may be caused and/or cured by the intercession of ancestral spirits. Thus, illness relates to religion, and curing is a major purpose and result of the ancestor rituals (M. Cohen 1984). Also related to the sense of well-being is the occasional feast to assure good fishing or harvests, particularly if threats have been made by the ancestors in dreams. The religious complex today contains elements that can be traced to the Amazon, to Europe, to Africa, and perhaps to Central American indigenous cultures as represented by the Miskito.

The Rites of Death

Premonitions of death haunt the elderly and the very sick, and preparations for death are often made in advance, including the construction or purchase of a coffin and burial garments, which may be proudly displayed to interested family and friends. People do not hesitate to talk about their own approaching demise—"They're preparing my passport now," was the way one informant expressed it. Sometimes personal portable property, such as tools, clothing, jewelry, household furnishings, and the like, will be distributed to favorites during the last few weeks or days before death.[1] And where the doomed one has a co-residing "partner," a marriage ceremony may be performed—often only hours before the last rites of the Catholic church.[2] All of this activity prepares the community, as well as the person who is dying, for the inevitable and serves to assuage the grief of those left behind, as well as to ensure that the spirit of the deceased can rest, or cease to "wander."

An untimely or sudden death is viewed with great suspicion and fear, for not only does it suggest that some human or spiritual evil influence has been at work in the community,[3] but that the spirit of the deceased is likely to be restless, returning to bother the living and, in some cases, even taking other lives (Sellers 1969). Much care must be exercised by the community to avoid the machinations of ghosts, and usually only formal rituals performed by the shaman, or *buwiye,*[4] and the family members succeed in placating them. These include, but are not limited to, Catholic masses, which are invariably supplemented by other, family-oriented rituals.

Once death has occurred, the fact will first be known to neighbors by the keening of the womenfolk. It may be further announced about the village by friends who pass from house to house beating drums, calling out the news as they go and inviting people to the wake. This "serenading" *(asederehani)* today may be commissioned and paid for by the family, or it may be omitted altogether. If the death has occurred locally, the body will be washed and dressed by relatives and compadres or comadres, placed in a coffin, and put on view in the best room of the house. The coffin, which rests on a table or bench, is surrounded by candles (two at the head, two at the feet, and one on each side), while glasses of holy water, pictures of saints, flowers and greens, and crepe paper streamers adorn a nearby table, set up as an altar, and the wall area behind it (usually a corner). The body is never left alone prior to burial, which by law in most tropical countries must occur within twenty-four hours, unless the deceased has been embalmed.

If the death occurs at night, the wake begins early the next morning and goes on all day, with burial in the late afternoon. A daytime death results in an all-night wake, with burial early the next morning. During the wake people come and go, prayers are said, and considerable drinking occurs. Sellers (1969) reported the telling of fables, or "Anancy" tales, generally accepted as of African origin. But these are usually not told until the ninth night (described below). *Punta* dancing was formerly one of the salient features of the all-night watch and is still considered mandatory in the more traditional villages of Honduras. Hadel (1972:98) has reported the same for Seine Bight in Belize, and Kerns (1983:154), working in Seine Bight a few years after Hadel, notes that older women made half-hearted and ineffectual protests against such frivolity. But my recent fieldwork in all three Central American countries shows that many of the more acculturated Garifuna believe *punta* dancing to be inappropriate until the ninth-night wake, and some prefer to omit it altogether.[5]

Bread, coffee, and sometimes sweets are served during the wake at noon and/or midnight. Friends and relatives accompany the body to the graveyard at the appropriate hour, stopping at the church or cemetery chapel for Catholic rites. The grave will have been prepared by male relatives or compadres while the body was being washed and dressed. All present watch as the lid is nailed down and the coffin lowered into the pit, and each mourner then throws a handful of dirt onto the coffin before leaving the cemetery. The mourners return to the deceased's house, where tubs of water scented with fragrant leaves are set out so they may wash.[6] Following another ritual snack of coffee and bread, they disperse. The complete seclusion of the closest relatives, mentioned by missionaries in Stann Creek in 1841, is remembered by some older informants but no longer occurs. Black and/or lavender mourning clothes may be worn by the close women relatives, especially in the Honduran towns and villages, but this custom is not always followed by the new generation.

In January 1984 I observed something in a Honduran Garifuna village that I had not previously seen: the funeral cortege was led to the graveyard by a small band consisting of a saxophone, a snare drum, and a cornet. The music, played in minor key, was pure Afroamerican (as opposed to Amerindian) and can only be classified as jazz-blues. McCauley (1981) describes a "lone saxophone" accompanying the body to a burial site in Santa Fé, near Trujillo. Because large numbers of Honduran Garifuna have lived temporarily in New Orleans over the past generation, it seems likely that this is an innovation deriving from their experiences there.

Funerals of the Island Caribs, as described by Rochefort (1666), included wailing, and De Vries (1857:56) mentioned "dancing, singing and drinking," but these generalities do not allow for specific comparisons with present-day customs except, perhaps, in a transformational sense. After nine or ten days the deceased was buried in the floor of the house, in a flexed, seated position. Prior to burial friends and relatives arrived, sometimes from distant places, to observe the corpse, lament the death, and offer food and drink to the spirit. After the burial the house was abandoned. Farabee's (1967a) ethnographic notes on various of the South American Arawaks, as well as the more recent work by Kloos (1971) on the Maroni River Caribs, detail several similarities, including burial inside the house (in the case of the Arawaks) and ninth-night wakes (among modern Caribs).

Today among the Garifuna the corpse is interred in (Catholic) hallowed ground following a wake attended by friends and relatives. Food and drink are consumed by the guests but not offered to the spirit until the first anniversary of death. The house is not abandoned, though some of the dead one's belongings may be destroyed or buried on the beach or in the yard. The ninth-night wake might be considered a symbolic retention of the longer period of mourning before burial that obtained with the Island Caribs, before laws were passed dictating interment within twenty-four hours. Its modern format, however, includes details primarily adopted from Europe.[7]

The Methodist missionaries in early nineteenth-century Belize were interested in recording and stamping out the work of the devil whenever they thought they had come upon it. In the case of the Black Caribs, they were convinced that the evil one was ever-present and thus have provided some invaluable descriptive materials on Garifuna ceremonies. For example, in 1837 the Reverend Greenwood reported the following from Stann Creek: "About a fortnight since near midnight on Saturday there was an assembly of about 50 in a private house, dancing, drinking and drumming, which they intended continuing til the dawn of Sabbath. This festivity was occasioned by the death of a child, whose corpse was decorated in the most gaudy manner, and surrounded with lights. The father was reasoned with upon the impropriety of such conduct. His answer was, 'It was their fashion'. Upon its being insisted that they should discontinue, the father wept, saying his child had not yet reached heaven" (MMS, box 225, no. 7).

In 1841 Rev. Richard Weddell, newly assigned to Stann Creek, noted that he was much affected by the Caribs' deep wailings and lamentations for the dead and that "it surprised me much to see them bring the nearest friends of the deceased to the Creek and washing them whilst others bore the corpse away to the place of interment" (MMS, box 225, no. 51). Afterward, the closest relatives were said to retire into solitude for two or three months. Another missionary, coming by chance upon another wake, rued what he termed the "excesses of riot and drunkenness." "The people (chiefly women) were praying over the dead, and in the house adjoining about forty men were smoking, drinking, and indulging in the most excessive laughter, while one in the centre of the room was making sport for the rest by the most ludicrous gestures." He then noted that the mourners prayed four times during the day and four times during the night, and when he asked if he might pray, not for the dead, but for them, he was surprised to find that his prayer counted for one of the four (MMS, box 225, no. 60).

In 1854 the Rev. Richard Fletcher observed an unusual event at a wake in Stann Creek: "They had the shape of a schooner marked out on the ground and masts driven in, rigged up, with the sails flying in the wind. A number of men running up and down the rigging and scores of people looking on, making a deafening noise. Such was a funeral wake and the person had only been dead for some hours before" (MMS, box 225, 4th folder, no. 13). This is the only description I have found in the literature of death being equated with a trip, and informants in Guatemala and Belize had no recollection of this, although "taking a trip" is today a common euphemism for death. In Trujillo, a *goleta,* or schooner, was occasionally burned at ninth-night wakes until the late 1950s. Friends and relatives brought pieces of wood and placed them on the beach to form the rough outline of the boat, and after masts and sails were added, the whole was set on fire. Bard (1855:68) reported that in the mid-nineteenth century the Miskito buried their dead in canoes. And while there was some Miskito intermarriage with the Garifuna at that time, the activity described by Fletcher and my informant seems quite different from the simple burial seen by Bard. Large canoes with masts are an important symbol in many Garifuna traditions, so it would not be surprising if they once formed part of the burial and/or ninth-night ceremonies.

Some of the missionaries' descriptions of "excesses of riot and drunkenness" fit not only the death watch but the even more important watch held on the ninth night after death, to bid the spirit a final farewell. For this, people come from distant towns, sometimes even from the United States if the deceased was a close relative.[8] The altar, with fresh flowers and leaves, now forms the focus for the event in the same room where the corpse had been laid out. (Foster [1981:3] refers to a model coffin being constructed to drive away the spirit double at the ninth-night wake, but I have never observed this.) Following eight days during which prayers are offered at dawn, dusk, and midnight, the ninth-night wake begins. There is a good deal of drinking, and the general atmosphere is one of merriment and celebration, although paid prayer leaders *(rezadores)* and grief-stricken relatives contribute a solemn note. Small clusters of men play cards on the porch or under a shelter which may have been specially constructed adjoining the house. In the yard, or in another shelter serving also as a kitchen, there is *punta* dancing to the accompaniment of rhythms beaten out on drums, wash tubs, or wooden boxes.[9] As the night wears on, one or more men relate and act out fables (Garifuna: *úruga*) to audiences who never seem to tire of hearing them.

Howland (1981:89), in a semiotic analysis, divides the Garifuna ninth-night wake into five components or sets of activity: (1) quiet talk by the intimate family and very close friends in the inner room of the main house; (2) story-telling in the main room of the house; (3) card playing on the porch of the main house; (4) cooking the food that will be eaten at midnight; and (5) dancing in the yard. She succinctly and, I think, correctly suggests that these are the features that make the wake contrastive with every other Carib event and that tell the ghost a wake is taking place and he or she must now leave this world.

At present along the Central American coastline only the Garifuna maintain the tradition of the ninth-night wake. Many among them, as well as among the general populace, believe the ritual is a survival of Vincentian traditions and of Garifuna origin. All ethnographers, starting with Conzemius (1932:154), have given similar descriptions for Central American Black Carib or Garifuna wakes. There is, however, no description of such wakes having been performed on St. Vincent, nor do the descendants of the Caribs still living on that island and in Dominica perform them. Taylor (1936:465), describing Island Caribs on Dominica, said that ninth-night wakes were the occasion for singing hymns, playing games, or performing ring-dances, the latter being of English origin and bearing no resemblance to *punta* dancing. Ross (1970) mentions candles, flowers, creole songs, storytelling, drinking rum and cocoa, and feasting on pork and cassava bread, but not dancing or card playing, as being typical of wakes among contemporary Caribs in Dominica.

Kloos's (1971:144–47) description of funeral customs among the Maroni River Caribs in Surinam best evokes what I have seen among the Garifuna. People there bring hammocks with them, and some sleep while the majority dance, sing, drink, talk, and play cards. There is much wailing among the close relatives and friends, and the older women lead in the dancing and the singing of songs that express grief and recount the life of the deceased. Kloos does not mention storytelling, however. The clothes and other possessions of the deceased are burned, and mourning begins for the primary relatives. Two additional feasts are held, one on the eighth day after death and another a year later to signal the end of mourning.

Wakes with Garifuna features have been reported for many eighteenth- and nineteenth-century West Indies slave societies, and Beckwith (1929:77) described virtually an identical pattern, including games and dancing, for early twentieth-century Jamaica. Baxter's (1970:211) account does not mention games and dancing, but Lekis (1960:137, 145) does speak of dancing at wakes in contemporary Trinidad and in Jamaica. Of course, similarities to the traditional Irish wake should be obvious to most readers (see note 7). It is clear that the death ritual contains many elements that derive directly from Christianity, including prayers, candles, holy water, and the symbolism of the number three and its multiple, nine. One might speculate that the Caribs adopted the custom from French missionaries on St. Vincent, who had succeeded in baptizing about 10 percent of the people before they were deported in 1797.[10] However, French Catholic funeral ritual seems not to have included several of the features mentioned, particularly the games, storytelling, and dancing. The latter were, however, part of wakes held in Wales, as well as in Scotland and Ireland before 1700, and it is possible that a previously existing local (Celtic) tradition was blended with Roman Catholic elements in the earliest days after the conversion to Christianity in this area (P. Morgan 1983:53–55).

Since there were close connections between Belize and Jamaica, it may be that the Garifuna adopted the whole funeral complex after their arrival in Central America, perhaps from other blacks with whom it is now clear they intermarried (see chapter 3). It is difficult to understand, however, why the Methodist missionaries in Belize did not report the same death rituals among the slave groups, unless they simply did not observe the latter. The missionaries were accused at the time of working primarily with free blacks and mulattoes in the urban areas and with Indians and Caribs elsewhere.

Stories told at modern Garifuna wakes, which might be expected to throw some light on past customs, are sometimes of the trickster, "Anancy," or "Brer Rabbit" type commonly found in Afroamerican cultures, while others are of European origin. Unfortunately, the storytelling tradition itself seems to be declining among the Garifuna, and to date no one has made a comprehensive study of this tradition, nor do we have a systematic collection of the stories themselves.

Ancestor Rites

The Island Caribs were said to believe that after death the spirits might become mischievous, annoying and even bringing harm to the living. To avoid this, the Caribs made spirit offerings of food and drink. Shamans *(buwiyes)* consulted the spirits from time to time on behalf of afflicted people, and the spirits were also helpful to the society at large in predicting the outcome of battles, counteracting sorcery, and exacting revenge on enemies. The spirits might speak through the *buwiyes* or through dolls or puppets made of bones of the dead wrapped in cotton, called *rioches* (Burton 1685:179). Sometimes, too, they would enter into the bodies of women and speak through them.

In this cultural domain, perhaps more than in any other, the question of African influence arises. It must be remembered that by the time of these earliest descriptions, there had already been considerable opportunity for the Caribs to have witnessed the behavior of many of the different blacks who were being brought to the Caribbean islands. Atwood's (1791:261–62) description of slave Christmas rituals in Dominica is suggestive:

> . . . they perform their offerings of victuals on the graves of their deceased relations and friends; a piece of superstition which all negros are addicted to, and which, were they to neglect doing, they firmly believe they would be punished by the spirits of the deceased persons. This offering consists of meat, whole kids, pigs, or fowls, with broth, liquors, and other matters; and is performed in the following manner: a man or woman accustomed to the ceremony, takes of each meat laid in dishes round the grave and pulling some of it in pieces, throws the same on the grave, calling out the name of the dead person as if alive, saying, "Here is a piece of such a thing for you to

eat; why did you leave your father, mother, wife, children and friends? Did
you go away angry with us? When shall we see you again? Make our provisions to grow, and stock to breed; don't let any body do us harm, and we
will give you the same next year;" with the like expressions to everything
they throw on the grave. After which, taking a little of the rum or other
liquors, they sprinkle it thereon, crying out in the same manner, "Here is a
little rum to comfort your heart," . . . and drinking some of it themselves to
the welfare of the deceased, they set up a dismal cry and howling, but
immediately after begin to dance and sing round the grave. The ceremony is
then concluded by every one scrambling for the remainder of the offering
left in the dishes. . . . they all depart to their houses, and continue their
merriment the whole day after.

Such fragmentary accounts present clear parallels to present-day Central
American Garifuna ancestral beliefs and rites. There is a series of ceremonies
that improve the environment for the living by virtue of the fact that they help
the spirits of the dead to achieve peace and contentedness in the next world. In
this sense, they may be seen as part of a continuum that begins with the wakes
held immediately after death and on the ninth night. A mass, followed by food
served at the host family's house, should be held one year after death, a rite
called *fin del año,* or *taguru ludu* in Garifuna, to mark the end of formal
mourning.

Within five years or so, a bathing ceremony *(amuiadahani),* also preceded
by a mass, is performed, at which the spirit of the deceased is offered bread,
coffee, and liquor, a complete set of clean clothing (hung on a clothesline in
the bedroom of the deceased's house), and water for a bath. Whenever possible, as in former times, a hole for the bathwater is dug in the floor of the
house or in kitchen, and as the water, poured in by each of the participants,
sinks into the ground, it indicates the spirit's use of it. Today, since so many of
the houses have cement or tile floors, a large washtub may be used instead.
McCauley (1981) reports that near Trujillo two tubs, one containing saltwater,
are set out to refresh the spirit. Kerns (1983:158–59) describes a somewhat
different set of ritual activities, with the hole dug on the beach rather than
inside the house. Arguments for greater antiquity may be made for each practice, but in the absence of early descriptions it is futile to speculate.

Eventually the spirit becomes hungry for the foods it once enjoyed, and it
lets its living kin know, usually in their dreams, that it wants a *chugu,* or *dugu.*
Taylor (1951:113–31) described such ceremonies in detail, and several other
observers have provided refinements and alternative analyses (M. Cohen 1984;
Foster 1981; Howland 1984; Jenkins 1983; Kerns 1983; McCauley 1981;
Sellers 1969; Wells 1982a). One result of the newer ethnographic work has
been to demonstrate the continuing strength and importance of these rituals,

even in the face of massive acculturation and modernization. It has even been suggested that the augmentation of incomes resulting from migration to New York City and elsewhere has stimulated an increase in the number of such ceremonies held in the home villages (Jenkins 1983). Milton Cohen (1984) says he attended a *dugu* in Honduras, the first in that village in twenty years. This coincides with my own observations; and as I indicate in the Introduction, I believe this increased incidence may also be interpreted as an expression of distress. Such ceremonies require a considerable financial outlay, and since none of the Garifuna of my acquaintance can be considered wealthy, the question remains as to why they choose to spend their money on rituals rather than on a new house, a car, or an air-conditioning system, all of which they have come to value as a result of their migration to the United States.

It is also interesting that the ancestor ceremonies generally require travel back to the home villages. Some say that since the spirits cannot cross water, ceremonies in their honor must be held at home. But it is also noted that spirits of persons who died in the United States or even on St. Vincent or Trinidad have managed to return to their home villages, although some doubt this and feel strongly that the body of one who dies in another place must be returned to the home village for burial.

Part of the *dugu* includes the symbolic invitation *(aduguhati)* to the ancestors by men who go out in canoes and return at dawn, signaling the beginning of the ceremony. At a rite near Livingston, Guatemala, in which I participated in 1984, an archway of palm leaves and crepe paper was set up on the beach to welcome both these messengers and the *gubida,* or ancestral spirits. Obviously, the urban U.S. setting of many Garifuna is simply inappropriate for a ceremony involving canoes, drumming, and singing, which may go on without interruption for three days and two nights. Today, these ceremonies are more generally held for the collective ancestors of a particular household or group of kin (although a *principal* recipient is usually designated) and, as such, serve as a means of reinforcing ethnic identity and kinship obligations among the living.[11] However, it remains difficult to separate the *dugu* from a curing ritual, for many times the decision to hold one is an effort to placate dead relatives who feel neglected by their descendants and consequently bring them misfortunes.

Sometimes the ancestor appears to someone in a dream or the *buwiye,* upon being consulted by the sick person, determines that the illness has a spiritual cause. In the absence of a *buwiye,* other mediums are sometimes able to diagnose and prescribe for illnesses caused by spirit intervention. People come from both Belize and Honduras, as well as the United States, to visit the Casa Blanca *(muna haruti)* in Livingston when their illnesses do not respond to other remedies. The same women who officiate as *rezadoras (aunaguli)* and in whom the spirits come to earth during the ancestor ceremonies are able to conjure the latter for information and advice on illnesses and other matters. In this they make use of induced trance, prayer, pictures and statuettes of saints, candles, "holy" water, alcohol (as libation for the spirits and to anoint the client), and tobacco—the latter being the only element not generally mentioned in descriptions of Latin American and Caribbean spiritualists (Garrison 1982; Goodman, Henney, and Pressel 1974).

A recent case involved a sixty-five-year-old woman whose daughter, living in Los Angeles, California, had pain in her legs and feet such that she was unable to go to work. Doctors had given her no relief. Recently the sick woman sent money to Belize to sponsor a ceremony on behalf of her mother's father and her mother's foster parents, her mother's mother having died at her birth. The *aunuguli* in Livingston determined that the spirit of the "blood" grandmother was jealous of the attention given the others and was unhappy over her own neglect. This spirit's only other child was hopelessly alienated from the Garifuna ancestral complex, so she had never even had a ritual bath. The spiritualist recommended that the latter be performed in Belize as soon as possible.

Once in progress, an ancestral ceremony may also be an occasion for spirits, who join the gathering by possessing one or more of the living participants, to treat the illnesses of guests. The women who harbor the spirits pass their hands over the bodies of the afflicted ones, sprinkle or rub them with rum, and blow gently on their heads, faces, and chests. The spirits also proffer advice, especially to the squirming but respectful teenagers, on how they should live, and they answer specific questions about the welfare of other deceased persons. When I inquired about the spirit of a young man I had known who had been shot while in New York City, I was told that he was "lost." The spirit went on to say that the young man had never been keen on these beliefs and rituals, nor had he sent money to his aged grandmother and other relatives. Interestingly, other Garifuna stated that the young man had probably died as a result of cheating on a drug deal, but this seems not to have contributed to the loss of his soul.

Methodist missionaries in nineteenth-century Belize were horrified by what they termed "devil dances," which they correctly perceived as being intended both to cure illness and to mourn the dead. They were as distressed by Catholic rites as they were by what they thought were indigenous customs, but, interestingly, they seem not to have realized that much of what they saw had Christian overtones, if not Christian origins. Also, they did not always distinguish among wakes and other occasions at which the dead were honored or invoked. Even today the few Garifuna Protestant converts insist that spirit possession and its associated rituals are the work of the devil.

In Belize and Guatemala foreigners' interference and remonstrances seem to have driven many ceremonies into the "bush," whereas formerly they were always held in the center of the village. In 1849, John Armstrong of Carib Town (Stann Creek or Dangriga) wrote, "This place is at present drained of its people who are gone to the Bushes to hold a feast to the devil who is their Sovereign Prince" (MMS, box 225, 3rd folder, no. 6). Herbert Wesley Haime, assigned to Stann Creek in 1850, also saw these rituals as occasions of dealing with the devil: "Even up to this time they worship the Devil under the title of Marfeu. To Marfeu they cause their children to be dedicated, to him they dance and pray in honour of him and to appease his wrath they have their feasts where their god is supposed to preside. Under the influence of drink they become enraged as though possessed and with actions that are frantic they strive to procure the devil's favour beating their heads and injuring their bodies till they fall one by one as though lifeless and thus they rest, satisfied that all is right" (MMS, box 225, 3rd folder, no. 16). This appears to be the first description of spirit possession among the Central American Garifuna, and it is remarkably similar to that of McCauley (1981) for modern Honduras.

Haime gave a more detailed description of such ceremonies in 1852:

I visited a house where preparations were being made for a Marfeu dance. The room [was] about 20 × 24 feet large. Upon the sides of the house were placed sixteen baskets made of wild cane, in each of which were placed calabashes. There were two drums. On the floor was a lot of sand obtained from the burial ground, which one of the natives called his "generation." Over this sand were two pieces of cloth and over all, two pieces of cane matting framing a square of one and a half feet. All this was to stay until next year, being placed thus early to inform Marfeu of their intention to dance to his honor. The calabashes are to hold the liquor.

A few days later, upon being told that a child had been afflicted by the devil, the missionary visited the family. The father said that his child was sick at Trujillo and that the spirits of the family were the cause of it. "Thus, the members of the family were called upon to prepare a feast whereof the dead might eat. Early in the morning the food was placed upon tables. Before two o'clock the dead were allowed to feast and after that the living. The father of the child and indeed the whole company were drunk" (MMS, box 225, 3rd folder, no. 36).

The same Mr. Haime attended another "Marfeu Dance" on May 4, 1853:

I found three men inflamed with drink looking more like demons than rational beings. These had their drums and were with their hand fiercely engaged in knocking out a tune. . . . Surrounding these were three rows of drunken women each holding a rag and a bottle containing liquor as insignia of their office. These women were scuffling to and fro in half circles. At the further end of the room were two sick children in hammocks which ever and anon were violently shaken by the women that waited on them during the dance. I diligently inquired why they held these snips of rags and the bottles in their hands and what it all meant but they would not tell me. At last the jumping stopped. For being very desirous to know, I inquired of the most active drummer but all in vain.

And in another case: "Upon the women scattering [after dancing] I found that they had carefully swept the clay floor, gathering the dirt into a heap. Over this heap they placed two strips of cloth and over that something in the shape of matting forming a square of a foot and a half. Upon further inquiry I found that they imagined that these children were thus afflicted by the devil or Marfeu [Mafuia, Mafia] and that they were thus engaged to . . . obtain cures for the children" (MMS, box 225, 4th folder, no. 3).

As early as 1835 a Belizean Methodist, Reverend Edney, described what he called the Caribs' "Great Triennial Feast," which they offered to their deceased relatives every third year. "They provide nearly everything they are capable of providing," he remarked. "This included fowls and hogs, as many as possible. When all are dressed they place them on tables made especially for the purpose. Then everyone leaves the house and the doors are fastened or locked. This is done that their long departed relatives may come and feast. They want to appease them so as to prevent them inflicting punishment on the living. When the deceased have eaten all they want, they open the doors and the living finish what remains" (MMS, box 134, May 1).

Let us compare these historical accounts with more recent ones. In 1969 Nietschmann attended a curing ceremony among Black Caribs at Orinoco in Nicaragua. The people called the ritual *Walagayo* (Cry of the Rooster), the name of a song describing how the rooster calls to the ancestors as it is about to be sacrificed. Nietschmann reports that during the three days and two nights "the interior of the house was filled with smoke and dancing bodies; arms joined, the dancers circled the room, singing. A pile of dirt that looked like a grave was heaped on the far side of the floor. In the center, the sick man lay in a hammock hung from the ceiling. He was wrapped in a white sheet, wore a bright scarlet sash across his chest, and his hands and feet were tied by strips of red cloth. A woman held a chicken by the feet, cut its throat and held it over a small bowl to collect blood" (1979:3). Nietschmann adds that there were six male drummers who led the dances, while women did most of the singing. The shaman squatted near the head of the sick man, blowing lungfuls of cigar smoke over him. Against one wall stood several tables piled with food and liquor.

Other contemporary accounts follow a similar outline but details vary, showing that modifications have occurred over time and in different places. Sometimes, after the spirits and the living have eaten, the remaining food is thrown into the sea, while at other times it is buried behind the *dabuwiyabe,* or ancestor house, where the ritual is performed. Livingston Garifuna scornfully say that in some places everything is consumed or carried off by the participants instead of being disposed of as the spirits direct. The pile of "dirt" is not taken from the graveyard but is really sand from the beach, where the ancestors are thought to linger. Although children are present and encouraged to come forth to meet and talk with their ancestors, the special "feeding of the children," described by several ethnographers (Coehlo 1955; Taylor 1951), is now more often omitted entirely, some say for hygienic reasons. In the traditional ritual, leftover food was placed on banana leaves on the floor, and the small children rushed in, upon a signal, to devour whatever each could grab.

The number of drums seems to vary from two to six, and the role of the women in what Howland (1984) calls "the choir" *(aunuguli)* is never well spelled out in the accounts I have seen. In my own observations, these women are essential, especially when there is no *buwiye.* They pray, lead the dancing and singing, and, most important, at least in Livingston, predominate among those who go into trance or become "possessed" by the spirits. Possession always occurs, and the success of the ritual is judged in part by how many ancestors "return" and by their behavior when they do. Occasionally a "nonprofessional," sometimes a man, is seized, especially if he or she is the descendant of a once strong *buwiye.* Howland's gloss of *aunuguli* as "choir" seems woefully inadequate in view of the multiple functions of these women.

Drinking is a necessary part of the ritual, but drunkenness, though treated gently, is frowned upon, both on the part of the spirits and the living. Those who are possessed may appear to be drunk, but the moment the spirits leave they become perfectly sober and go about their duties. Kerns (1983) found that most of the *aunuguli* are women middle-aged and older, which generally coincides with my observations. However, in Honduras selected young men and women may be ritually administered alcohol to induce trance (McCauley 1981). In 1985 I observed a fourteen-year-old girl during her first trance experience; she had not imbibed any liquor, so far as I could determine.

Alcohol plays an important role in Garifuna ritual in other ways as well. White rum is thrown out of the doors and windows at the start of the ceremony to attract the spirits, and it is also sprinkled upon the dancers and the drummers, as well as upon and under the drums themselves. It is used to cool and sooth the possessed, to cure those seeking relief from physical and psychological ills, and to anoint the sacred table at the end of the ceremony to determine whether the offerings have been acceptable to the spirits. For the latter, rum is poured in the sign of the cross, then lighted, and the table is tipped from side to side. If the flames leap up properly, all is well; if not, the entire ceremony may have to be repeated—in which case another *buwiye* may be sought.

Dobbin (1983) compares the "Jombee Dance" of Montserrat to similar forms known among various other West Indian societies, including the Garifuna of Belize. A table is set with food for the spirits, most of which is later eaten by the guests. Rum is drunk and used ritually almost as described above, and ecstatic dancing both honors the dead and aids in healing the sick (note the parallels with Atwood [1791]).

By 1985 there had occurred several changes in the ceremonies I first observed in Livingston in 1956, some of which my informants seem not to have noticed or remarked on.[12] First is the current use of a uniform dress code, not only for the chief functionaries and family members, but for guests. The spirit being honored designates (either in a dream or through a possessed person at another ritual) a color or color combination and even a specific textile pattern, such as green and white checks or solid orange. Women then have dresses made of the spirit-selected cloth, in slightly varying styles, at a cost of about Q.8.50 (one quetzal officially equaled U.S. $1 in 1986; Q.3.50 was the minimum daily wage) or Q.7.00 if they make it themselves. Short-sleeved shirts of the same material are worn by the men, and a distinctive neckerchief completes the outfit for both sexes. Guests are not required to wear these clothes, but they show their support and respect by doing so; after the ceremony they may be used for everyday wear.

The *aunuguli* dress uniformly in another color and pattern, which is not distinctive for the particular spirit being honored, but they change into the spirit's preferred costume during the actual feasting. Most of today's ceremonies in Livingston do not include a *buwiye*, but in one *dugu* I witnessed in 1984 in which a *buwiye* participated, he did not wear the traditional red sashes across his chest or red strings on his wrists. In fact, the symbolism of the color red—important both to the Island Caribs and to West Africans—seems lost, at least in Livingston, although Wells (1982c) describes its continuing significance in Belize. In Honduras, as in Belize, special red clothing is worn, but only for the most sacred ceremony of *dugu*. Dresses or shirts of white muslin are stained red with achiote by the close relatives of the honorees. These garments are saved for repeated use at other *dugus* and may be loaned to friends and relatives; they are never worn for any other occasion. Special colors and clothing used in symbolic ways are characteristic of many well known Caribbean rituals, including *Shango* in Trinidad (Lekis 1960:129) and *Vodun* in Haiti (Courlander 1960; Metraux 1959), and are ubiquitous in modern Afroamerican rituals as practiced in New York City (Garrison 1982).

Food and drink provided to the Garifuna spirits and company in modern times include, in addition to the basic cassava bread *(areba)*, cassava wine *(hiu)*, chicken, and pork, every imaginable item from the contemporary diet— fish, rice and beans, plantains, fresh fruits, candies, cakes, soda pop, raisins, cheddar cheese, and more (see chapter 5). Each ancestor is presented with what he or she liked best in life, as well as with new foods highly valued today.

For a full-fledged *dugu,* a special cook may be engaged, who brings in as many assistants as necessary.

The food tables are not kept behind closed doors to allow the spirits access, as they were previously. Rather, candles are placed at each end of the tables, they are prayed and sung over, and then (in Livingston) the women who are possessed by ancestral spirits eat on the latters' behalf, served and watched over by loving relatives of the honorees. When they have finished, a portion of food is buried or flung into the sea for those spirits who chose not to enter the feast hall or who have been doomed to wander on the beaches. Only then are the remains distributed to the guests. To call this a "Thanksgiving" feast (Macklin 1976) does credit neither to the Garifuna ceremony nor to the American harvest celebration of the same name. Still, English-speaking Garifuna increasingly use this term to explain themselves to outsiders.

The Catholic church no longer forbids its members to participate in a *dugu,* as was once the case throughout the area;[13] but contemporary church policy is to discourage what several priests described in 1984–85 as a "waste" of foodstuffs. Unfortunately, from the Garifuna perspective it is precisely the element of sacrifice that gives meaning to the whole system; so, for them, a rite cannot be effective unless a certain amount of food is set aside for the *gubida.*

Believers, Nonbelievers, and the Specialization of Labor

A full-fledged *dugu* today is inevitably attended by Garifuna from many places, who return from foreign cities where one might expect that ancestor rites from a distant time and place would have been forgotten. In fact, those Garifuna who reject the concept of the *gubida* tend more often to be of the generation now approaching their last years of life. Many of the more widely traveled Garifuna of the past fifty years, especially those who were in more or less constant contact with American or English employers, are openly skeptical, if not contemptuous, of the whole ritual complex. The particular brand of Christianity practiced seems not to be a determining factor, for even some of the few Protestant converts may secretly attend or sponsor ancestor rites, in spite of the heavy Catholic overlay in the rituals.

Education per se also does not seem to be correlated with belief or disbelief, for even some Garifuna with university degrees from the United States profess respect for the mysticism involved and faithfully attend rites when they can. In one instance, I sat all afternoon in New York City listening to a *buwiye* and a medical doctor—both originally from Belize—exchange views on symptoms and curing methods. Each was granted an area of expertise that the other could not match, and they reached agreement on the idea that they should refer to each other the patients they could not cure.

Locally educated Belizean Garifuna, by contrast, have insinuated that the

entire complex has today become "big business." This view was also vocifer-
ously expressed by a *buwiye* in Trujillo in 1985, who thought Livingston and
Belizean Garifuna had lost the essential holiness of the ritual in their efforts to
outdo each other in the amount of money spent. Indeed, there has been a
proliferation of new expenses, as anthropologists have recently discovered and
reported (e.g., Jenkins 1983; Kerns 1983). The specialization of labor, for
example, now entails the hiring of cooks, musicians, and caretakers, not to
mention the cadre of women whose role it is to become possessed and relay
messages from the spirits to the living. The fact that today these same women
may also be those who diagnose illnesses and prescribe the rituals seems suspicious to some Garifuna. There is some concern as well that there are relatively
few *buwiyes* anymore, and more and more of the ritual is left in the hands of
the newer specialists. Trujillo has four *buwiyes* at the present time, but they
must also service nearby towns and even travel to the remote villages in Mosquitia. There is a famous woman *buwiye* in Dangriga, Belize, and a young
protégé of hers in Masca, Honduras. Two *buwiyes* living in New York City on
occasion return to conduct ceremonies in Central America.

Becoming a *buwiye* is a long and arduous process, and it is believed that
there is a supernatural, hereditary factor involved, so that not just anyone can
aspire to the role. Traditionally, a child born with placental material over its
face (a caul), or one who shows unusual sensitivities or awareness when very
young will be watched and discussed as a possible future *buwiye*. If he or she
is the descendant of an illustrious *buwiye,* the expectation will be even stronger.
Later, if and when such an individual has a bout of stubborn illness, it will be
said that the spirits are calling their own and that if the designee does not
accept his or her fate, death will result. The required knowledge is generally
said to be acquired over a period of years, often through a series of visions or
dreams. In fact, a young or new aspirant usually has some tutelage from the
buwiye who has diagnosed the problem and suggested that the cure is to give
in to the spirits. Then the neophyte begins to "work," and if people find comfort
and their ancestors express satisfaction with the rituals dedicated to them, the
new *buwiye* begins to earn a reputation.

Not everyone who sponsors a *dugu* can afford the expense of retaining a
buwiye, especially when it involves bringing in that person from elsewhere. In
Livingston, most rituals today are conducted by the *aunuguli,* whose special
skills are widely sought and much appreciated, though they are not so "holy"
as the *buwiyes*. It is generally accepted that not everyone is equally susceptible
to spirit possession, but the necessary behavior can be learned if one has the
personality traits required. McCauley (1981) seems to doubt the genuineness
of these trances; however, though some individuals may be able to fake their
performances, for the most part I believe a state of altered consciousness is
achieved. One close friend confided to me that she stayed away from these

ceremonies after having been seized as a young woman. The experience frightened her so much she did not want to repeat it. She described a feeling of powerlessness over her bodily movements but was aware of and remembered clearly all that happened during her trance.

Because no tests of the trance state are practiced, it is certainly possible or even probable that some of the behavior associated with possession is in fact calculated and conscious. But even when it is, the performance is so carefully orchestrated, the behavior so consistent with that expected of the particular spirit on the basis of his or her remembered personality during life, the words spoken so appropriate, not to mention all-knowing and wise, that one cannot help but admire the artistry even if one might not bow before a supernatural presence. Few "mistakes" are made, and these can usually be explained in some fashion. Those who attend *want* to believe that their recently deceased loved ones have returned, and it is a thrill when they "appear." People laugh, cry, dance, hug and kiss, and generally behave as they would at a family reunion. And when they receive advice, blessings, and sometimes become cured of aches, pains, and other troubles, it is hard not to believe. The pretense of belief is, therefore, always there, even for those who might be skeptical. No one at a *dugu* suggests that not all is as it seems. In a sense, it does not really matter, and the fact that the *aunuguli* are able to carry it all off with aplomb and skill makes their fees seem very small.

It is tempting to compare family behavior at a *dugu* with everyday behavior. Most observers of Garifuna life recognize that there is considerable hostility among family members. Not only are marriage bonds brittle, but siblings seem bound together primarily by common ties to their mother and/or father, with ties to the mother being by far the stronger. Once the dominant parent or parents are dead, siblings may have little to do with each other. In my earlier work I was convinced that the mother-child bond was a difficult, if not impossible, one to break. More recent observations show that even if this was once generally true, it no longer holds. In the case of one family well known to me, the mother has completely lost track of three of her four grown sons. They do not send her money or letters, and they never return to visit, even for family ancestral rites.[14] I am told that this state of affairs is not unusual.

As noted earlier, parents often threaten their grown children, not only with disinheritance, but with abuse and ill fortune from the hereafter (once they have achieved that place and power). Babies are cuddled, showered with kisses, and indulged when they cry, but not for long. Toddlers may be shunted off to grandparents, aunts, older sisters, or more distant relatives, and their favored position is lost as soon as a tiny new rival makes an appearance. I have observed a crying two-year-old, frightened by having had his feet pecked by chickens, ignored for fifteen minutes by his mother, who was only a few feet away. By the age of eight or ten, the Garifuna child is expected to work, to obey, and to repress most childish fears and/or happy fantasies. Chances are that after the age of about two years, children will be moved from household to household until the day arrives when they move off on their own. Although this encourages "individualism" and "adaptability," these characteristics might instead be interpreted and labeled as "selfishness" and "fickleness" on the parents' part. (Chapter 7 describes and explores this theme further.)

No wonder, then, that the *dugu* is a popular retreat, even though the ancestors may be stern in their warnings about poor behavior and sometimes reject the offerings and the ceremony in its totality. On the whole, however, ancestors are pleased, and when they "return" there is great happiness and even elation among the living. Indeed, times remembered may be even better than they actually were, especially in a society in which close relatives bicker and spend much of their lives separated from each other. The *dugu* is a family feast in the truest sense of the word, better than a feast where only the living appear, for it is the dead who create the sense that something special, intimate, and wondrous is taking place. The rite is the tie that binds; for the moment, all the relatives are united and working together for a common cause. There is no other Garifuna occasion that accomplishes this.

As suggested in the Introduction, the recent increase in Garifuna ancestor rites throughout the Central American area, as well as the apparent revival of interest among those who have migrated to New York and other foreign cities, might be interpreted as a sign of increased distress and inability to cope with the demands of a harsh exterior world. Of course, some Garifuna acculturate very quickly and have blended imperceptibly into the American black or immigrant West Indian populations in New York City, but the large majority are still on the fringes of poverty, even after reaching what they have long thought was the Promised Land. Under these circumstances, a return to or an intensified interest in religion should not be surprising. And when the religion of choice also unites them with loved ones in ways they may never have experienced before, it is bound to exert a powerful attraction. After communion with both the living and the dead, one can perhaps better face the uncertainties and disappointments of a cold and hostile world. The symbolism of food as a life-giving force even after death, and the importance of ritual food sharing among the living, are discussed further in the next chapter.

NOTES

1. In spite of this apparent acceptance of the inevitable, there is a reluctance to make written wills in regard to real estate, including houses, house lots, and agricultural lands. This results in tensions, anxieties, and often open disputes among siblings both before and immediately after the death of parents who have owned property. Every family has tales, which sometimes persist for two or more generations, about how wily

and opportunistic individuals have succeeded in bilking coheirs out of their rightful shares. There is also the fear that if "vexed," the elders will sell their own excess property, thus having nothing to leave to their children. Grown children are reluctant to press their elders to make wills or even verbal declarations about their desires for fear of precipitating such sales through their appearing to be greedy or guilty of wishing to hasten deaths.

2. In Livingston the local priest told me that since the Catholic church has discouraged the concept of "last rites," he is frequently called upon to administer to the merely ill. But, he says, when the sheets on the bed are clean and the house filled with elderly crying women, he knows that death is presumed imminent.

3. The fear of magic and sorcery is strong. Today, in Guatemala, the latter is almost always referred to as *obeah* (see Gonzalez 1970a) and as such is nearly identical with that widely reported for the Afrocaribbean. In Honduras, the term *obeah* is hardly known, but it is accepted that certain acts by living people, as well as by spirits, may bring misfortunes on others. Early accounts of Island Caribs in St. Vincent in the seventeenth century describe similar beliefs and practices. Rochefort (1666, 2:283) observed, "when any one dies, his Friends and Relations are wont to consult the Sorcerer how he came to his death; if the Sorcerer answers, that such or such a one was the cause of it, they will never rest till they have dispatch'd him whom the [sorcerer] hath nam'd to them."

4. Foster (1981) renders *buwiye* as "priestess." Although these leaders may be either male or female, I encounter more who are male. The word "shaman," besides being gender-neutral, seems to me to represent better than "priest" or "priestess" what the *buwiye* actually is. The curing aspect, in particular, is characteristic of the shaman role as generally used in anthropology. "Priest" implies a quite different relationship between the people and the supernatural.

5. Because the *punta* dance is so common at wakes, Beauçage and Samson (1964) and Hadel (1972:100) assume it to be religious in nature. Its similarity to secular dances from elsewhere in the Afrocaribbean, as well as the fact that the people disclaim any sense of sacredness, lead me to reject that interpretation. In Livingston the *punta* dance occurs on any occasion and has become a popular diversion among tourists. Taylor (1951:100) noted its erotic nature and linked its popularity at wakes with the fact that the Black Caribs "look upon this rite as a sort of farewell party to the spiritdouble of the deceased." My interpretation agrees with his.

6. The Island Caribs removed the "scent of death" from themselves by washing with certain roots prepared by the shamans. Today the leaves of the sour orange are used, and the practice is not thought to have spiritual significance. The people now say they do this to remove the dirt from their fingers after they have placed a handful of soil into the grave.

7. Irish settlers were established in the eastern Caribbean, especially on Montserrat, by the middle of the seventeenth century and were prominent among the British of St. Vincent in the eighteenth century (Pares 1956:202). Messenger (1973:54) claims there were more than 20,000 Irish in the Lesser Antilles by 1643. During the eighteenth century the British troops in the Caribbean were largely made up of recruits from Africa or from Ireland, and Irish "adventurers" often found their way to both Jamaica and the Bay of Honduras, where they took wives from among the native Indian,

Zambo, and mulatto populations (Lloyd 1954:165). It is not unthinkable, then, that Irish funeral customs should have been observed and sometimes imitated.

8. Perhaps because so many people live and work elsewhere, and because the rhythms of life are now more governed by the employed person's workweek, most "ninth-night" rituals are actually held on a convenient Saturday and may be delayed as long as a month after death to allow absentees to make travel plans. The timing also allows the participants to either rest or travel on the following day before returning to their homes and/or work sites.

9. Several ethnographers have stated that drums are never used at wakes (Hadel 1972:100; Howland 1981; Sellers 1969; Taylor 1951), but I have frequently observed them, though at other times tubs or boxes, and sometimes only clapping hands, are used as rhythmic aids. Upon questioning, some elders say the occasion is too sad to use drums but indicate that the younger people prefer them. Others simply shrug and say that not everyone owns a set of drums and in their absence anything will do. In contrast, drums are essential for the ancestor rites, and the drummers are paid for their services and the use of their instruments.

10. The Spanish made lists of those people they transferred from Roatan; and in addition to name and age they recorded whether the person was "Catholic" or "Carib." Although it can be argued that these people were not actually practicing Catholics, they were certainly counted as converts by the church, and it seems unlikely that they would have accepted baptism without having been exposed to some of the church's teachings. Other references to their pre-deportation Catholicism include: Authentic Papers (1773:42); W. Young (1764:9); and Coke (1793:267).

11. Foster (1982) has criticized an earlier article in which I stressed the importance of these rituals in the latter regard (Gonzalez 1959b). His contempt for what he calls my "conclusions deriving from an alien mode of production" does not alter my view that these rituals do bring together kin who may not have interacted for some time and that they educate the children concerning their own ancestry on both sides. Obviously, rituals can and should be analyzed from several different perspectives, and I do not consider Foster's interpretation to be in conflict with mine in that respect. Although I laud his sympathetic approach to the sacred nature of the *dugu,* I fault his procrustean analysis, which conveys a certainty of symmetry and order my observations do not confirm.

12. What the Garifuna are willing to reveal to outsiders depends on how long and how well they know the observer. The process of revelation continues in my own case, and I have discovered things after twenty-eight years that I had not been permitted to witness before. In part this is related to my status as a female elder (see Kerns 1983) and in part to the fact that I have been around the Garifuna long enough to know people who have become *gubida.* When the latter call upon someone by name, as has happened to me, this induces a respect and acceptance among the living that even the most skillful outsider could not contrive.

In 1984 I was called upon by a spirit to participate in a ceremony as a member of her immediate family. This required my active participation in ways never permitted during observations over the preceding quarter-century. As a dancer and hostess I became one of the dispensers of liquor and learned by experience the informal rules by which the drummers, singers, and guests are to be served. I witnessed disputes among family members and representatives of the spirits over how much money should be paid to the latter. I also was instructed on how to serve food to the spirits and learned that some of the latter actually arrive at the ceremonial house the night before to guard against theft of the food and liquor stored there. They demand that the women in whose bodies they reside for the night be paid for their services — an unexpected innovation for which the host family in this case was unprepared and which they disputed (to no avail).

Naturally, the fact that I have been specifically addressed by a spirit also places a considerable financial obligation upon me, which skeptics are quick to note. But in this I was treated no differently than more affluent relatives, who are also likely to be beseeched directly by the *gubida*.

13. In 1866 Caribs in Mosquitia complained bitterly that the Catholic Mission ". . . les quitó sus fiestas de mafia con que aplacar la cólera de sus muertos [had stopped the rituals by which they appeased the anger of the dead ones]" (Alvarado 1905:99). The Caribs have repeatedly been evangelized by Catholic missionaries, most of whom have despaired of ever really eliminating the indigenous religion. Nevertheless, today probably more than 90 percent of the Caribs consider themselves Catholic, and most see no conflict between that and the rites described here. The Caribs were first visited by French Jesuits on St. Vincent, then by Franciscans in Trujillo, and also by the famous missionary Padre Subirana in Mosquitia in the 1850s. Neither Catholics nor Protestants have ever been able to eliminate the *dugu*, but Catholic ritual eventually modified it, as I have tried to show.

14. Theoretically, these people should be drawn back by the spirits, even though they are out of contact with their living relatives. There are numerous "prodigal son" stories, in which long-lost persons return to their natal villages without announcement after having dreamed of a grandmother or other dead relative, often on the eve of a *dugu*.

5

Foods and Their Acquisition

Diet

"You are what you eat" is not only a nutritional or physiological maxim. Dietary patterns are usually considered of fundamental importance in defining and promoting ethnic identity and solidarity, and favorite foods are perhaps more capable of evoking ethnic nostalgia than any other single item. The Garifuna diet today is more varied and no doubt less nutritious than that of their Island Carib ancestors, yet, it bears an unmistakable resemblance to the former while also reflecting the various exotic cultural influences experienced over the past 400 years.

Where and when did the Garifuna adopt what they today consider to be "their" cuisine? What items, if any, distinguish them from others and mark them as a people apart? Is diet really the important ethnic marker assumed by both social science professionals and laypeople? Garifuna food habits have received some attention from scholars in relation to sickness (Gonzalez 1963) and to patterns of protein-energy malnutrition among children (Jenkins 1980). Staiano (1981) uses a semiotic approach in analyzing food taboos, and Palacio (1983, 1984), taking a completely different tack, discusses the relationship between food and personal interactions in a Belizean Garifuna village.

The emphasis in this chapter will be on the role of food in creating, preserving, and transmitting notions of ethnic solidarity.[1] For this purpose, it is important to consider the use of foods in three contexts: secular celebrations, everyday nourishment, and religious ritual. It is almost impossible to discuss these as discrete categories, for all three are closely related, both practically and conceptually. It is my contention that the Garifuna are likely to borrow exotic food items first for secular celebrations such as birthdays, graduations, club meetings, and so on. These foods become known to them in their non-Garifuna associations, either at home or abroad; tamales, mortadela sausage, cheddar cheese, and Kool-Aid are examples of fairly recent acquisitions. Then, after having been consumed at celebrations, such foods may be served at home on special occasions when finances permit. Finally, after their deaths, individuals will be offered their once-favorite foods at the ancestor feasts, thus completing the process by which these foods become ritual components.

Food as an offering to deities or supernatural beings is common in many religions, and the rituals involved come to be associated closely with ethnicity. Anthropologists have long considered that the older and more basic the food is to a particular culture, the more likely it will be to figure in ritual, folklore, and myth. Among the Garifuna this is not always the case. In chapter 4 I discuss how the Garifuna *dugu* utilizes foods in both symbolic and practical ways to reinforce ethnic solidarity (see also Jenkins 1983), but the majority of these foods are relatively recent additions to the Garifuna cuisine. The following description is taken from field notes written in 1985 in Trujillo, Honduras.

At 11 the drumming was suspended and the tables began to be prepared. Banana leaves went down first, then 10 × 10 inch pieces of *areba* (cassava bread) were laid all over the tables. The food prepared by the host family was brought in and large pieces of meat were placed on each piece of *areba*. There was a pig's head, cut in half lengthwise, pigs' feet, heart and liver; also three whole chickens, mounds of *hudutu baruru* (pounded plantain), tamales, *atol de arroz* (sweetened rice beverage) in small plastic cups, sweet potato pudding, *tableta* (coconut ginger candy), and coconut bread. Over these went other (mostly plastic or paper) plates of food brought by relatives and guests. Each of these held a single portion of several foods, as if serving a meal. A typical plate would include fish or meat (sometimes egg), with rice or a rice and bean mixture, boiled green bananas, fried plantain, a slice of tomato or shredded cabbage. Several layers of these plates accumulated. On top, placed helter skelter wherever there was room, were fruits and candies, the whole now rising some twenty-four inches above the table top.

The offerings described in my notes are included in Table 5.1, arranged in categories following Palacio's (1983:153) analysis and with the probable period of each item's adoption noted. Today, any one of these foods may be found daily on ordinary Garifuna dining tables; seasonal availability and household finances determine the selection and variety offered. At certain times of the year avocados, breadfruit, oranges, grapefruit, melons, pineapple, turtle eggs, and other items may make their appearance. Turtle, manatee, and forest game, such as agouti *(Dasyprocta* agouti; Spanish: *tepesquintle),* are rarer but much appreciated when available. Processed items are clearly modern, but many of the others, even the staples, were not found in Island Carib cuisine. Palacio

Table 5.1 Modern Ceremonial Foods, Classified by Time of Probable Adoption

	Prehistoric	Sixteenth century	Nineteenth century	Twentieth century
Uwi	fish iguana crab fish roe	chicken eggs pork	lobster white cheese	bologna
Breadkind	*areba* *malanga* cassava gruel sweet potato pudding sweet manioc		plantains tamales green bananas rice and beans banana fritters tomato slices rice gruel	spaghetti white bread cabbage
Sweets		mangoes watermelon	coconut candy cashew fruit	cookies hard candy
Beverages	*hiu*		rum coconut water	Kool-Aid Coca-Cola orange pop beer

(1983:153) states that bleached white flour, rice, and fish are the important everyday staples in the Belizean village in which he worked, followed by green bananas and plantains, especially when boiled and pounded with coconut milk—a creation known as *hudut* ("it has been pounded"). My observations for Guatemala and Belize show the situation to be the same there, although manioc or cassava *(Manihot esculenta Crantz)* is more important in Honduras, being eaten boiled as a vegetable when the "bitter" hydrocyanic acid is at a low level. The use of these varieties (often termed "sweet" in the anthropological literature), as well as other roots such as *yautia* (also known as *tania* or *malanga [Xanthosoma sagittafolium]*) and sweet potatoes *(Ipomoea batatus)*, reflects national or regional rather than merely ethnic preferences, however.[2]

Fish (including shellfish) and cassava were the basic staples of the early Island Carib/Arawak peoples and of their Island Carib descendants. Both items figure prominently in Carib creation myths (M. Gullick 1980) and are described by all the early observers. According to Sturtevant (1961:70–71), early Caribbean peoples grew maize, but it was less important than manioc or cassava and sweet potatoes. He also points out that the yam *(Dioscorea)* is often mistakenly thought to have been found in America by the early explorers. Possibly it was confused with what Hodge (1942:192) listed as a native wild yam *(Rajania cordata)* among foods eaten by Dominican Caribs in the 1940s. Watts (1985) also lists *canna* as having been among the culinary roots of the Arawak/Carib peoples. Early chroniclers mention many of these roots, as well as hot peppers (capsicum), peanuts, beans, and what Rochefort (1666:294–95) called "pulses" or "pease," among which he listed "small millet." The indigenous pineapple was said to be a favorite fruit and was cultivated along with guavas, guanabana (soursop), mamey, and papaya. The last, like oranges, grapefruits, citrons, figs, bananas, and plantains, was not indigenous but apparently diffused from the Mediterranean via Spaniards at an early date.[3] Cacao, indigenous to Mexico or Central America, was important as a trade item with the Europeans, but it is not clear whether it was grown pre-historically in the West Indies. The coconut, today a very important flavoring and the principal source of oil, is not mentioned, apparently because it had not yet diffused to the area. Interestingly, it is also ignored by Palacio (1983), even though present-day cookery would be almost impossible without it (M. Lewis 1975). The early accounts also mention wild honey and groundnuts, or peanuts.

Grime (1979:19–26) lists the following as having been brought to North America (and/or the Caribbean) by slaves: okra, akee *(Blighia sapida Konig),* pigeon peas, marihuana, senna *(Cassia italica),* yams, broadbeans, sorghum, and plantains. Bananas and/or plantains seem to have been introduced so early that many of the first accounts assume they were native to the area (Grime 1979:149; Smole 1976:218). All but akee and senna are known, though not necessarily cultivated, by contemporary Garifuna in Central America. Mangoes, sugarcane, and coffee should also be listed as imports that were adopted at an early date, as well as arrowroot *(Maranta arundinacea),* for which St. Vincent is today known commercially.

Fowl and pigs had been adopted in St. Vincent at least by the middle of the seventeenth century. Spaniards left the latter on many of the islands to breed in the wild and serve as an emergency food source in the event of shipwrecks (Watts 1985:2). Interestingly, both chickens and pigs are today indispensable to the Garifuna ancestor rites, being sacrificial animals, but there is no clear evidence as to when they were first used as such or, for that matter, as food. It is difficult to assume anything other than African influence in this regard.

Before the introduction of domesticated animals, hunting and fishing provided the needed animal protein. It is not clear from the historical sources (see chapter 1) how important hunting was for either the Island Carib or the Black Carib in St. Vincent, although lizards, agouti, and birds are mentioned by many chroniclers as having been common prey. Elizabeth Wing (1968:104) found significant quantities of bones of opossum, agouti, iguana, and the rice rat *(Megalomys)* on St. Lucia and Grenada. Land crabs were widely dispersed on the islands, other shellfish were caught just offshore, and fishing occurred on both rivers and in the sea. Her findings from St. Lucia, Barbados, and

Grenada suggest that the diet varied from island to island and was strongly influenced by the microenvironment. Thus, land animals, supplemented by sea turtles and reef fishes, were most important on Grenada, while reef fishes and sea turtles were more common on Barbados. Wing found the greatest diversity on St. Lucia, where the early Carib/Arawak peoples were equally dependent on land vertebrates (especially rats), sea turtles, and reef and pelagic (deepwater) fishes. This rich diversity provided the protein that made the manioc-based diet not only well balanced but capable of supporting a relatively dense population (cf. chapter 1). Several investigators have suggested that around A.D. 1000 the land crab *(Gecarcinus lateralis)* declined in importance due to overexploitation and/or increasing aridity, leading to a pan-Caribbean shift to coastal and marine foods (Goodwin 1980:59; Jones 1980:264; Wing and Scudder 1980:245). Unfortunately, too little work has been done on St. Vincent itself, the rivers of which may have made its environment superior to that of other islands.[4]

The diet on St. Vincent in 1797 was not transferred intact to Central America. Since the people departed with very little, it is useful to consider what the British themselves and those dependent upon their largesse were eating at the time. Food scarcities were rife in Britain because of poor harvests in 1795 and 1796 (Chambers and Mingay 1984:264). Barley and rye, as well as potatoes, were being urged upon both the more affluent and the poorer families. Still, every effort was made to provide an adequate diet for British military and naval forces, since it was increasingly recognized that mortality and desertion rates could be partially controlled by providing a liberal food ration and a judicious allotment of liquor. A 1796 document (Dundas) lists good amounts of beef, wheat, potatoes, and beer as daily rations. A more varied diet was recommended in 1808, including pork, peas, oatmeal, sugar, butter, and cheese, in addition to the items mentioned previously (M.A. Lewis 1960:404). This was certainly comparable to—in fact better than—the diet of the working and farming people in England at the time.

It is also interesting to consider what foods the British provided to slaves, who like soldiers and sailors were of low social status yet had to be kept reasonably healthy due to their economic importance. In 1816 male slaves in Belize were said to receive five pounds of pork per man per week, as well as yams, plantains, rice, flour, and salt (CO 123/25). Mrs. A.C. Carmichael's (1833, 1:183) description of the diet of slaves on the eve of emancipation is also illustrative and more detailed. Babies were fed sweetened arrowroot, flour, or oatmeal pap from the age of two weeks, while adults ate salt fish, salt pork, pigs' feet, souse, fowl, turtle, jackfish, plantains (roasted, fried, or pounded), boiled or roasted sweet cassava, pigeon peas stewed with peppers and herbs, and "biscuit." Of course, this account was written more than a generation after the Carib deportation by a woman who, for the most part, romanticized, though she did not fully condone, the slave system. Still, the foods listed probably represented what was customarily available in the islands, even though the everyday slave diet was probably not so plentiful as the description suggests.

The list of provisions sent along with the St. Vincent outcasts is remarkably similar to Mrs. Carmichael's, and the diet of present-day Garifuna, especially in Belize, is drawn from an almost identical inventory (Palacio 1983). The fact that the British and their slaves occupied both areas is certainly not coincidental. Although the Garifuna dry fish for sale and eat it when necessary, they far prefer fresh fish and will go out of their way to obtain the latter, either in the marketplace or through their own efforts. The only time I ever observed salt pork being prepared or consumed was in the house of an "English" black from Roatan who was living with a Garifuna woman.

The foods missing from Mrs. Carmichael's description are bitter manioc, or "cassada," as the English called it, and coconut. Since the latter is used almost exclusively for its oil or for added flavor or texture, it is sometimes not thought of as a food.[5] But in any case, the general adoption of coconut in the islands seems to have occurred at least 250 years after Columbus. Taylor (1949:383) reported that Père Breton saw only two coconut trees on all of Dominica. Bitter manioc, which requires laborious processing, was apparently not a favorite food among most of the already overworked Caribbean slaves.[6] Its American origin also meant that it was unfamiliar to Africans in the earliest days, although it was later introduced to that continent and today is a staple in some areas. Sweet manioc, which requires only peeling and boiling, may have been more popular, but it is not mentioned by Mrs. Carmichael nor by others of the earlier travelers.

The lists of supplies sent to Roatan (see Tables 2.1–2.2) give an idea of how Europeans in the Caribbean perceived of the diet of the native peoples and perhaps how they influenced it. Most of the items were foreign to the area, including processed foods such as "biscuit." Yet the notion of bread leavened with soda or baking powder seems not to have been common among the Caribs at the time. Today, those who remember stories about the deaths of hundreds of their ancestors on board the British ships often mention "flour poisoned with lime," which they claim was fed to the people on the way over.[7] Today, wheat biscuits, tortillas, and pancakes with baking powder or soda, as well as coconut bread made with refined wheat flour and yeast, are considered "typical" Garifuna foods and figure prominently in everyday meals. Informants believe their own people have always made them.

The inclusion in the Roatan cargo of "cassada," maize, sweet potatoes, yams, and peppers for planting, as well as graters and iron griddles, suggests that some thought had gone into providing the Caribs with what they were accustomed to eating. Of the staples, only peanuts, said to have been important to the Island Caribs, were omitted; today peanuts are eaten occasionally as a snack food. It is curious, however, that other items were included that may have been part of the Garifuna diet at that time but are seldom, if ever, eaten today—for example, guinea corn (sorghum) and jerked meat (probably beef), called "tasso" (Spanish: *tasajo*) by the eighteenth-century British. Yet there was no mention of rice, beans, or plantains, which are the staff of life today throughout Central America. Perhaps it was thought these were easily procured in Central America. Rice is not mentioned for St. Vincent at all, so it may have become a staple only after 1797. It was never a common item of the British diet, although it was fed to their West Indian slaves, as documented by Mrs. Carmichael and others. Of course, rice was eaten by the Spanish from the beginning of their sojourn in the New World, so the Black Caribs might well have adopted it from them after arriving in Honduras. Maize is used to some extent today, but it is not considered a staple. Sweet potatoes and yams are still common, and okra, pidgeon peas, and peppers were still grown in Livingston kitchen gardens in the 1950s, though they are less popular today as these gardens have been abandoned. Hot peppers are no longer a highly desired condiment, the famous pepper pot of the Island Caribs having been replaced by "boil-up" (Garifuna: *falmou*), a still delicious but now comparatively bland concoction of fish, tubers, and coconut milk. *Cassirepe,* the boiled juice of bitter cassava, an essential ingredient of the pepper pot, is now rarely made.

The supplies left with the Caribs on Roatan included sugar and cocoa but in amounts that seem minute by today's demands (see Mintz 1984). Although cocoa is still enjoyed on special occasions, coffee and various "bush teas" are more common. A good deal of sugar is used to sweeten these beverages, as well as the cassava starch pap given to babies and invalids, and sugar is also added in large quantities to gruels, or *atoles*—probably adopted from the Spanish and Central American Indian cultures, although something similar may well have been eaten by the Island Caribs, since gruels are also common in the Amazon today (Dole 1978). The Garifuna prefer to make these foods and beverages with manioc or rice starch, while maize remains the favorite with their contemporary neighbors.

The Garifuna sweet tooth is also accommodated by various cakes or "puddings" made of sweet potatoes, rice, or leftover bread. *Tableta* is made by boiling grated fresh coconut, ginger root, and brown sugar until they hold together; the mixture is poured into a greased pan and cooled, then cut into squares (or pieces may be broken off). The product is much sought after by tourists, who buy it directly from the cook or her small children, who hawk it near bus stops, boat landings, and even in the streets of Tegucigalpa. The identical candy is still made in Jamaica (Cassidy 1961:200).

Finally, potatoes, which were a staple item for British sailors, were not provided to the Caribs either as food or as seed, perhaps because they do not grow well in lowland tropical soils. Potatoes fed to the navy undoubtedly were supplied from Ireland, whence came many of the soldiers and sailors as well. The Irish "provision trade," as it was called, was largely supported during the eighteenth century by the needs of the British West Indies colonies and the military. Before the War of Independence in the United States, large amounts of foodstuffs were also imported into the Indies from the "northern colonies" (Liverpool Papers 1778–79, F.8).

Public health officials and anthropologists of functionalist persuasions have sometimes assumed that dietary preferences change slowly and with great difficulty. The present study suggests that this is far from true, even though it cannot be denied that foods become important symbols of ethnicity and that individual preferences based on the customs by which one has been raised may be psychologically very important in establishing and maintaining a sense of security and well-being. But as we have seen, most of today's favorite foods among the Garifuna were unknown to the people encountered by Columbus, though these foods are shared with other modern Caribbean peoples, most of whom are descendants of slaves. For example, *hudut* (pounded plantain) is known as *fufu* in Jamaica (Cassidy and Le Page 1967:191) and is found today throughout the West Indies as well as in parts of Africa.

The prehistoric islanders of the Caribbean, whose penchant for fruits was commented upon by Rochefort (1666), did not have several of today's greatest favorites—the mango, the papaya, and the watermelon. The banana, perhaps even more common than plantains today, may have become popular in Central America only at the beginning of the twentieth century, when thousands of rejects were available for carting away in every port in which the fruit companies operated. Bananas are usually boiled and eaten as a starchy vegetable accompaniment at meals rather than as a sweet snack, as most fruits are consumed. Indeed, ripe bananas are seldom to be found in Garifuna households, even though children love them.

In addition to the dietary changes brought about by the deportation and contacts with Europeans, we must also examine the impact on the Garifuna diet of the early English slave culture and the association with the Miskitos in Central America. As we have seen, the foods eaten by slaves and the list of items sent with the Black Caribs on their deportation show striking similarities. Further adoptions undoubtedly occurred as the Black Caribs encountered the slave culture again in Belize. Little food was grown in that territory, by uneasy agreement with the Spanish, who suffered the British a foothold on condition that they only cut wood and not establish a permanent settlement. Thus, most food was imported, which meant flour, salt pork and beef, butter, oatmeal, and various legumes. A new Carib dependence upon wheat flour, ubiquitous in the British colonies, was almost certainly developed after 1797. Today, Garifuna in Belize, in contrast to those in Guatemala and Honduras, are fond of dishes such as pickled pig's tail and English baking-powder scones ("biscuits," in American English, which have national rather than merely ethnic significance in that country.

There are no native African staples in the Garifuna diet today, but the same can be said for the entire Caribbean area. Sorghum, native to Africa and still widespread and basic in many African cultures, is grown in some parts of Honduras but not by the Garifuna. Even among the people who do cultivate this grain, it is definitely not a favorite food and tends to be considered of low status, fit only for animals or for people in extreme need (De Walt and De Walt 1984). Typical African preparations, many involving fermentation, for example, are unknown in Central America. And even in many parts of Africa, the more affluent, especially urban, populations prefer (white) wheat bread to unleavened breads of sorghum. Cassava, maize, rice, and wheat—none of which are indigenous to the African continent—have become ubiquitous today among black peoples on both sides of the Atlantic.

The parallels between the foodways of the contemporary Miskitos and the Garifuna, owing to their long if uneasy association, their proximity, and their sharing of a similar natural and social environment, is especially notable. For instance, the green banana, like the plantain, is also important in the diet of these Indians, perhaps due to the large quantities of rejected fruit available from the fruit companies, as mentioned earlier. Both also make use of manioc, but the Miskitos do not manufacture *areba*—they merely boil the sweet variety, much as do other Hondurans and Nicaraguans. The Miskitos share with the Garifuna a fondness for fish, but it is the perception of both groups that the Miskitos eat far more meat than the Garifuna do, especially wild game and turtle.[8] Coconut milk or cream is important in both cultures as flavoring and to give body to soups and sauces. Since the coconut had likely reached Central America before the conquest, but was unknown in the Caribbean until after Europeans introduced it there, it is possible that the earliest Black Carib immigrants to Central America adopted the coconut from their Miskito neighbors. The Miskitos, like the Garifuna and the creole of Belize, are fond of stews combining fish, coconut milk, plantains, green bananas, manioc, and other root crops, but they call the dish "rundown" rather than "boil-up" (Nietschmann 1979:37).

Both the Miskitos and the Garifuna ferment fruits such as pineapple to make a mildly alcoholic beverage, but according to Cassidy (1961:204), a sweet fermented banana or plantain beverage, flavored with ginger, is common in Jamaica as well. During the Christmas season the Garifuna produce a pungent wine from the *Rosa de Jamaica,* known in English as sorrel, or Rose of China *(Hibiscus rosa-sinensis L.)* Both groups chew starches to start the fermentation process for wines or beer, a trait ubiquitous among Amerindian populations in the tropics but falling into disfavor now as new hygienic rules are learned. The Miskitos seem more fond of fermented foods, converting many fruits and vegetables to this state, sometimes wrapping the roasted, mashed item in leaves and burying it until it has soured (Conzemius 1932:97). As among the Garifuna (see Table 5.1), green bananas and plantains may be boiled, mashed, and formed into tamales or small cakes that are wrapped in leaves and steamed, boiled, or roasted. In all of this it is difficult to know the direction of the diffusion of these foodways. Because our information from early St. Vincent is so scanty, it is tempting to assume that the Garifuna learned much of their cuisine from the Miskitos. But it is significant that in spite of the fact that the two groups share so many foods and dishes, the overall configuration is quite different, suggesting the importance of food *patterns,* by contrast to the mere presence or absence of certain items, in denoting or assessing ethnic differentiation.

The Garifuna diet will no doubt continue to change as new foods become available or as some items become difficult to obtain. It will be interesting to observe the future of the most salient Garifuna food symbol of all, *areba.* The basic technology for making bitter manioc *(Manihot esculenta Crantz)* into unleavened flatbread has not changed, though recently there have been improvements in grating and baking techniques introduced by development agents. As the men who make the traditional basketry implements for compressing and sifting the manioc pulp die, and as the art disappears, substitutes will probably be adopted, as they have been elsewhere.[9] Throughout the Caribbean manioc grated on perforated tin slabs has long been squeezed through ordinary white cloth by non-Garifuna peoples, and today it is made in factories for sale both locally and in the United States. But nowhere else outside of parts of lowland South America does it have the ritual and ethnic meaning with which the Garifuna endow it.

In this connection, it is important to discuss what appears to be a pattern reversal among the Garifuna and to assess what that means in relation to culture change, diet, and ritual. Few of the women in the larger towns where Garifuna live still know how to make *areba,* and it has consequently become both scarce and expensive. In Livingston it is now primarily a ritual food, used only at ancestor rites and on a few other special occasions. Ironically, Palacio (1984:20–22), himself a Garifuna, devotes considerable attention to its manufacture yet does not even list it among the foods commonly eaten in 1983. Hadel (1972:44) says that women in Seine Bight (Belize) made it only occasionally when he was there in the late 1960s.

In Honduras, by contrast, *areba* manufacture has been stimulated by the recent introduction of improved clay ovens with waist-high built-in griddles about three feet in diameter—the appropriate size for making *areba.* In some towns a gasoline-driven grater has been introduced, which reduces from three to two days the time needed to make a batch of the bread and saves many woman-hours of heavy labor. Although the machine I saw was temporarily in disrepair, it was said that it could grate 100 pounds of manioc roots in fifteen minutes at a cost of one lempira (U.S.$0.50). It would ordinarily take two or three women working together for three or four hours to accomplish the same work by hand.

A large potential market may exist for this special food item among the Garifuna who now inhabit towns and cities in Central America. Older women who have the skill enjoy considerable status, as noted by Palacio (1984:22). Those who adopt the new technology and succeed in turning a good profit will be emulated by younger women who might not otherwise have cared to engage in this work.[10] Some rue the fact that the reduction in the amount of labor required will alter the cooperative relationships so well described by Palacio (1984), making the manufacture of *areba* an individual specialty enterprise. But the camaraderie of cassava making would have been doomed anyway, along with the entire traditional technology. It remains to be seen whether *areba* processing will continue to be associated with manioc cultivation as before, or whether farming itself will become a distinct occupation. My observations and interviews in the area lead me to believe that the latter will occur and that most of the farmers will be non-Garifuna.

Food Production

Agriculture in the form of shifting cultivation has long been part of the Carib/ Arawak way of life. Like most other tropical forest peoples, and in contrast to the Antillean Arawak groups, the men cleared the plots and the women did most of the rest of the work, including harvesting and transporting the produce back home. In addition to providing for their own subsistence, the Island Caribs and Black Caribs marketed some of their produce. In about the middle of the eighteenth century, cash crops began to be planted in St. Vincent, and men became more involved in the production process, some even acquiring slaves to work in the fields (chapter 1). Tobacco, coffee, cotton, cacao, and silkgrass[11] were mentioned as items traded to the French at Martinique (Miller 1976:69). William Young (1971:99) noted that Carib women brought poultry, fruit, and cassava bread to market in Kingstown, and a painting by Brunius in Harvard University's Peabody Museum West Indies Collection shows a "French mulatress purchasing fruit from a Negro wench" in St. Vincent in the late eighteenth century. A handwritten note attributed to F. W. Putnam, former curator of the museum, identifies the "Negro" as a Black Carib (Peabody Museum File 975-5; 30/9416, A–D). Miller (1979:76) notes that the Caribs also kept cattle, sheep, and goats.

The skills acquired in this aspect of their economic system served the Caribs well upon their arrival in Central America. After the difficult months on Roatan, they were welcomed at Trujillo, where for many years food supplies had been so scarce that provisions had to be imported from Havana (*Gaceta de Guatemala* 1802:292, 309).[12] There was even some consideration given as late as 1803 to bringing slaves from that port to produce food. But the Black Caribs almost immediately produced a marketable surplus (Anguiano 1813; Rúbio Sánchez 1975, 2:474–75). Their triumph was certainly due in part to the predominance among their cultivars of manioc and other tubers, as well as unspecified "vegetables."[13] These root crops, especially manioc, grew well even in the shallow, acidic tropical soils found on the Honduran coastline. Indeed, manioc will grow within meters of the sea in what appears to be pure beach sand. Furthermore, these crops required relatively little labor and were largely managed by women, so that the men were free to take wage-paying jobs or to otherwise occupy their time and energies. In addition to whatever remunerative work they could find, most of the men also fished. Within a few years of their arrival in Trujillo, an article in the *Gaceta de Guatemala* (October 8, 1804) reported that 114 pounds of turtle (shell? meat?) had been exported from Trujillo from the "fishery established by the Caribs."

Another, possibly crucial factor also must be considered. In 1803 the Spanish authorities in Guatemala decided to distribute lands to members of the local militia in Trujillo and elsewhere, encouraging them to grow crops and raise animals. Although Caribs are not specifically mentioned as being beneficiaries of this plan, *los morenos franceses,* as well as the Spanish colonists, were included (Peralta 1898:566–67, quoting Antonio González, July 5, 1803). Given the evidence that Black Caribs served in the militia, and the extreme interest in agriculture on the part of the authorities, it is possible that some of the Caribs were also given land. Yet references to the hardships they suffered at the hands of the Spanish in Trujillo may indicate that they were not considered in the same light then as the French blacks, who had won many accolades for their military prowess and were considered to be more civilized at that time than the Caribs. This issue cannot be resolved on the basis of evidence I have seen so far.

Whatever the situation in regard to land tenure, in time the list of Black Carib agricultural products in Central America lengthened, presumably to meet the demands of the local population. In the 1840s Ephraim Squier described various native cultures he encountered along the Central American Caribbean shore. In regard to the Caribs he said, "All along the coast, generally near the mouths of the various rivers, they have their establishments or towns. These are never large, but always neat, and well supplied with provisions, especially vegetables, which are cultivated with great care. They grow rice, cassava, sugarcane, a little cotton, plantain, squashes, oranges, mangoes, and every variety of indigenous fruits, besides an abundance of hogs, ducks, turkeys, and fowls, all of which they export in considerable quantities to Truxillo [*sic*], and even to Belize, a distance of several hundred miles" (in Bard 1855:316–17). The account is reminiscent of those from eighteenth-century St. Vincent (Miller 1979:70).

At the present time, Garifuna agriculture is minimally important in Belize and Guatemala. In the former, the British were enjoined by their agreements with Spain from producing any food locally, for fear that they would become permanently settled there (Fowler 1879:48; Anderson 1970:30). Although some clandestine gardening did occur, major agricultural efforts would have been difficult because woodcutting, the principal industry, required the men to spend ten or eleven months of the year in the forests, and most of the women remained in the city. After 1787 the British succeeded in obtaining Spanish permission for the settlers to grow subsistence crops, but by then the habit of importing foods from abroad was well ingrained, and it persists to this day (Dobson 1973). Nevertheless, the earliest Black Carib immigrants to Belize, like their kinfolk in Honduras, did supply Belize City with "vegetables," fowls, and pigs. Only in the past generation have many or most given up the practice (Hadel 1972:44), the food-producing niche now being filled by Mennonites, Hindus, and Mayan and Kekchi Indian immigrants (Wilk 1984). Belizean Garifuna livelihood today depends almost exclusively on wages earned either abroad or in professional urban occupations, such as schoolteaching or govern-ment service (Cosminsky 1976; Saint-Louis 1977).

Among Guatemalan Black Caribs in the early days, agriculture was also performed by the women, although I have not found a single reference to their having marketed a surplus outside the town. Rather, they became known at the turn of the century in the nearby port of Barrios as sellers of dried fish. According to my informants, in addition to drying fish caught by the men, every woman had a slash-and-burn plot for subsistence crops. So long as there was no competition for land or fish and the population remained relatively small, these activities were sufficient to supplement the wages brought in by the men from their temporary or seasonal migrations (see Gonzalez 1969). Women, as well as men, did grow bananas as a cash crop during the boom along the coast in the 1880s and 1890s, but the sale of bananas dropped off in the early part of the twentieth century and disappeared entirely by about 1940. In the 1960s, however, as emigration to the United States became an increas-ingly popular alternative for men and later for women, even subsistence fishing and agriculture steadily declined.

Simultaneously with the increased Garifuna migration came an influx of Kekchi Indians, population pressure having driven them from the interior Guatemalan provinces, especially from Alta Verapaz. By the early 1970s they were serious contenders for the "empty" forest areas where the Garifuna had for so long practiced their shifting cultivation.[14] The newcomers soon staked out permanent plots, building houses and fences, thus precluding even temporary use of the land by others. As will be shown in chapter 7, this effectively slammed the door behind the Garifuna emigrants, forcing them to adopt perpetual migration as the norm. This is not to say, however, that the Garifuna uniformly perceive this as detrimental. Few men or women in Livingston today see agriculture as a desirable occupation.

The agricultural situation in Honduras is and has always been more favorable than in Guatemala and Belize, so far as we can tell from the historical and ethnographic information available. Beauçage's (1970) detailed description, and his assertion of its primacy for modern Garifuna, struck me as odd at the time, since my research showed a very different picture for the other countries in which Garifuna lived. Even if he were correct for the 1960s, I was skeptical of his view that agriculture had been the primary source of livelihood for all Black Caribs in past generations and that only with recent modernization had things changed. Bolland and Shoman (1977:91) operated on this assumption in their work on Belize, asserting that the Caribs had originally been a "self-sufficient peasantry" but had been pushed off their lands in the twentieth century so as to create a ready labor force on the coast.

How do we reconcile these two views? As suggested earlier, the Caribs were looked upon as an agricultural people when they first arrived in 1797, and their produce fed thousands along the coast for a century. But at the same time they engaged in many other activities with a view toward earning a cash income (in chapter 6 these will be described in greater detail). Suffice it to say that the Mosquito social, political, and natural environments were all more conducive to combining these various activities than were the areas west and north of Trujillo. Furthermore, the woodcutting and banana operations, once important for the wage opportunities they offered, declined in Mosquitia earlier than in Guatemala and Belize. Thus, the population emigrated, abandoning settlements at Carataska and Brus lagoons. Only in the series of villages between Trujillo and Plaplaya in Mosquitia does one find today a fair number of Garifuna *men* in the prime of life who admit to farming as a regular occupation, although there are still some older men and women of all ages who cultivate their small plots in nearly every area.

It is significant that until recently there have been large tracts of land available all along the coast for the small farmer to cultivate on a shifting basis, even when these tracts have had other, registered owners. At various times in the past the owners—in rare cases individual Garifuna—have come forward to enforce their claims, usually when the land became valuable for some purpose other than subsistence cultivation. In recent years this has frequently been for raising cattle (De Walt 1983), an industry that has existed along the coast ever since the early British occupation in Mosquitia, from whom the Miskito acquired cattle. The first Carib immigrants, some of whom may have had cattle in St. Vincent, soon acquired a few animals from their neighbors in the Trujillo area (Rúbio Sánchez 1975, 2:398). Today, in communities such as Santa Rosa de Aguán and up the coast as far as Tocomacho and Plaplaya, there are Garifuna who raise cattle—sometimes only a few head but in some cases on a large scale. The object is to sell the live animals to itinerant purchasers, who drive them along the beach to sell to cattle owners near Trujillo. On occasion, small-scale milk production for local sale is combined with the raising of animals for beef. A concomitant of this is the development of a "horse culture." In Santa Rosa de Aguán I saw numerous young boys and men riding bareback for sport as well as business; and even women sometimes ride horses along the beach to go to market or to visit in another town.

Another important characteristic of the ecological setting in Honduras is that in several areas the villages are located near lagoons that are connected by creeks and rivers to the gardening plots and pastures. Davidson (1976) has discussed this type of location as one of several favored by the Black Caribs upon arrival on the coast, for women, as well as men, could paddle canoes to and from the "bush." [15] This transportation system makes it possible to farm areas farther from their homes than is possible in Guatemala, Belize, and even Trujillo, where access to plots is only by foot. [16] Thus, the Black Carib may rotate their fields more often without moving their villages or setting up temporary camps, which was sometimes done in the past in other areas.

Land shortage was frequently mentioned by the Garifuna as a problem, but, ironically, only in the urban areas such as Trujillo, Livingston, Punta Gorda, and Dangriga, and usually by nonfarmers. Like everyone else, perhaps, these people wanted the best of both worlds—the comfort and convenience of a town and the wide-open spaces of the countryside. In the smaller villages and hamlets the people not only voiced no complaints about land but asserted that there was much more available if people would have only moved farther from the major towns. Of course, they also pointed out that traveling to markets was difficult, so that most agriculture was undertaken primarily for subsistence, with cash requirements being met by remittances from emigrants.

In Trujillo and its environs lands were granted communally to the Caribs in 1885, but the records I have seen do not show clearly just where these were or their extent (Vallejo 1884). There was a crisis in 1903–4 when a group of Garifuna men journeyed to Tegucigalpa to seek a presidential confirmation of lands they claimed had belonged to their ancestors from time immemorial. After lengthy surveys and considerable protest from other claimants, a large area was awarded to the Comunidad de Morenos de Río Negro y Cristales. Shortly thereafter, however, a good portion of this land was rented to the Truxillo (*sic*) Railroad Company for a trifling sum. There is no doubt that some of it was and is still farmed, but even at the time of the dispute the claimants had some difficulty finding a sufficient number of men who would declare themselves farmers, as required by the government adjudicators. Of course, the prejudices of the larger society were reflected by the Caribs' failure to include women in this effort—not even listing them as cultivators.[17]

Both men and women work these lands cooperatively today, but only small plots are planted, mostly by older people who do so for their own subsistence. Farming is considered onerous and not likely to lead to a comfortable life. This also reflects a worldview that values mobility. Women today increasingly are on the move, a pattern once characteristic only of the men. And, as we shall see, the effective range of their traveling has been greatly increased, to the extent that horticulture is no longer really a viable supplementary activity. Even kitchen gardens, ubiquitous in Livingston and elsewhere in 1956, have mostly disappeared in the larger towns.

Food Supply and Population Size

Food supply, of course, is determined both by indigenous production and by marketing systems that contribute to the availability of items not locally grown, for one or another reason. These two factors together determine population size in any given environment. Before concluding this discussion of the relation of foods to ethnicity, it seems useful to consider some of the arguments with regard to the number of people—Island Caribs, Black Caribs, and Garifuna— who have lived on St. Vincent, Roatan, and along the mainland Central American coastline.

If population segments are to be recognized as ethnic groups, they must maintain both sociocultural boundaries *and* a sufficient size—the latter here defined as whatever it takes to exploit successfully a specified ecological niche and to reproduce the group. The concept of *niche* in sociocultural analysis was borrowed from the science of ecology some time ago and has been used, in one form or another, since the early writings of Forde (1937) and Kroeber (1939). More recently, various anthropologists have further developed niche theory in attempts to explain or interpret resource competition among ethnic groups (Barth 1956; Despres 1969; Bennett 1976), differential settlement patterns within an ethnic group (Whitten 1974), and the process of social change (Eighmy and Jacobsen 1980; Love 1977). I am not aware that it has been extensively used as I use it here—primarily in relation to occupational stratification among ethnic groups. This is, of course, similar to resource competition if one thinks of jobs as scarce resources.

Recruitment to an ethnic group or to a niche may be through sexual reproduction of the members and/or immigration and "conversion" of outsiders. The latter strategy was unsuccessfully used by the Shaker sect; more often, some combination of the two obtains. The merging of present-day South American Carib-speaking groups whose size has dwindled below functional

levels has been documented by several anthropologists.[18] It is my view that the
Black Caribs in Central America incorporated blacks from outside their ranks
from the beginning of their sojourn there, and it is clear that the Island Caribs,
whose numbers must have been diminished by disease and warfare after the
original European incursions into their territory, did the same two centuries
earlier.

Thus, following Eighmy and Jacobsen's (1980) ideas, we might argue that
optimum exploitation of a niche is assisted by population expansion, especially
when the carrying capacity of the territory has not been reached and defense
of it against outsiders is necessary. By contrast, when two or more *separate*
groups attempt to occupy the same niche, ethnic competition within it may be
exacerbated by the threat of an insufficient food supply. When this occurs,
those groups with superior food-producing technology and/or access to outside
sources of food would have an advantage. "Access" implies both the availability
of a regular supply of staples as well as the wherewithal to acquire them. Over
time, the Carib food preferences just outlined have been conditioned by both
the changes in the natural environment in which the Caribs have found themselves and the foreign foods to which they have achieved or been given access.
The concept of carrying capacity, borrowed, like niche theory, from the ecological literature dealing for the most part with (nonhuman) animal populations, may be relevant to this discussion.

A good bit of attention has recently been given to the problem of determining the carrying capacity of various environments under different sociocultural circumstances (Hames and Vickers 1983), and the matter becomes
important in assessing Island Carib and later Black Carib adjustments on
St. Vincent, Roatan, and along the mainland coast where these people eventually settled. Levin (1983), basing her ideas in part on the pioneering work of
Carneiro (1961), offers interesting and important speculations concerning the
Island Caribs. Given bitter manioc as the staple food, she believes St. Vincent
before Columbus might have provided enough calories to support a population
of some 35,000 people. However, the highest population figure ever suggested
by any European observer was 10,000 Caribs in 1735 (Hawtayne 1886:196),
and the scant archaeological and historical evidence available makes even that
number seem high. Levin concludes that a lack of protein, not calories, was
the primary population-limiting factor. This is an example of what Hames and
Vickers (1983:19) cite as *monocausal determinism*. Quite apart from the epis-
temological and practical problems inherent in such reasoning and in demonstrating cause and effect in an empirical setting, I think it can be said that the
St. Vincent Caribs probably had adequate supplies of protein (see chapter 1).
It is important here to consider both land and sea fauna, as well as domesticated animals acquired after contact with Europeans.

This contrasts dramatically with what we see today, for local river and sea fishing cultures have experienced severe declines nearly everywhere due to multiple strains brought about by increasing population size, both locally and worldwide. The smaller and less technologically sophisticated populations have suffered most. Along the Central American coast the activities of non-Garifuna and often foreign shrimp boats, which have plied the offshore waters increasingly over the past decade, have seriously compromised Garifuna fishing. The shrimp boats' nets capture even the small fish, which die before they can be thrown back. Since they are the food for larger fish, the latter have apparently sought other feeding grounds. This situation is exacerbated, as we will see, by the disturbance of spawning patterns.

Fishing, less productive than before, continues to be technologically unsophisticated and is, overall, less important in the total economy, although it remains, at least between Omoa and Trujillo, an important male enterprise that confers considerable ethnic distinction on the whole group (see Craig 1966:64) and individual prestige among the more skilled and successful. Most fishing today is done with hooks and lines or large seines placed just offshore, the latter requiring a cooperative effort of five or six men. Circular nets, some six to ten feet in diameter, are also used by individual men who cast them while standing up in their dugout canoes—a feat that makes the uninitiated gasp.

At one time river fishing must have been prevalent among Black Caribs in Central America, for some informants still can describe how to use the juice of a local vine to stun (some say kill) the fish. In addition to that technique, now outlawed, the Caribs used harpoons, arrows with three prongs, basketry traps, and nets, the latter being placed across the streams and slowly dragged upward to trap the fish in shallower water (Dudek 1985). In Livingston in 1956 the Caribs still plied the rivers at night, carrying torches to attract the fish, but this technique has now fallen into disuse, along with most other traditional fishing technology.

The riverine environments in Central America have been severely altered in recent years by the digging of sand to use in making concrete, now a major construction material both in the immediate vicinity of each river and throughout the several Central American countries. This activity disturbs the spawning of the fish. Formerly, as on St. Vincent, many of the ocean species laid their eggs upstream, but now most no longer do so. The result is that there really are fewer fish in both the rivers and the sea, just as informants invariably claim. But in addition, with the advent of commercial fishing and larger coastal populations generally, the rivers have been overfished. The Honduran and Guatemalan governments have taken conservation measures, primarily by forbidding all river fishing during the months of May, June, and July—the spawning season.

Even the largest of the Garifuna fishing canoes are limited to shallow waters, since they have no way to anchor in deep water (Craig 1966:83). Most fishing therefore occurs now, as in the past, along the seashore, not far from each village. When possible, fishermen travel to the reefs and keys that stretch along the Belizean coast and near the Bay Islands.[19] Farther down the coast in Mosquitia there are numerous lagoons that have long been favorite fishing grounds. Lobsters, shrimp, conch, and other shellfish are still harvested, though the high price of the first two on international markets makes it difficult for the people to eat them—most are sold to non-Garifuna, to local restaurants, or to exporters.

On St. Vincent in the difficult years just before deportation, fishing along the rivers was apparently more important than in the sea. Poisoning or diverting the streams through traps were the most common methods (Coke 1808, 1:250; Anderson 1983:66). Fish lines and nets of silkgrass were also mentioned by La Borde (Jesse 1968:118), and the botanist Alexander Anderson noted that in the eighteenth century the Black Caribs used pineapple leaves for this purpose (R. A. Howard, personal communication). But the most crucial fact is that when the river fish spawned, they were easily gathered. According to George Davidson (1787:15–16), hundreds of Caribs turned out to harvest them, thus providing a surplus, which when dried could be stored and used during periods when, for whatever reason, fresh fish and meat were not available. This may have been particularly important during the Carib War, when large numbers of men were involved in fighting and when their needs were increased by their French allies, who also had to be fed. C. Gullick (1978) has been particularly concerned with the carrying capacity of the Carib territory at that time, but he, like Levin (1983), erred in not considering this major source of food. The evidence suggests that the Caribs of the late eighteenth century were highly productive and capable of amassing considerable surplus food supplies (Miller 1979:69).

Not enough is known about the availability of game, fish, molluscs, and landcrabs on St. Vincent during the eighteenth century to provide any quantitative information, but Davidson's account of plentiful fish in the rivers suggests that protein was not a problem. Certainly there was some seasonal variability, but preservation by drying must have provided a stability that Levin did not take into account. These sources of protein would have been enhanced by the introduction of domesticated fowl, cattle, sheep, goats, and pigs.

If fish were as plentiful as the accounts suggest, then other factors should be examined, including the possibility of conscious population control. There is absolutely nothing, either in the early literature or in the recent ethnographic accounts, however, to suggest that the Caribs ever practiced late marriage, coitus interruptus, abortion, infanticide, or any other method of family planning. The long nursing periods, which effectively reduce fertility in many other societies and which are not popular today with the Garifuna, may have been practiced by the Island Caribs, although there are no data to support this view. Today, as McCommon (1982) suggests, the entire culture seems oriented toward achieving maximum fecundity and population increase.

What, then, prevented the Island Caribs and their Black Carib descendants from achieving a higher population on St. Vincent? Levin's argument does not take into account the elements of warfare, which preceded the coming of the Europeans, and the fact that Caribbean land and fishing grounds were not particularly crowded before the sixteenth century. It may be that expansion into the area from South America was proceeding, only to be cut off by the diseases and general violence of the European conquest. There was simply no good reason for 35,000 Caribs to crowd together on one island so long as there were other islands to be exploited. The nature of their sociopolitical organization probably did not lend itself to the effective management of a population that large. As among the Yanomamo today, if and when internecine conflict occurred, small groups could easily break away, going to another island to live but returning for friendly visits or for raiding.

All of this fits nicely with Carneiro's (1970) theory of environmental circumscription, but as we shall see there are many causal factors. After European intrusion into the area the Carib population was increasingly restricted, and we might ask why they did not then achieve a population size of 35,000 on St. Vincent, which was one of the two islands supposedly left in their control. Again, I would point to sociopolitical constraints, plus the fact that their resource base itself had begun to erode. There was a steady encroachment even on St. Vincent by Europeans who not only acquired Carib lands and competed with them for the wild game and fish available but introduced new diseases. Even before that time, of course, new crops and domesticated animals had been introduced. No new grain or vegetable staple was acquired, however, though eggs, milk, and meat should have made animal protein even less of a problem. But after English settlement and the introduction of large-scale sugarcane cultivation, Black Caribs may have provided much of the food for slaves. Use of their surplus in this way may have had unintended implications for population size unless the Caribs were importing foods with the money earned from sales, and there is no evidence for this. Rather, Carib earnings seem to have gone for manufactured items such as guns and ammunition, cooking pots and griddles, clothing, and various luxury items, including pipes and personal ornaments. Later, toward the end of the Carib War, as suggested in chapter 1, they may have been pressed for caloric sufficiency, particularly since they harbored many outsiders and were under seige.[20]

Roatan, by contrast, was not nearly so hospitable an environment, at least in terms of its natural endowment. Immediately upon landing, if we can trust the account listing the provisions landed for their use (see Table 2.1), the Black

Caribs had food stores sufficient for several months, as well as seeds and cuttings for planting, tools for building canoes and clearing land, and fish hooks and lines. The waters of Roatan and nearby Guanaja (Bonacco) abound today with fish and shellfish, and there is no reason to assume the situation was different in 1797. Although they had large amounts of oatmeal, flour (presumably wheaten), and "farina" (probably cassava meal), the supply would not have lasted more than about four or five months. Planting should have been accomplished almost immediately, then, in order to harvest by the time their supplies ran out. The fact that this was a difficult, if not impossible, task is suggested by Major Wilson's desperate plea to his superiors in London to send another supply ship to Roatan as soon as possible (WO 1/82:719). By the time the ship carrying food, livestock and poultry, clothing, tools, arms, and ammunition was ready to leave England (see Table 2.2), word arrived that the Caribs had joined the Spaniards at Trujillo (WO 1/692:96). Consequently, the supplies never left port—possibly an example of how bureaucratic delays sometimes change history!

Although the Caribs seem to have initiated the exchange that led to their leaving Roatan shortly after their arrival there, they apparently did not actually arrive on the mainland in large numbers until October 1797 (Dambrine 1797). Thus, they survived for some five or six months, presumably on the stores provided, plus fish and whatever short-term vegetable crops they might have been able to grow or to gather. They may also have been able to beg some provisions from the Spanish and/or other blacks who might have been already resident on the island. Grains and staple roots such as manioc must have been scarce by that time, particularly if the Caribs had not been able to store and ration their supplies. And many people must have died on Roatan, since the number reported when they arrived in Trujillo was about 350 less than the number reported to have landed in Roatan in April (see Table 1.1).

All observers, from Anguiano (1813) on, have commented on the fecundity of the Black Caribs and the Garifuna. Population estimates cannot always be believed, especially during the period in Trujillo when the local observers wished to convey their fear of being overwhelmed by what was turning out to be not quite so desirable a set of neighbors as they had first believed. Table 5.2 gives estimates for different places and time periods, based on what evidence is in the various records. By anyone's calculation there has been a remarkable population increase since the Caribs' arrival in Central America, which I attribute to several factors.

First, upon arrival nearly every woman was of child-bearing age, and given the high mortality among infants during the St. Vincent-Baliceaux epidemic, nearly all adult females must have been at risk of pregnancy since they would no longer have been lactating. There may have been as many as 500-600 babies born within the first year alone; hence, the figure of 4,000 recorded in

Table 5.2 Carib/Garifuna Population Estimates

Year	Source	Belize	Guatemala	Honduras
1801	Vallejo (1843)			4,000 (Trujillo)
1806	CO 123/14	15		
1823	Juarros (1823)			300 (Trujillo)
1829	MMS	1,200		
1842	Young (1842)			1,500
1844	Rignaux (1844)		500	
1861	FO 53/7; Valois (1861)	2,380	500	
1881	Hadel (1974)	2,037		
1897	Morlan (1897)		2,000	
1921	Hadel (1974)	3,197[a]		
1946	Hadel (1974)	4,711		
1956	Hadel (1974); Guatemalan Census	6,154	1,762	
1960	British Honduras Census	4,147[a]		
1975	Guatemalan Census, 1974		3,101	
1980	Cruz (1980), based on Davidson (1976)			60,900
1984	Palacio (1985)	10,600		
1985	Gonzalez fieldnotes		3,000	

[a] Persons fifteen years of age and older.

1804 (Vallejo 1893) may not have been so far off as it first appears. This would have been even more likely had the Caribs by then absorbed many or most of the French and English blacks already in the area.

A second factor relates to the resistance of the immigrant group to yellow fever and malaria, the two most dreaded diseases in the area. The Caribs, along with other blacks, would have fared better as a population than the whites and mestizos, for reasons stated earlier.

Third, polygamy, which demographers have long recognized as being associated with high fertility, persisted in the area. The number of females exceeded that of males in all of the census materials preserved, although disease on Baliceaux tended to even out the numbers somewhat. But polygamy and a relaxed attitude about sequential unions ensured that no woman would be left without a sex partner for any reason. As McCommon (1982) discusses at length, the Carib culture was and remains today highly oriented toward a free, open, and long-lasting sex life for men and woman, a love of children, and a sense of pride (among both men and women) in having produced many offspring. That children may have been more of a liability than an asset in their earlier years is suggested by Sanford's (1971, 1974) analysis of the institution of child-keeping and child-lending. Once grown, however, many offspring were a definite economic advantage, for some would migrate and send back goods and/or money, while others would stay on and help with the work of maintaining the household (Gonzalez 1969).

A fourth factor enhancing population growth in Central America was the availability of land, fish, and wage labor. The Caribs would have had little problem feeding themselves once they reached Trujillo. Although analysis of the soils today shows them to be relatively poor, acidic, and low in potassium,[21] evidence abounds that the Caribs, unlike the European immigrants, were good farmers. Manioc was especially suited to this type of soil, and the Caribs also managed to grow a variety of other root and tree crops. For at least 100 years the Caribs were held to be the best workers along the coast for most unskilled, and some skilled, jobs (see chapter 6).

Last but not least, we must consider the migratory pattern established early in the Caribs' Central American sojourn. Not only did the emigrants send back money and goods for the benefit of those who remained at home, but they themselves were not a drain on the local resources and facilities. This allowed a larger total population size among the ethnic group at large—a phenomenon seen also in other Caribbean nations with heavy out-migration during this century. Another reason the carrying capacity of any particular local area cannot be perfectly quantified is that it is not possible to keep track of how many persons are "outside" at any given time. Much of the migration today is undocumented, and people are reluctant to discuss their absent loved ones' activities for fear of deportation and/or other unspecified reprisals they imagine will await them if discovered.

Migration will be further discussed in most of the chapters that follow, for it has become a fundamental, if controversial, determinant of the Garifuna lifestyle today. Although it has brought countless benefits in the past, many are now looking upon it as their primary misfortune and possibly the instrument of their annihilation as an ethnic group.

NOTES

1. Nutritional quality of the diet will not be a major consideration here except in the grossest sense. My judgment that today's diet is less nutritious than that of the seventeenth and eighteenth centuries is subjective and largely based on the degree to which "junk foods" have been adopted, as well as on the extreme obesity typical of many of the Garifuna women. Frying has largely replaced boiling and roasting, and refined sugar is consumed in enormous quantities. The Garifuna diet is high in coconut oil and lard, which is probably related to a reported high incidence of high blood pressure (Elington 1985). Protein malnutrition occurs frequently among preschoolers (Jenkins

1984), although the use of Incaparina, a high-protein cereal product, may be responsible for a reduction in both morbidity and mortality in this age group, at least among Guatemalan Garifuna. Of course, having the cash to purchase such supplements is itself a result of the out-migration described later in this chapter.

2. The question as to whether "bitter" and "sweet" manioc are the same or different species has long been settled — both are *Manihot esculenta*. However, some varieties contain far more hydrocyanic acid than others, and roots taken from the same field, and sometimes from the same plant, according to my informants, will vary. Cassava breeders at CIAT (Centro Internacional de Agricultura Tropical) in Cali, Colombia, are not sure what causes this variation, but it may relate to the amount of moisture that reaches that particular root. In any case, indigenous peoples, as well as the anthropologists who study them, have long been aware that the roots lend themselves to different uses depending upon how "bitter" they are. Some control through selection is possible, and it is clear that Black Caribs and Garifuna prefer the bitter varieties for making *areba*. These are also sometimes said to be superior in that insects are less likely to attack them in the fields (but see CIAT 1983:28–50).

3. It may be presumed that the Africans were in no position to pack their bags with seeds before leaving, so Europeans, in effect, did that for them. In order to feed their slaves, various plants were introduced into the Americas. Sorghum, an African grain, had become the major staple in Barbados before the end of the seventeenth century (Sloane 1707:xv), and slaves planning an escape from that island might well have taken some seeds with them. In any case, judging by the seeds sent along at the time of the deportation, Caribs were eating all of the items mentioned in addition to "guinea corn" (sorghum), okra, and so on. Sorghum is not presently cultivated by Garifuna in Central America.

The British noted that the Caribs had huge stores of "grain" in their huts when the latter were destroyed. Even though Rochefort (1666) spoke of maize, peas, and millet, the basis of their diet has long been thought to have been bitter manioc, as it is in the Amazon and was until recently in Central America. If they were eating the grain, it seems strange that no recipes were given by Rochefort or others, although they did describe ways of preparing manioc and other root crops. The Caribs may have been growing much of the grain for sale to the French and especially to the British, who were always short of food for their slaves.

4. New discoveries of journals kept by Alexander Anderson, keeper of the Royal Botanic Garden on St. Vincent in the 1790s and keenly interested in the ethnobotany of the Black Caribs, provide a glimpse of other dietary and medicinal plant usages. Richard A. Howard of the Arnold Arboretum of Harvard University is presently editing Anderson's unpublished notes made on trips he took to the Carib territories. Publication of this material should greatly enrich our knowledge of the foodways and plant usages of the Black Caribs just before their deportation.

5. To make coconut "milk" or "cream," small amounts of water are poured over grated fresh coconut, which is then squeezed to extract the oil and flavor. The result, depending on how much water is added, is a thick or thin milky white liquid. The ingredient is so much a part of tropical West Indies cuisine that it is now sold in the frozen food sections of urban supermarkets in those countries, as well as in stores in

parts of New York, Miami, and Los Angeles. Coconut "water" is the clear juice of the green fruit; mature coconuts, from which milk is extracted, contain little water.

6. Recently Dr. Lydia Pulsipher directed me to a photograph of a drawing at the John Carter Brown Library at Brown University which shows scantily clad, light-skinned people with the tightly curled hair typical of Africans engaged in cassava processing on Montserrat. All the steps, as well as the appropriate equipment and utensils, are shown in meticulous detail. She had assumed these were slaves, but it is possible they were Caribs, indeed even Black Caribs (see the *Gazateer Americana,* vol. 3, p. 225, 1763).

7. In 1887, in the United States, advertisements for Royal Baking Powder warned the consumer that "impure" brands might indeed cause illness or worse. Although the use of leavening is the most likely explanation, there is one other remotely possibility. Lloyd (1965:43), quoting Lind, an eminent eighteenth-century physician, notes that cream of tartar was sometimes used "as a preservative against many of the diseases of mariners." It was both cheaper and more palatable than other acids, including vinegar, which at that time were thought to protect against fevers. One-half pint of vinegar per man per week was part of a sailor's rations in 1808 (M. A. Lewis 1960:404).

8. This perception was shared by the Spanish (Ladino, Indio) population of Honduras but not by the Miskitos with whom I talked. I am unable to say whether it has any objective basis.

9. The traditional "snakelike" basketry press, still used but becoming scarce among the Garifuna, is identical to that described and pictured by Farabee (1967a:36) for the Central Arawaks of the Amazon area in 1918, and it is still found among various indigenous groups in Colombia, Brazil, Venezuela, and Surinam. Farabee also showed a basket with a tumpline for bringing produce in from the fields which is identical to one in a painting by Brunius. Similar baskets were made in Central America as late as the 1950s but are no longer available. Only people aged forty or over seem to remember the word for these—*gadauri.* Efforts in 1985 to acquire even an old *gadauri* for the national museum in Tegucigalpa were unsuccessful.

In June 1984 the *Garifuna News,* published in Los Angeles, carried a notice to the effect that the Garifuna communities in Nicaragua could no longer produce *areba* because they lacked the traditional equipment. Readers were asked to send names and addresses of anyone with skills in making the sifters and squeezers so as to help preserve the Nicaraguan Garifuna culture and heritage. It seems likely that factors other than technological stagnation are more important in explaining the decline in *areba* manufacture.

10. Most women younger than thirty have no idea how to proceed. In recent years one of the qualifications for selection as a Garifuna holiday "queen" in Belize has been the ability to cook several "typical" dishes. Were they to declare *areba* making an essential skill, I daresay there would be few candidates.

11. Silkgrass *(Aechmea magdalenensis)* is a species of bromeliad having thick, fleshy leaves from which fibers were made (Craig 1966:35).

12. There were complaints of food shortages on the coast near Trujillo dating from the time the British were expelled and the Spaniards began to settle there in 1789 (see AGCA A1.12.7/469/48 for 1793; Peralta 1898:373–74 for 1803; AGCA 1.23/4641/224

for 1804). Later, in 1804, things were said to be improving in regard to agriculture at Trujillo (Peralta 1898:378), thanks to the efforts of the Caribs. See also Sorsby (1972:145) for some discussion of the problem.

13. The term "vegetable" seems to have referred to any cultivated nontree crop except the grains commonly used in making flour, such as wheat, barley, oats, and so on. "Vegetables" included roots as well as "fruits" such as eggplant, okra, and the like, which is consistent with the concept "vegetable crop" as reported for modern Belize by Palacio (1983).

14. Perhaps because of their preference for shifting cultivation, as well as because it was primarily the women who did the farming, the Central American Black Caribs frequently neglected to claim and register the lands they used. In 1885 an Austrian immigrant sought four *caballerias* (1 *caballeria* = 4,279 acres in Central America) along the Río Dulce near Livingston. The map accompanying his petition noted that the land in question was "vacant, possessed without title by various Caribs" (AGCA, Izabal, Paquete 7, Expediente 9). This was typical of the attitude in Central America and was comparable to that in St. Vincent. See Cruz Sandoval (1984) for a description of the situation for Honduran Indians today.

15. It is interesting that in Guatemala and Belize women seldom paddle canoes, and it is sometimes thought that they cannot or should not do so. This is in contrast with nineteenth-century accounts that mention women bringing produce, including stems of bananas, to market in this way (Charles 1890:118–19). Beauçage (1970.65) doubted the veracity of these accounts, but my own observations in Honduras convince me that women are perfectly capable of handling canoes by themselves and that they often grow and market bananas and other produce. Presumably women in Honduras, and especially in Mosquitia, retain a skill that was once more widespread but has disappeared among their more western and northern relatives. The frequent absence of men for long periods of time in Central America may have first motivated the women to become skilled in paddling, as there is no mention of them doing so while on St. Vincent.

16. The lands near Punta Castilla, bordering the lagoon of Guaimoreto, were once used by Black Caribs from Trujillo and neighboring communities. Travel to those plots was usually by sailing canoe, for distances were greater than in Mosquitia, and paddling speed was directly related to the number of hands available. Agriculture, unlike fishing, was and is an individual or family enterprise. Women frequently go to the fields alone or with a youngster or two. When a man's assistance is required, as for clearing and burning, he may accompany his "partner" or go alone. The only time I have seen truly communal labor was by a group of women during harvest on behalf of a church organization.

17. The original of this document is held in Trujillo by the president of the organization, which still exists ostensibly to keep watch over these lands. That there is some need to do so is suggested by a major dispute that has erupted in Honduras over the apparent illegal appropriation of a part of these lands by some members of the Honduran military, who sold them to an American, who in turn sold them to the U.S. Army for purposes of establishing a military base. The controversy has been aired in the United States as well, but usually only in relation to the legality of the means by which

the United States acquired the land. The U.S. Supreme Court refused to hear the case brought by the American who claimed he did not receive fair compensation for his "farmlands." The Catholic church and some other interested groups have tried to pressure the Honduran government to consider the case and redress the wrong to the Garifuna, but they have not been successful to date.

18. At a seminar on Carib political and social organization at the Forty-fourth International Congress of Americanists (Manchester, England, Sept. 1982), this matter was discussed at length by a group of distinguished scholars, all of whom had worked among Carib-speaking groups in South America. Wagley (1940) was one of the first to document the process.

19. Two small fishing communities have sprung up on the Cayos Cochinos off the coast of La Ceiba, Honduras, since the mid-1950s, much to the distress of American investors hoping to attract tourists to a "purified" tropical paradise (i.e., one in which the natives, if any, do nothing but sing, dance, and wait on tables). "Captain" Horton Kivett, one of the expatriate entrepreneurs, informed me that he intends to evict these "squatters," who have been nothing but a "nuisance" to him for years. He seems to have neither understanding nor compassion for the peoples' plight in the face of inexorable modernization, nor does he apparently respect Honduran law, which severely limits the measures that can be taken against squatters.

20. The accounts seem contradictory. Some observers noted the Caribs' "emaciated state" upon surrender, yet others commented upon the huge stores of grain found in the huts. It is possible that starvation set in only as a result of the burning of the domestic establishments, for several months passed before the last Caribs were rounded up and sent to Baliceaux.

21. Six soil samples from an area behind the town of Trujillo that was said by local people to be good agricultural land were sent to the University of Maryland Cooperative Extension Service for analysis. Phosphorus was consistently low or very low in all samples, but potassium and magnesium varied from very high to very low, with the highest values from samples of topsoil taken on the surface, where burning had more recently occurred. The samples showed a generally acidic character, with pH values ranging from 4.9 to 5.6, the higher (less acidic) values being those from the surface. Manioc is one of the few crops that can do well in such soils (Nicholaides et al. 1983).

6

Work Identity and Ethnicity

Ethnicity and Reputation

A fundamental component of ethnicity is reputation, that is, what significant outsiders believe about the people who form a specific group or category within a larger social universe. In a plural society, the ethnic components probably never reveal themselves fully to each other. A kind of collective "presentation of self" occurs in which each group defines the way it wishes to be perceived by others. Of course, the way in which the members of any given group are viewed may not conform to either their self-perception or to their intended projection of self. The situation is further complicated by the observation that the ethnic presentation of self by individuals is, if not infinitely variable, at least extremely flexible, depending upon the immediate situation. That this process is both reciprocal and culturally and situationally determined has been repeatedly demonstrated, to the extent that some might say it is self-evident (see Royce 1982 for a comprehensive review.) However, the way in which it operates at any given time is not always clear.

In the case of the Caribs, certain behavior patterns were differently perceived and/or interpreted by Europeans associated with them at different times and in different places, resulting in several ethnic profiles. The question then arises as to what the Caribs were (are) "really" like and how one can best interpret the various accounts describing them. How much of these descriptions derives from the different ways in which Caribs presented themselves, and how much from the expectations of the Europeans—which in turn were formed by their own cultural background as well as their immediate goals of conquest? Washburn (1959) has provided an informative analysis of the mind-set of the British who first encountered native peoples of the Americas. They were either judged to be inhuman savages beyond the hope of Christian salvation or, as portrayed in Aphra Behn's novel *Orinooko,* as the most noble and persecuted of human beings.

One is tempted to believe that reputation is defined in an entirely subjective manner. Yet psychologists suggest that the ideas others have may indeed affect a group's self-image such that behavior patterns become congruent with the way in which others see them, as in a self-fulfilling prophecy. Learning theory has long provided an explanation of how individual behavior patterns change in response to the expectations of dominant individuals or groups. But Pavlovian explanations cannot account for how cultures change the way their individual members learn to behave toward this or that outside group. To the extent that certain actions bring gratification, the elders will teach the young to emulate them, and/or the young will do so anyway, thus establishing a "typical" pattern with positive value attached to it.

As plural societies form, usually through the processes of conquest and colonization, the several segments must find ways to maintain their cultural integrity while achieving some level of acceptance by the other segments. Furnivall (1977) has suggested that the "marketplace" has been the primary arena in which interethnic relations become established in plural societies. In the case of the Caribs, who sold their goods first and then increasingly their labor to the Europeans, this conceptualization seems especially useful. Their work identity became nearly synonymous with their ethnic identity, for apart from a few missionaries, outsiders never saw, much less studied, their home identity until the third decade of the twentieth century brought ethnographers to their doorstep. Furthermore, as Mead (1961) noted in her Manus restudy, a group's work identity is a creation of both outside (or foreign) expectations and the efforts of individual workers to gain acceptability in the labor market.

In this chapter, I will examine the work identity of the different Carib "types" over time and try to show how these developed and how they relate to the present ethnic situation. Discussion will relate almost exclusively to male work patterns and reputations, for the simple reason that women's interactions with the outside world are less often mentioned in the historical sources.[1] It is clear that from early St. Vincent days all three Carib societies or types engaged in agricultural and marketing pursuits. These activities have been discussed in several of the preceding chapters, since they are basically domestic in nature and had a profound impact on the development of certain aspects of Garifuna ethnicity, particularly in the realms of family and household (Gonzalez 1969) and religion (Kerns 1983). But it was mainly men who interacted with outsiders and thus made the impressions by which the group's reputation was formed.

St. Vincent — Raiders and Traders

If we hark back to the original Arawak/Carib encounter, the two groups apparently intersected primarily through the exchange of goods, or trade. Loven (1935:679) suggested that at the time of Columbus the Caribs were acting as middlemen in the trade between the Arawak-speaking Tainos of the Greater Antilles and various groups in South America. This accords well with the descriptions of Morales and Arévalo-Jiménez (1981), who have reconstructed extensive trading networks between the Lesser Antilles and South America, and with conclusions drawn by Taylor and Rouse (1955). Later accounts of Vincentian Island Carib trade with Martinique and Trinidad, and Central American Black Carib trade with Belize, indicate a continuation of the long-distance trading role up to and after the time of the deportation.

Supposedly, the early trade erupted into violent conquest, resulting in the merging of the populations through rape and/or marriage of the Arawak women by Carib men, although there is no archaeological or other solid evidence for this conclusion. There may have been such an Amazonian pattern, perhaps related to long-standing ethnic rivalries, and institutionalized so as to make success in raiding and taking captives a means of asserting manhood. The assumption might be that it was then transferred to the Caribbean area, where it amounted to territorial conquest, the Caribs gradually displacing the Arawaks from all but the more northern and larger Greater Antilles (Jamaica, Hispañola, Puerto Rico). We must await solid archaeological evidence to resolve this question.

I have seen no discussion as to what happened to the Arawak men, although conventional views of the nature of Amazonian/Caribbean warfare suggest they were systematically eliminated by their conquerors. Presumably the conquest occurred only incrementally, small groups of Carib men swooping in and overcoming the Arawaks, island by island. Their numbers must have been small, otherwise a serious imbalance would have occurred in the Amazon area they abandoned. It is also possible, though I have not seen the idea discussed, that the early Carib traders had wives on both the islands and the mainland, the latter being their primary place of residence. Some of the male Arawak captives might have been returned to the mainland as "slave" labor, which would have alleviated the shortage caused by the Carib trading and raiding patterns.

The relationship between the Carib/Arawak or Island Caribs and the earliest blacks in the area was created and configured by the latter's exchanging their labor for sanctuary among the former, albeit sometimes under duress. African male captives were put to work by the Caribs in their agricultural and other enterprises, perhaps thus permitting Carib men to spend more time off-island. Eventually this practice became merged with kinship obligations, as the newcomers married Carib women.[2] As local groups increased in size, African intermarriage might have been one of many possible disrupting factors leading to dispute and eventual fissioning, much as Chagnon (1968) has described it for the Yanomamo.

From about 1700, and continuing until the time of the deportation in 1797, Europeans commented on the presence of what they perceived to be two ethnic groups among the indigenous people of St. Vincent (see Chapter 1). Descriptions show that the two were considered as quite different sorts of human beings. Island (i.e., Red or Yellow or "pure") Caribs were thought to be quiet, peaceful, timid, and harmless—generally friendly to Europeans and their establishments. Thus, an observer in 1772 expressed surprise that some Yellow Caribs had "perpetrated cruelties on negro slaves" (CO 101/16/209). This, it should be emphasized, is quite a different profile from that attributed to the Caribs earlier, which led to their name becoming synonymous with "wild, cannibalistic, warlike savages" (Boromé 1966:33). It is difficult to understand what lay behind this change in European attitudes. Was the Island Carib culture so altered by Black Carib competition and hegemony that it affected the personalities of its members?

Perhaps the explanation is to be sought in European racism, which favored the "noble savage" over the "blackamoor." The Island Caribs' image seems to have suffered (though European contemporaries must have considered it more flattering) by comparison with the Black Caribs, who were thought of by opponents and allies alike as fierce, aggressive, independent, proud, and clever. It was repeatedly noted that, above all, the Black Caribs feared being enslaved, so to distinguish themselves from slaves being brought to St. Vincent by the French and increasingly by the British after 1763 they began to shape their children's heads in imitation of their lighter-skinned cousins (see chapter 1).[3] Skin color then, as now, was associated by the Europeans with ethnicity, and no one seems to have considered the possibility that the two Carib groups may have had more in common than either did with the intruders.

In this regard, there is no doubt that both groups were expert canoemen and were equally perceived as such by Europeans. Red Caribs living on the windward side of Dominica were hired by French planters to carry produce to Roseau in the first half of the eighteenth century, and this was probably common much earlier (Dalrymple 1763:449). Similarly, Black Caribs from eastern St. Vincent performed the same service for the British (W. Young 1764:10; Shepherd 1831:179), and those Caribs left behind in 1797 apparently continued in this employ. Day (1852, 1:95) included a drawing of canoemen loading a hogshead of molasses from shore to ship off Rabacca, St. Vincent, in 1846. Negroes and "Red Carib Indians" were said to man these "moses-boats."

The pre-Columbian trading patterns typical of St. Vincent and other Island

Caribs were transformed by the Black Caribs into an active interisland exchange with the French on Martinique, St. Lucia, and Grenada. In addition, the women sold produce locally at Kingstown and Calliaqua (Coke 1808, 1:182, 197), as is portrayed in one of Brunius's paintings at the Peabody Museum at Harvard University.

At the time of the deportation from St. Vincent, the Black Caribs, in contrast to the Red or Yellow Caribs, were characterized by the British as devious, devilish, cruel, and inhumane—in a word, *savage*. Yet only a few months later, after they arrived in Central America, they were sought as allies by both the Spanish and the British, who now found them clever, independent, brave, and skillful in warfare. Curiously, on St. Vincent they were generally respected as being hard-working, though in 1797 the Spanish at first thought them unaccustomed to hard work.

Only the above brief sketch is possible for St. Vincent because of the paucity of descriptive material. But beginning in 1797, and continuing to the present day, the record is clearer for Central America. Accounts of European military officers, government officials, travelers, missionaries, and anthropologists abound. In the argument that follows I have mustered all the references I have been able to find so as to describe the way in which the Black Carib immigrants developed an ethnically distinctive reputation and to show how their modern descendants, the Garifuna, have used and changed that reputation.

Central America—Soldiers and Smugglers of Fortune

The Spanish officer who recorded the Black Caribs' names and other personal data upon their arrival in Trujillo told his commanding officer that the men were surprisingly knowledgeable when it came to handling arms, yet the people in general, he thought, were not accustomed to hard work (Pérez Brito 1797). He added that they would be useful nevertheless in certain crafts such as basket making, and he predicted that they would soon adapt to their new milieu. In line with this, before the middle of the nineteenth century the Central American Black Caribs did achieve a reputation as skillful, dedicated, tireless workers—one that they have unfortunately lost today.

One of the first accolades recorded about the Caribs was from Gen. Tomás O'Neille, who fought for the Spaniards at the turn of the nineteenth century. He noted, in a letter written about 1800, that the Caribs under his command "fight desperate" (quoted in Burdon 1933:71–72). Apparently others thought so too, for in 1812 Gen. Pedro Gutierres, commander of the Caribs in what was called the Battalion of Olancho, noted that both the enemy and their fellow troopers were frightened by the demeanor of these "wild" soldiers (Gutierres 1905). Throughout the last days of the colonial period, Caribs manned Royalist garrisons in Trujillo, Omoa, San Felipe, Tegucigalpa, and

Guatemala City. Apparently, by then their fighting behavior had changed, for in 1827 García Granados specifically noted that Carib soldiers were "more civilized" and militarily superior to those soldiers in his company who had been recruited from among Belizean slaves (García Granados 1952, 1:104). Immediately after Independence, the regular garrison at Tegucigalpa was reduced to fifty men, but the Caribs who were there were retained (S. Gutiérrez 1822:100).

The Caribs' reputation for military prowess extended from St. Vincent and the Carib War through at least the first three decades of the nineteenth century in Central America. As we have seen in chapter 2, they continued to hire out as would-be revolutionaries during the 1820s and early 1830s, but after their defeat by Morazán's forces in 1832, we find very few references to them in the literature on military matters.[5] Oral tradition among some Garifuna today is that Morazán traversed the Shore between Trujillo and Plaplaya, recruiting men for his Nicaraguan and Costa Rican campaigns after his defeat as president of the Federation. The stories usually claim that some Carib men were impressed against their will, though many escaped. I have so far found nothing in Morazán's memoirs or other written accounts of the period to confirm this. There is also a common belief among present-day Garifuna that they fought *with* Morazán from the beginning of his liberal assault on Arce in 1826. The written record belies this view.

In addition to their skill as warriors, the early Central American Caribs were known as expert seamen. They were in demand as crew on European-owned sloops and schooners that plied the waters of the Bay of Honduras both before and after Independence (Gibbs 1883:166). But most Carib men had their own canoes, the largest of which, called "creers" (or *creaus;* Craig 1966:55), were fashioned from massive hardwood trees such as mahogany, cedar, and San Juan. These capital investments allowed them to reach sites where they could sell their labor; and they also used the canoes in fishing and turtling (sometimes as far away as Bluefields, Nicaragua), in ferrying people and goods from ship to shore and back, in long-distance transportation of people, in carrying their wives' and the latter's produce to market, and in smuggling British manufactured goods out of Belize for resale in the Spanish (and later Central American) provinces.

The Carib man's skill in handling canoes in all sorts of weather and waters was recognized and respected well into the twentieth century. Numerous accounts mention traveling from one or another place "in an open Carib boat"; almost everyone utilized their services between Belize and the San Juan River in Nicaragua. They sailed and paddled with extreme dexterity, navigating by the stars at night and by coastal landmarks by day. There was not a point or cove or river they had not explored. Pim (1863:273) described a twenty-two-hour canoe journey from Greytown along the Nicaragua coast, up the Colorado River to Ft. San Carlos on the Lake of Nicaragua. Six Carib paddlers performed almost unbelievable feats, including cooking the travelers' lunch during their only (two-hour) stop. When Pim complimented them on their hard work, they claimed they often worked much harder and longer at mahogany cutting. In addition to their strength and endurance, experience allowed them to beach their canoes in the often treacherous surf—a skill that is today fast disappearing, even though it is still attributed to them.[6] All of these skills, of course, were invaluable in escaping pursuers, whether government authorities or pirates.

Knowledge of seacraft and the sea included fishing, although it is probably inappropriate to think of Carib fishing at any time as having been a full-time occupation. Rather, fishing was, and to a large extent remains, part of their domestic life, which on occasion is extended into more formal working situations. Little boys begin fishing from docks with simple lines at an early age, and by five or six they venture out in small canoes to try their luck offshore. Older boys and men also fish—sometimes today merely for fun but also to provide food for themselves, their families, and other kin. There was always a market, either among their own people or others, for any surplus, and some men began to supply fish regularly to the general non-Carib population almost immediately after arriving in Trujillo in 1797. But it probably never occupied them full-time, and few, if any, thought of themselves as "career" fishermen. It was simply part of every male's repertoire of skills.

Perhaps more important, in the nineteenth century fishing in canoes was often a cover for smuggling or spying. If caught, a man could show his catch or gear and insist that fishing was his only motive for being at sea. The authorities were well aware of this game but could do little to stop it, for fishing was a valuable and ubiquitous activity, necessary for everyone's subsistence. Even today, when men traverse the shore in canoes for other purposes, they constantly note and discuss among themselves the presence or absence of fish in the various locations.[7]

Smuggling in the Caribbean and along the Spanish Main, and the participation of indigenous groups in the process, is a topic upon which a separate book might well be written. Suffice it to say that all European national authorities fought against it but to no avail, for "free trade" was seen as a right by many of the European creole settlers, and it might be said that smuggling was one of the primary mechanisms of economic and political modernization in Europe at the time. The Black Caribs, along with the Miskitos, were quickly recruited by both the English and the Spanish to carry consumer goods, arms, ammunition, escaping slaves, and later undocumented aliens, all along the coast. Petty smuggling of canned foods, medicines, liquors, soaps, and marijuana continues to the present day.

In addition to making canoes for their own use, Black Caribs made them for others, especially rural creoles in Belize and mestizos and blacks elsewhere. This was a skill retained by the Dominican Caribs as well, the men being famous for their products until recently (Taylor 1935:267). Dugouts came to be known generally in Belize as "Carib craft" in the early nineteenth century and were distinguished from the Miskito *pitpan* by their shape. Craig (1966:55) states, "By the 1840s, Black Carib fishermen from Trujillo to Stann Creek were supplying doreys to the creole and white inhabitants who had formerly depended on [the Miskitos] to provide them with these dugout canoes." Caribs also repaired boats and vessels of larger dimensions, the shipyards at Livingston achieving considerable reknown early in the twentieth century.

In effect, during the first half of the nineteenth century the Caribs largely controlled small-scale private transportation facilities up and down the coast. True, there were packets owned by Belizean and Guatemalan merchants, or the various governments, but these plied more often between New Orleans, Jamaica, or Havana and the Honduran Bay and Shore. Their schedules were irregular at best, and their cost and inconvenience outweighed any relative comfort they might have provided. Besides, smaller craft were more maneuverable along the coast, with its shallows, sandbars, and rocky protuberances, as well as in the lagoons and connecting waterways. This Black Carib "monopoly" lasted from about 1825 to 1870, when the number of private boats of all sorts increased as the fruit trade with the southern United States flourished.[8] During anthropological surveys in 1985, Garifuna canoes, now mostly with motors, were still the only means of reaching certain parts of the Honduran coast.

As noted above, before the arrival of the Black Caribs, Miskito Indians had provided similar transportation services, but there is no evidence that the latter used sails, nor were they considered as reliable as the Caribs on the sea. Miskitos also cut wood, often alongside Caribs, but they seem not to have crossed the breach between occasional, supplementary wage labor and an economic dependence upon it (Helms 1969a, 1971). As the different Miskito factions increasingly fought among themselves for an illusory royal throne and empire, the Caribs gradually came to replace them in most parts of the local labor market; and in so doing they became more and more firmly attached to the Western capitalist system.

As the Miskito image changed from fierce warrior and entrepreneurial raider and trader during the seventeenth and eighteenth centuries to that of backward and harmless savage in the nineteenth century, the Caribs' established reputation and continuing behavior patterns allowed them first to fill the "fierce" role and then to move steadily into other roles that were more respectable in European eyes. They became known as industrious, intelligent, temperate, and reliable laborers, and accounts increasingly used the term "civilized," by which was meant Christian, fully clothed, fluent in a European language, and sometimes literate (Baraud 1947:336). Most important, perhaps, was the fact that the Caribs had become consumers of European goods. Even the British, who once spoke highly of the Miskitos as their allies, now derided the latter's nakedness and their constant requests for rum, as they simultaneously praised the Caribs. Although the British Methodist missionaries on the coast in the 1830s and 1840s despaired of converting either group, they were clearly more comfortable dealing with the Caribs and accorded them more respect. This complete reversal in their positions of 1797 is apparent in descriptions from the latter half of the nineteenth century and persists to the present day, although there are signs that the Miskito reputation is again changing in the direction of so-called civilization.[9]

Wage Labor— Wood and Bananas

Although the first wage labor to which Carib men applied themselves in Central America was soldiering, woodcutting occupied them almost as early and continued to be their primary source of wages until the end of the nineteenth century. Whereas logwood (for dyes) had been the main target for Belizean woodcutters in the early centuries, mahogany (for furniture) became the rage in Europe after about 1750. For some time both woods were sought, but as cheap and vivid aniline dyes became available after the middle of the nineteenth century, the logwood trade declined and almost entirely disappeared.[10]

Mahogany cutting was difficult work, requiring physical strength, skill, and sophisticated decision making. Appropriate trees had to be selected, and these were scattered throughout the forest, rather than in stands. To be commercially viable, mahogany must be distributed at least two trees to an acre. The Honduran Mosquito coast had an unusually high mahogany density, but a large percentage of the trees were infested with termites, which reduced the value of the wood and consequently made labor costs higher (Von Hagen 1940:250). Once the trees were located, often in dense forest, they were carefully hewed to fall in such a way that they could be dragged to the closest river, then floated to the coast. Once there, they had to be prepared for shipment to Europe or made into lumber for local use. In 1838 teams of men worked different sections of the forest and were paid monthly wages plus rations (MMS, box 225, no. 15). Bard (1855:320) said that half the wages were paid in goods, such as clothing, ornaments, dishes, and pots and pans, a fact that clearly affected the entire domestic way of life and helped perpetuate the flow of labor to European enterprises as the Black Caribs' wants escalated. It is precisely such consumption patterns that have made archaeological techniques valuable in reconstructing ethnic differences in settlement patterns along this coast (Gonzalez and Cheek 1986).

In the last years of the eighteenth century, having cut much of the virgin wood in the north, the Belizean cutters began to search for new stands in the Stann Creek area. As noted above, they needed all the labor they could get, and Carib men filled that need and filled it well (see chapter 3). Stann Creek and Punta Gorda were certainly settled permanently when Carib women journeyed northward to be closer to their men, who were often in the interior for up to ten months of the year. Unlike the slave and creole and Miskito populations, there is some evidence that Carib women and children occasionally accompanied the men to the lumber camps, at least in the earliest days. Thus, speaking of Stann Creek in 1830, one Methodist missionary commented, "It is principally to this place that the Mahogany cutters in Belize have recourse in order to obtain labourers for the interior, therefore many of the Charibs old and young and of both sexes we see only three out of twelve months, and even then only for a few weeks" (MMS, box 139, no. 11).

By 1834 the Belizean merchant Marshall Bennett, in concert with Central American Federation President Francisco Morazán, began woodcutting operations in Honduras near Trujillo and eventually as far east as Brus and Carataska lagoons. Other individuals had already begun similar operations in the vicinity of Omoa (Griffith 1977:226). Caribs are known to have moved immediately into these works, and from all accounts they were the mainstay of the operations there. Even though there had been Carib settlement in Mosquitia earlier, certainly it was augmented at this time. Although it seems to have been entirely coincidental, the 1832 flight from the more settled areas of Trujillo, Omoa, and Livingston (as described in chapter 3) benefited Bennett's Mosquitian plans. At about the same time, Bennett and his Guatemalan partners began similar woodcutting operations in the Río Dulce area. They were not so fortunate in finding labor there, as most of the Caribs from Livingston had fled to Belize. The Caribs were, however, persuaded to return in 1836 (AGCA B119.2/56992/2521/1).

By 1898 Central American wood had ceased to bring such high prices in Europe, due both to competition from cheaper fine woods from Asia and Africa and to a decline in the quality of the Central American shipments. The largest old trees had been systematically removed over the preceding century, leaving only younger ones with smaller diameters. The established Belizean cutters and merchants—now the local elites—looked for new ways to invest their money and energies. Sugarcane had been tried periodically but had been more of a "boom-or-bust" industry (Helms 1969a); only in the northern Corozal district did it become a lasting enterprise in the twentieth century. Cohune nuts, valuable for their oil, were a minor commercial crop around the turn of the century in the Stann Creek area, followed by grapefruit orchards, which still provide some jobs for Carib women. However, the fact is that Belizeans tended to lose out on the biggest boom—another luxury food crop that came to be known as the green gold of the tropics.

Bananas and Prosperity

The Honduran coast in the late nineteenth century was flooded by waves of immigration, the largest of which consisted of Americans, though others came from Europe and the Middle East. They began a boom that many thought was to be a permanent development, one that required large amounts of labor, both on the plantations and on subsidiary works such as docks, housing projects, railroads, and the like. Following on the heels of independent growers and traders working originally out of the Bay Islands, there developed a corporate banana empire stretching from Belize to Bluefields.[11] The United Fruit Company, founded in 1899, began loading its ships at Belize, Livingston, Omoa, Puerto Cortes, and Tela in 1901, and at Trujillo a decade or so later. The Standard Fruit Company replaced the family-owned Vaccaro Brothers from New Orleans who had settled, along with other Italian-Americans from the same U.S. city, at La Ceiba. Names like D'Antoni, Oteri, De Lerno, and Macheco are still remembered with nostalgia by some older Garifuna men. La Ceiba itself had been founded only about twenty years earlier by French fruit growers from Roatan (Périgny 1911), but in 1899 the Vaccaros obtained the first governmental concession in Honduras to plant and export bananas on a large scale (Lainez and Meza 1973:120). In 1911 Samuel Zemurray, who had immigrated to Mobile, Alabama, from Bessarabia or Russia gained control of concessions around Omoa and Puerto Cortes and formed the Cuyamel Fruit Company.

These large companies built upon and then destroyed a system that had evolved over half a century. Small growers, sometimes selling as little as one bunch at a time, brought their fruit to the coast to meet small buyers, who at first used small schooners to take their cargos to New Orleans, the primary market for bananas in those days. This was popularly known as *poquitero* (one who deals in small amounts) trading. In 1899 there were said to be 114 companies, only 22 "of some consequence," importing bananas into the United States from the Central American Caribbean coast (F. Adams 1914:70). In the early days Caribs not only grew fruit for sale but were on hand to tend to the difficult loading, for larger vessels could not come close to shore in many places and canoes or lighters were used to ferry the produce across the breakers.

To give some idea of the immensity of the boom, consider the following. In 1876 the Bay Island of Utila, then the primary producer, shipped 52,926 bunches of bananas. The United States purchased some 16 million bunches from the more than 100 Central American companies still in business in 1898 (Lainez and Meza 1973:119). But in 1903 the United Fruit Company alone shipped 22 million bunches to the United States from the Honduran area (Rose 1904:108).

As the three large companies prospered, they expanded by absorbing or driving out smaller companies and then centralizing their operations in the few ports mentioned. Small-scale purchases declined as the companies planted conceded acreage, usually along railroads, whose construction was the primary "carrot" used in negotiating with the governments of the various countries involved.[12] Caribs, some of whom had formerly planted bananas for sale, increasingly left their village homes to find work on the docks, in the subsidiary railroad and machine shops, and even on the plantations. Some Caribs achieved skilled labor and white-collar positions, but most were unskilled laborers, especially stevedores.

The boom drew large numbers of workers from nearby areas, but even as early as 1903 the companies complained that there was a shortage of workers on the coast and that they were being forced to pay excessively high wages. Some noted, "The trouble is to get the native to work after he becomes possessed of a few dollars. As soon as he has a little money he goes off and drinks it" (MMS, box 226, 1903). Such comments were aimed primarily at the mestizos, locally called Indios in Honduras and Ladinos in Guatemala. Caribs, by contrast, were more highly respected. The designation *moreno,* which had been used on the coast since at least the eighteenth century, now became synonymous with Carib and reflected their conceptual differentiation in the minds of local persons from other population segments, including black newcomers.

Since the new demands for labor could not be satisfied by Central Americans alone, the companies began to agitate to bring in laborers from the nearby Caribbean islands and the South American coast. Against the wishes of the Honduran government, which was opposed to the immigration of blacks, they brought workers in from Jamaica, Colombia, Panama, the Caymans, and Belize. The United Fruit Company had already established itself in all of these places except the last. Most of the newcomers were English-speaking blacks with experience in the banana industry, so they became preferred workers, both on the plantations and on the docks (Procuraduría General de la República 1979). As they took more and more of the jobs, Caribs turned increasingly to the coastline itself, eschewing plantation work as fit only for "black" people and/or "Indios," with whom the Black Caribs chose not to identify themselves. Perhaps because dock work was less regular, and also because it was on the seashore where Caribs were at home and could easily travel, they came to predominate in the labor gangs of ports such as Barrios, Cortes, Tela, and La Ceiba. It was probably a good strategy under the circumstances, for such specialization did allow them to retain and circulate job information within the ethnic group and to recommend their relatives and friends in an effort to bypass or at least compete strongly with the new blacks in their midst.

Even though matings across the ethnic boundaries occurred, the Caribs usually denied having anything to do with these *Ingleses,* as the English-speaking blacks were generally labeled. And children of mixed couples, if they were raised as Caribs, soon forgot their non-Carib forebears. Like other *morenos,* they emphasized their own South American origins, pointed out that their ancestors had never been enslaved, and carved out a distinctive heritage that denied any African element, even though both their culture and their physical type bore unmistakable witness to the contrary. This attitude, of course, had older roots, starting on St. Vincent when they had endeavored to distinguish themselves from slaves by shaping their infants' heads. The tendency for white employers in Central America to look down on blacks and former slaves in particular must have exacerbated the negative feelings with which they were perceived by Caribs on their arrival. Pim (1863:312) noted that the Central American Carib was insulted by any suggestion that he had an African background. A mild antagonism persists today, at least in Honduras and Guatemala, as young *Ingleses* ridicule the "primitive" language of the Garifuna, who respond that they are not speaking a bastard tongue like Creole!

It seems to be the case that the fortunes of the Black Caribs peaked at about the same time as those of the fruit industry on the coast. Whatever criticisms can be made of the companies' impact on the national economies of the area (and there are many), Garifuna informants from the 1950s to the present unanimously extol life during the first three decades of the twentieth century, saying that they never lived so well before or since. Not only was there sufficient work for all, but the major companies actually paid higher wages than other employers (Checchi et al. 1959:102). In addition, their commissaries provided higher quality goods at lower prices than could be obtained elsewhere, and the railroad network gave them reliable and inexpensive access to major coastal towns, as well as to many of the villages along the Honduran coast that had once been reachable only by canoe or on foot.

In Trujillo some of the fine old houses in the Carib barrios were built in the 1920s with money earned in the banana industry—the dates were often commemorated in the cement floors or steps, and some can still be seen today. The Truxillo (*sic*) Railroad Company, a subsidiary of United Fruit, rented land in that area from the Carib community, paying what today seems a shockingly trifling sum. But the land was not being fully utilized anyway, and the rent the Caribs received from the company exceeded what they earn today from renting the same land for agricultural purposes to a few members of the Garifuna community. In addition, the railroad company built and equipped the first school located in the Carib barrio of Cristales. Colonialistic and patronizing though they seem today, these policies did promote development of a stable, educated working class, from which might have sprung a middle class had not the system collapsed as a result of banana disease and the interruption of trade during World War II.

If they were not already partisans of big business, most Caribs became so during this period. They tended not to be involved in the labor unions and strikes that beset Honduras in succeeding years,[13] and for the most part they have associated with the more conservative political parties in all three countries in which they live.[14] Even today, most Garifuna regret, but do not seem to resent, United Fruit's pullout, which included the destruction of the entire railroad system linking Mosquitia to Trujillo and the western coast. Garifuna apparently accept the general philosophy expressed to me by one United Fruit Company official in 1956, that "the Company is in business to make money."

It is not surprising, then, that the attributes assigned to Carib workers were, for the most part and up to that time, positively phrased by the employer class. Caribs had earlier been favorably compared with Belizean blacks or creoles (García Granados 1952, 2:104; Pim 1863:312), with Guatemalan Indians (La Compagnie Belge de Colonisation 1844:158), and with Miskitos (Douglas 1868–69:29). One visitor in the 1870s said, "The Carib males rival the Chinese in industry, and in honesty they surpass the world" (Boyle 1874:209).

At the same time that their reputations were high among Europeans, the Caribs were looked down upon by the other more humble people of the coast. Honduran Indios despised them because of their skin color and their different living patterns. Belizean creole blacks considered them backward, if not primitive, in line with their own postslavery Anglophile worldview. As late as the 1950s I was told by a Belizean creole public health nurse that Caribs in her country practiced cannibalism and ritual sacrifice of babies, that they were thieves and liars, and that they were dirty and smelly. Virginia Kerns told me privately that she had heard the same in the 1970s. Methodist and other nineteenth- and early twentieth-century missionaries continually berated the Caribs for practicing polygamy, for their ancestor rites, and for what was considered lewd dancing. Yet the first and last of these behaviors were equally characteristic of slaves and lower-class creoles.

The United Fruit Company, having formed close ties with its former competitor, Cuyamel Fruit, moved out of Trujillo, Livingston, and Belize in the late 1930s but continued loading fruit from Barrios, Cortes, and Tela for another generation. La Ceiba, controlled by the Standard Fruit Company (later Castle and Cook), survived longer, and even today both bananas and pineapples are shipped under the Dole brand from that port. Most of the loading is now mechanized, however, and there are fewer jobs than before, or at least they seem more difficult to find. Checchi et al. (1959:101) state that some 10,000 jobs were lost along the north coast of Honduras during the 1950s, a trend that has continued, even though the total population of the coastal cities

Table 6.1 Growth of Honduran Coastal Cities in the Nineteenth and Twentieth Centuries

Date	Trujillo		La Ceiba		Tela		Puerto Cortes	
	Total	Urban	Total	Urban	Total	Urban	Total	Urban
1791	812							
1801	6,480	480						
1838		1,000						
1842	2,500							
1881	6,186	4,723						
1887	6,186		1,963					
1901	4,040		3,379					
1905	3,294		3,096					
1910			2,954		2,876		3,004	
1916	4,238		6,926		4,455		4,410	
1926	6,040		12,136		7,184		8,065	
1930	8,865	5,989	13,073	10,237	9,935	6,041	9,597	6,014
1935	10,408	3,370	13,073	10,237	14,460	6,893	11,306	6,479
1940	8,313		15,124		17,457		12,614	
1945	7,547	2,957	16,152	12,185	21,633	10,454	13,932	7,955
1950	13,125	3,016	20,949	16,645	24,899	12,614		
1961	9,781	3,491	32,328	24,863	31,375	13,619	28,958	17,048
1974	20,441	3,961	47,835	38,788	46,521	19,055	44,108	25,817

Sources: 1791 (Sorsby, 1972:149); 1801 (Anguiano, cited in Vallejo 1892:127–31); 1838 (Roberts, cited in Squier 1855:102); 1842 (Young, cited in Squier 1855:102); 1881–1974 *Direccion General de Estadisticas* 1974.

has increased (see Table 6.1). A few Garifuna along the coast are government employees in both white-collar and laboring positions. But many others live by selling their services or on remittances from relatives overseas. Today, Garifuna in Honduras no longer even think of bananas or other fruit as a viable industry in which they can make a living. In fact, most young men aspire to occupations that will take them out of their country—either forever or until they can return as affluent retirees.

New Horizons—In Search of a Living

Since the beginning of World War II, when nearly everyone could see that the banana industry was in serious trouble, Black Carib men have looked to the international labor market. They began by joining the U.S. and British merchant marine corps when those countries were enlisting most of their able-bodied male citizens in the armed services. Most of the Caribs started out in menial positions: cooks' helpers, waiters, engine room and deck maintenance, and so forth. In time many of them moved into responsible and well-paid jobs that lasted until they reached the age of retirement. Usually they joined the National Maritime Union, which taught them new behavior patterns in relation to saving, spending, and safeguarding their collective position as workers. Their experiences in foreign ports gave them a new view of cultural differences, human rights, and the opportunities open to different peoples of the world. Without any doubt at all, these experiences affected the relations between the sexes, children's and teenagers' aspirations, and finally, the Caribs' sense of citizenship in broader contexts than their own village or ethnic group. In fact, they became conscious of the power of ethnicity in the modern world—something of which their ancestors had been only dimly aware, if at all, even though they had utilized the principle with great success.

In Honduras, Guatemala, and Belize large numbers of citizens of all social classes and ethnicities are presently choosing to leave their country for a better life elsewhere. Although numerous Guatemalan Indians have had their lands, livelihoods, and lives threatened, and can thus be considered political refugees, there is no evidence that any Garifuna fall into that category today. Rather, the Garifuna who leave are seeking jobs. According to recent information, many Honduran and Guatemalan Garifuna are now flooding the Belizean coast, while at the same time Belizean Garifuna are leaving in droves for New York and other U.S. cities.[15] My ethnographic work in 1984–85 leads me to believe that those flocking to Belize are there seeking (a) to improve their English and (b) a clandestine overland route to the United States. Thus, they can be considered part of a larger, regional exodus. Even though the general pattern seems to be a continuation of one established much earlier (Gonzalez 1969), I believe the earlier balance achieved through periodic returns to their native villages has now been severely altered. Chapter 7 will deal with the concept of home identity and with how that has changed through time.

NOTES

1. Women did contribute to cash income but most often by selling agricultural produce as well as fowl and pigs. They also processed and sold cassava starch, coconut oil, and dried fish, as described in chapter 5. And, on occasion, we learn about them as wage earners; for example, there are references to women working at the cohune plant in Stann Creek in 1920 (Great Britain 1920:45), on sugar and banana plantations in Honduras, and as domestics in the coastal cities shortly before the turn of the century (Morlan 1897:33). But the evidence is too fragmentary to reconstruct a satisfactory picture. See chapter 7 for further information on women's roles.

2. Readers may wonder whether at least some of the immigrant blacks may not have been women who were taken as wives by Carib men, although this has never, to my knowledge, been mentioned by other scholars. Reducing the possibility is the fact that

more male than female slaves were imported for heavy plantation work at that time. Also, the surviving domestic technology is almost exclusively South American "tropical forest," which suggests a continuity of womenfolk and women's culture throughout the various population shifts.

3. In the two or three sketches or paintings that have been identified as portraying Black Caribs on St. Vincent, none show the peculiar head deformation referred to in many of the written accounts. We know that European painters often romanticized their subjects, however, and it may be that they thought the appearance of head deformation too grotesque to record. Brunius's paintings show Black Carib men wearing headscarves—perhaps to hide their heads? It is also possible that only some Black Caribs actually did it, and that head deformation had largely gone out of fashion by the end of the eighteenth century (see Anderson 1983:67). At least two travelers commented upon head deformation among some adult Carib men in Central America as late as the 1860s (Douglas 1868–69:29; Pim and Seemann 1869:308).

4. I use the term "European" to designate culture rather than provenience of the observer, many of whom were U.S. citizens.

5. There are two exceptions to this. Davis (1896:23) included a photo of what he called the "Guatemallecan" army garrison at Livingston. It is clear that the entire group of twelve men is black, most likely Carib. Also, during the "Soccer War" between Honduras and El Salvador in 1974, it is rumored that Garifuna were employed by the military to relay radio messages, using their own language as a secret "code," just as Navajos were used by the United States during World War II. Today some Garifuna do serve in the armed forces in both Honduras and Guatemala, but their numbers are small. It is not a profession much discussed or aspired to by young men.

6. I know this by unfortunate personal experience. It is curious that today the Caribs have lost, if they ever had, the knowledge of how to sail against the wind by tacking. This is because they do not construct their sails with battens to control luffing, nor do they use a boom. Non-Carib sailors in the area tell me they have tried to teach modern Garifuna the appropriate principles, but they seem uninterested—perhaps because motors have become fairly common. Older Garifuna insist that at one time they could sail against the wind, but I have not yet found anyone who does so or who can give me details on how it was done in the past. It is difficult to imagine the Caribs traveling the distances they did without this knowledge, although they may simply have put in to shore when the wind was against them and started out again when it changed.

7. In 1983 four large fishing trawlers were given by the Danish government to a fishing cooperative at Trujillo. Most of the members of this organization are Garifuna and they travel long distances to find fish, which they sell from their large cold-storage rooms at Trujillo. In addition, refrigerated trucks belonging to the coop go out twice a week or more peddling the fish in other cities along the coast, especially La Ceiba and San Pedro Sula. Ironically, the technology of large-scale fishing, including the use of radar, for which these boats are intended, is almost totally unknown to the Garifuna fishermen. As a result, the boats are underused; much of the "catch" is purchased from smaller fishermen along the coast, even as far away as Nicaragua. There is an expectation that Garifuna men should know everything necessary to make a success of fishing and boat handling; unfortunately, the boats are not well maintained and will probably

not last. Since the U.S. boycott on trade with Nicaragua, many Honduran fishermen—especially from the larger companies that handle lobster and shrimp—are profiting by purchasing Nicaraguan catches at a low price and reselling them in the United States as their own.

8. It is not generally known that this trade actually began in the 1840s, when settlers from Grand Cayman came to Roatan and started planting coconuts, pineapples, and plantains, as well as bananas (MMS, box 225, no. 24). It was said that at the time there were only about 1,200 inhabitants on the island, mostly blacks. Trade fell off during the American Civil War and then began to boom around 1870.

9. They achieved worldwide prominence when they clashed with the Sandanista government of Nicaragua and were assisted in their resistance and flight tactics by the CIA. Various agencies, both public and private, are now dedicated to helping them achieve a basis for a sustainable independent existence as a modern ethnic group within both the Honduran and Nicaraguan republics. Whether they can survive their experiences in Nicaragua remains to be seen. Although Marxist governments have repeatedly attempted to stamp out rather than nurture ethnicity, there is some evidence that the Nicaraguan revolution may be trying a new tack. I have been informed that three communities of Black Caribs who had nearly lost their identity before the revolution are being helped to achieve status as Garifuna within the Nicaraguan polity. The less well settled and acculturated Miskitos seem to have exerted more independence and perhaps for that reason felt their very existence threatened by the new regime.

10. Logwood is today virtually unknown to ordinary people anywhere in the world. Henderson (1809:52) gave a good description of both mahogany and logwood cutting as it was done in Central America at that time. Logwood is a low, prickly tree resembling the hawthorne. It thrives in low, swampy grounds contiguous to freshwater creeks and lakes, toward which the roots extend, and matures in fifteen years. Most logs taken were only a few inches in diameter, though the trees sometimes reach five to six feet in diameter. When treated with alkaline, logwood produces colors ranging from red through purple and black; acid brings out various shades of yellow and was also said to "fix" colors, giving them greater brightness and durability (Howard 1796–98:65).

11. It would be of no use to attempt to tell the whole story of the rise and fall of the banana industry in Central America. Of the numerous works that can be consulted, Kepner and Soothill (1935) is one of the most complete; but see also F. Adams (1914), Lainez and Meza (1973), Rose (1904), May and Plaza (1958), La Barge (1962), and Procuraduría General de la República (1979). None of these can be said to be without bias, but La Barge is perhaps the most scholarly. Clearly, the subject arouses extreme passion, and much more data on the banana industry remain to be discovered, analyzed, and interpreted.

12. The Central American republics were desperate for railroads to link the populous highlands with the coasts, and thus with the world. The United States and European countries were also eager to have some way to ship goods cheaply from the Atlantic to the Pacific, and numerous schemes and serious attempts were made to finance and build such railroads, starting at least as early as the 1860s (De Silva Ferro 1875). However, not until 1879 did Minor Keith, with British capital, succeed in building a working railroad in Costa Rica. It took until after the turn of the century, how-

ever, for the other Central American countries to follow suit. The fruit companies needed good transportation to get their fruit to the coast quickly after harvest, and they persuaded their host countries to grant them extensive concessions of land for both plantations and railroad beds, with the promise that they would complete the tracks all the way from the ports to the capital cities.

13. Although they did not convert to their religion, perhaps they learned it was sometimes to their benefit to respect the established law and order from the Methodists in Belize, who started the first schools in Stann Creek and Punta Gorda in the 1830s and 1840s—schools to which Caribs from Guatemala and Honduras also sent their children for more than 100 years.

14. This is not to suggest that they vote as a block or that all hold identical political beliefs. However, it could be argued that it matters little which party is in power in these countries and that the Garifuna, like nearly everyone else, either vote for the candidate who seems to promise most at the moment or stick to their party out of a kind of team spirit. There is a group of younger Garifuna in both Belize and Honduras who espouse a more radical stance, but their primary goal seems to be ethnic recognition and development rather than social revolution for the country as a whole. Guatemalan Garifuna, as will be discussed in Part 3, seem almost to have abandoned any hope of improving their lot by political or other means aside from emigration.

15. Dr. Joseph O. Palacio, a Garifuna, has recently begun a study of documented and undocumented immigration to Belize (Palacio 1985). His estimates are nearly incredible, but most represent persons of non-Afroamerican race and culture who take up farming in their new home. Some Garifuna, like Belizean creoles, have become highly educated white-collar and professional workers, and a few continue to work in farming, either on plantations or small plots, while the majority eschew such work and choose emigration as a solution to their income needs.

7

Domesticity, Personality, and Perceptions of Self

The Nature of the Data

We have seen how the Island Caribs, Black Caribs, and Garifuna were perceived by various of their Amerindian, European, and creole neighbors, as well as by the peripatetic strangers who traveled among them or observed them from afar. Now we will examine the more intimate side of ethnicity: the institutions that regulate how people behave toward each other, as well as the values and attitudes they have about themselves, their fellows, foreigners, and alien cultural systems. Although in a sense we are examining two sides of the same coin, it is important to emphasize that the two faces are not alike.

I find some discussion of personality unavoidable in this regard, since the concept of self, or personhood, would seem to be closely related to ethnicity. As Carter (1982), following Mauss (1969), notes, societies impose the attributes, capacities, and signs of personhood upon particular human actors, as well as upon collectivities of human actors, such as ethnic groups. He also points out that in some cases personhood may be denied to particular human actors in whole or in part—as has frequently been noted in chattel slavery (1982:118). But there are numerous accounts in the ethnographic literature suggesting that denial of personhood, or "peoplehood," to collectivities other than one's own has been a frequent phenomenon. Although Tuan (1982:139ff.) asserts that non-Western societies have a less intense awareness of self and less of a sense of individualism, I know of no society that denies peoplehood *to itself* as a collectivity.

The ethnic group as a whole may exhibit characteristic ways of experiencing reality. This chapter will deal with how the ethnic identity or personality is learned and managed, leaving for other chapters the questions of how it is *structurally* generated, organized, ascribed, sustained, and sanctioned (Worsley 1984:245). An adequate social scientific analysis of personality should include not only a description of the prevalent lay or folk categories in common use but a more objective measure of the underlying behavior patterns presumed to be diagnostic criteria in assessing personality. Beyond that, it is important to describe the domains of culturally defined social relations that underlie and shape personality, especially those we have customarily called "kinship" and "residence" (Ostor, Fruzzetti, and Barnett 1982:4). Child-rearing techniques, including formal education, have long been considered of great importance in establishing personality traits and behavior patterns.

Needless to say, the written historical record is not revealing of personality per se, nor even of much that can be translated as such, largely because those who were doing the writing probably did not think of the "natives" as persons in the sense in which I use that word. Although domestic life is not much better documented, there is some information for the Island and Black Caribs on family and household structure, though there is little mention of children until the ethnographic accounts of the twentieth century.

Following in the literal footsteps of Claude Lévi-Strauss (1966) and/or in the spirit of Clifford Geertz (1973) or Victor Turner (1967), some symbolic anthropologists working in the lowland South American area have used the analysis of myth to understand the cosmology, values, and even personality characteristics of the people who tell, listen to, and live by myths (M. Brown 1984; Seeger 1979; T. Turner 1969; see also Bloch 1974). Unfortunately, collecting myths among the present-day Garifuna has been a disappointing endeavor. Douglas Taylor (1946a, 1946b, 1952), primarily a linguist, recorded a few tales in the 1940s and 1950s, mainly in Dominica, but his interpretations were straightforwardly descriptive and entirely neglected symbolic meanings. His 1951 work on the Black Caribs of Belize contains a short appendix entitled "Lore and Learning," but it consists primarily of proverbs, riddles, color terms, and the like. There is no mention of tales or myths, and the few dreams he related have to do with the ancestor rites and presumed control over the behavior of the living by the dead. Taylor (1951:7) recognized his omission of folklore and urged that other ethnographers record the songs "before it is too late."

Hadel (1972) followed Taylor's lead for his doctoral thesis, unfortunately still unpublished. He recorded eighty-four Belizean songs in Garifuna and provided English translations and a content analysis based upon the latter. Dary Fuentes's (1981) compilation of "popular literature" from Livingston contains interesting selections, including some with European motifs (e.g., *La Llorona,* or the Sirene).[1] Others are reminiscent of Africa, with animal tricksters, or of Amerindian origin myths, much like some of those recorded by Taylor (1946a). Most of the songs relate to everyday life and, like calypsos throughout the West Indies, frequently spread the latest gossip. Lilian How-land of the summer Institute of Linguistics in Guatemala also has an unpub-lished collection of songs and stories from Livingston that she was kind enough to share with me. I have relied heavily upon all of these works in the pages that follow, especially since my own attempts to collect songs, delayed until my 1985 fieldwork in Honduras, proved extremely frustrating.[2]

Projective tests to assess personality traits have been carried out among the modern Garifuna in only a few instances of which I am aware. I administered the Goodenough Draw-a-Person test to all Garifuna primary school children in Livingston (Guatemala) in 1975 and again in 1985, as well as in Trujillo and the nearby villages of Santa Fé and Guadelupe (Honduras) in 1985. Munroe and Munroe (1971) and Mertz (1977) have focused on the psychological im-pact of certain sociocultural patterns among modern-day Garifuna, both of them concentrating on males and cross-sex identity behavior. One of the reasons the Garifuna have attracted such studies is the fact that so many of them have lived in largely father-absent homes for several generations. In addition, there persists among them the institution of the *couvade*, in which the genitor experiences some of the pregnancy symptoms of the mother. This is apparently a survival from Island Carib times, and something they share with numerous South American lowland groups (Coehlo 1949; Rivière 1974). Elements of the *couvade* can be discerned in the expressed ideas and actions of even well-educated young Garifuna.

In 1956–57 I noted that it was commonly believed, by both men and women in Livingston, that the father's behavior could influence the course of delivery, as well as cause severe and sometimes permanent damage to the child. For the most part, however, such beliefs have largely disappeared today or can be said to fall into the grey area of "superstition"; that is, most Garifuna say they do not really believe the stories they have heard, but like many Americans who say they do not believe in ghosts, they may appear to do so when it fits their purposes or when they can think of no other explanation in seemingly bizarre individual cases. Thus, a young female research assistant confided to me that the first inkling she had of her own first pregnancy in 1978 was when her boyfriend's persistent nausea was said by a Garifuna shaman to have been caused by his having impregnated someone. I am sure neither she nor her lover was aware that their ancestors, the Island Caribs, had believed in a similar "mystic" relationship between the begettor and the begotten (Taylor 1950:343).

The Munroes (1971:16) found that forty-five of their forty-nine male infor-mants in the early 1960s in Belize had experienced pregnancy symptoms. Furthermore, father-absence during the childhood of male subjects was posi-tively correlated with the frequency of pregnancy symptoms they experienced in later years (1971:20–21). Although high levels of aggression are frequently noted among males in the United States who grow up without fathers, the Munroes (1971:23) note that Carib males seldom engaged in actual physical aggression with each other. Kerns (1983:77) states that "adults may threaten attack but they rarely come to blows." People "fight" by bitter name-calling, cursing, invidious gossip, the composing and singing of derogatory songs, or as a final resort, magical formulas to get even with their enemies; but they are not known for assault and battery, much less for murder.[3] Even with the increased consumption of alcohol seen today among both men and women, physical violence is rarely used to settle quarrels, except among children and sometimes teenagers. Kerns describes a mother who encourages her child to "fight back." I have more often seen mothers intervene, sometimes with a certain amount of violent behavior on their own part, to separate furious and impassioned youngsters intent on slugging it out. The beating of wives is so rare as to cause considerable gossip and outrage when it does occur. The Garifuna are, in fact, best described today as a gentle people, even when their outward demeanor may suggest otherwise.

This is in marked contrast to the "fierce" reputation the Black Caribs had both before and immediately after the deportation from St. Vincent. Their wartime killings, in fact, seem to have been carried out with considerable passion, if not viciousness. They struck fear into the hearts of all who faced them in the Lesser Antilles and later in Central America, inciting even the hardened Gen. Tomás O'Neille to warn the Miskito king that the Caribs "fight desperate" (Burdon 1933:71–72). According to Anderson (1983), violence within the group was also common, murder being the frequent outcome of quarrels, even among brothers. Husbands, he said, were exceedingly jealous of their wives, "and nothing but death of both suspected parties could atone" (1983:66). This contrasts sharply with marital behavior today (see note 3).

Mertz (1977) approaches the question of the effects of father-absence quite differently. He tries to ascertain the degree of the male children's "psychological differentiation," an important element in the human (and perhaps mammalian) maturation process. This concept deals with the individual's development of a sense of separate identity, including the ability to function autonomously— first of the mother and then of other members of the society. The development of more structured, specialized psychological defenses is characteristic of those who are more highly differentiated, and in general it is assumed that greater psychological differentiation is healthy and necessary for normal functioning of the individual, at least in Western society.[4] Mertz chose to study the Garifuna because studies among father-absent children in the United States had suggested that less-differentiated functioning in children is linked to family structures characterized by a "female-salient surround" in which there is an absence of strong male role models, thereby inhibiting the developmental task of separating from the mother (Witkin and Berry 1975:57).

Mertz concludes, however, that even when Garifuna fathers were physically absent, their influence remained strong enough that the boys were not hindered in their psychological growth. In other words, their degree of psychological differentiation was not significantly different from that of males in other cultures. As a side issue, however, Mertz (1977:20–21) notes that the single most important relationship for growing boys was with their older siblings, especially brothers, but sisters as well. Unlike the Munroes, Mertz did not study actual behavior patterns or further test for aggression or other such tendencies.

Because of the many uncertainties as to the meaning of the concept of psychological differentiation, I was more interested in using the Goodenough test as a possible means of judging the relative influence of the two sexes, through the available role models, upon the growing child. Earlier (Gonzalez 1970a) I had suggested that what we were calling "matrifocality," or "mother-centeredness," might be expected to affect children in testable ways. The results of my 1975 study show that Garifuna boys (as well as girls) in Livingston were more likely to draw figures of the female sex first, even at ages when boys in other cultures overwhelmingly drew males first (Gonzalez 1979). This was more in line with the Munroes' findings than with those of Mertz, and my 1985 test results, including those from Livingston, support this conclusion.

All the psychological studies have pointed to child-rearing techniques and domestic structures as major determinants of what we may loosely term "personality,"[5] including not only such things as aggression but gender- and age-related behavior. The previous chapter outlined the reputation, including certain personality characteristics, enjoyed by the Island Caribs, Black Caribs, and Garifuna among their contemporaries and among historians working with contemporary records. As has been shown, the extant early descriptions largely relate to men and to the workplace rather than to women and/or the domestic or home environment. Furthermore, only ethnography (or cross-cultural social psychology) is likely to shed light on the present-day Garifuna perceptions of self, and then only by inference, unless the investigator has consciously gathered information on the subject.

This chapter will present what little evidence exists for how the Island and Black Caribs thought of themselves, especially in relation to those domestic and supradomestic[6] institutions (such as schools) that shape personality. I will present data that show how these institutions have been rapidly changing over the past generation. Finally, I will discuss the Garifuna self-image and those behavior patterns that seem to distinguish them today from other groups.

Island Caribs and Black Caribs

There is virtually no evidence upon which I can base my conclusions here, but we can speculate as to how the Island Caribs perceived themselves. The very notion that they might have had a self-perception was beyond the thinking of most Europeans of the conquest period, who either portrayed them as "Wild-men" (Burke 1972–73) or as "Noble Savages" (Behn 1973), neither image buttressed by any kind of reliable behavioral descriptions. The ethnocentrism of the Europeans permitted them to portray the indigenous peoples of the New World only within the framework of their own experience.

Toward the end of the St. Vincent period, we begin to find statements or descriptions alleged to have been taken from observations of actual events or from personal interactions. One of the most salient points, made over and over again, is that the Black Caribs were proud of their separate ethnic identity and fiercely rejected the idea that they had anything in common with the African slaves of the area. As we have seen, head deformation, apparently unknown among lowland South American groups, was said to have been adopted by the Black Caribs in order to distinguish themselves from the slaves. Increasingly throughout the eighteenth century Europeans distinguished between the Black and Yellow Caribs by the fierce demeanor of the former. Note was made of the continually belligerent countenances of the women as well as the men, though there is no mention of women having actually fought in any battles, even in self-defense (Coke 1808–11, 3:265).

Anthropologists who have tried to reconstruct the sixteenth-and seventeenth-century Island Carib social organization from contemporary accounts have encountered inconsistent and sometimes contradictory clues. This undoubtedly stems from imperfect observation, misunderstanding of non-European social systems, and an urge on the part of the observers toward establishing *the* custom and ignoring variations in pattern, at least some of which may have been due to ongoing change in response to conquest conditions. It is thus risky to rely too heavily on any single historical observation, but I will try to present an ethnological analysis, based on clues from eye-witnesses, archaeology, linguistics, and what we know about social organization in general.

It is generally agreed that the descriptions of the Jesuit missionary Raymond Breton (1665) are probably the most reliable for gaining an idea of the structure, if not the nature, of the Island Carib domestic establishment. He was the only one among the early chroniclers who ever actually lived among the Caribs, staying on Dominica for some eighteen years. He described settlements of several households clustered about a larger communal house which served as a ceremonial center and the place in which men relaxed and took their meals, and in which they and the adolescent boys also slept. This description is consistent with the plan of the settlement excavated by Adelaide and Ripley Bullen (in 1970) on St. Lucia, as well as with many descriptions from lowland South America.

Dreyfus (1982:6), who is more familiar with the historical works on the Island Caribs than any other anthropologist to date, says, "The social system can be defined as comprised of networks of local groups, interconnected by marriages and other exchanges. Most of the local groups were exogamous and were constituted by one uxorilocal, extended family whose headman was the father of married daughters. Some of the villages were larger than others; the largest were those whose headmen were also renowned war chiefs and who played an important political and ritual role, as suppliers for anthropophagic ritual performances."

The headman in each such community was polygynous, perhaps as were some of the other men, although it is not clear to what extent polygyny was common. Each woman occupied a separate house with her daughters and young sons. Breton (1958) reported that after marriage—often, if not preferentially, to a patrilateral cross-cousin—most men lived with their in-laws. This may have been a temporary arrangement, in the manner of bride service, but in most cases it appears to have been permanent. In the event of a man taking a second wife, unless she were the sister of the first wife, uxorilocal residence would have been awkward. Yet given the mobility of the men in trading and raiding, some may have had wives in several different communities, visiting each in turn or as their travels took them. Breton (1958:24) stated that when men went to other islands they left their wives at home, taking up with local women "for as long as they expect to remain there." Labat (1970:77), by contrast, specifically mentions women and children traveling with their men, at least on occasion.

As Helms (1981) suggests, this pattern is, superficially at least, not unlike that described by me for the Black Caribs of Central America (Gonzalez 1969). However, the institution of "war" and the presence of war chiefs, as clearly outlined by Dreyfus (1982), molded the character of the villages and of the social organization in ways not found after the deportation. The most effective chiefs had more wives than the commoners, as well as the right to virilocal residence for themselves and for their sons. Their daughters' husbands also lived with them, unless these women were themselves married to chiefs. Thus, the villages of the most successful warriors were larger than others, as were their networks of relatives, affines, and allies (Dreyfus 1982:7).

The European incursions into the Leewards may have reinforced the above patterns, at least at first, because of the increased level of warfare, trading, and slaving—all of which had previously existed but now took on new meanings in relation to the newcomers. The latter included not only white men from several nations but Africans, the earliest of whom were introduced into the area in 1504 (Dreyfus 1982:14). It must be emphasized that from the perspective of the Island Caribs or Kalinago (modern-day Karaphuna/Garifuna/Garinagu)[7] and other groups native to the West Indies, both whites and blacks were potential allies or enemies, and members of both groups might themselves be taken as slaves. They soon discovered, however, that only the whites purchased (i.e., bartered for) people to be used as slaves and that they accepted

Indians and blacks, but not whites, in that capacity. Thus, captives might now be sold rather than eaten or kept for their services. Presumably both male and female Indians had some exchange value, even though males were probably most in demand.

Male Roles. What does all this suggest for the Island and Black Carib family, homelife in general, and resultant personality formation? In the absence of more precise data, we can only imagine that at best the role of adult men must have been difficult. Fierceness, as among the Yanomamo today, would have been encouraged and valued. The threat to the warrior of himself being captured and either sold or eaten must have been constant and fear-instilling, and many men must have sallied forth never to return. We can only deduce that the Island Carib men were outgoing, self-confident, and not to be intimidated by the strangers who so arrogantly sought their land and their labor. Taylor (1946c:182) interpreted the early accounts as suggesting that the Island Caribs emphasized "rugged individualism," even though Glazier (1980:448) disagrees that there is any evidence of this. As a recent Asian writer has noted (Tuan 1982:39), it is Western culture that encourages an intense awareness of self and an exaggerated belief in the power and value of the individual. Macfarlane (1978) believes the English were among the first Europeans to develop individualism as a character trait, although it seems to have been highly valued in ancient Greece (Tuan 1982:156).

Historic descriptions of Amerindian and African cultures do not give us much evidence about personality, and Tuan's conclusion that the social unit has always taken precedence over the individual or self in both areas seems credible, though it is based upon too little data to be persuasive. Rivière (1984:98) notes that the Guiana Indian *appears* to have an individualistic bent but only, he believes, because societal and individual relationships are of the same order of complexity in that system, with society being no more than the aggregate of individually negotiated relationships. These apparently divergent views may actually reflect the likelihood that at a certain level of sociocultural integration individualistic behavior is congruent with the needs and shape of the entire social unit. Individualism, then, is to a certain extent "in the eye of the beholder," which might help to explain the difference between Glazier's and Taylor's conclusions.

It is reasonable to suppose, however, that in the eighteenth century there may well have been differences in the ways in which Amerindians and Africans viewed themselves and the world. Indeed, it would be strange if there were not. Although captive black men were sometimes absorbed into Island Carib communities as slave-husbands (see chapter 1), we have no way of knowing if they were permitted to participate in the slaving-raiding-trading forays. Most likely it was only the second generation and beyond who were treated as full

members of the society, and to the extent that personality is culturally determined, the behavior patterns of these mixed-bloods should have been similar
to those of their Indian ancestors. By the middle of the eighteenth century,
however, there may have been an influx of African-born men who escaped
from other islands or arrived with the "Brigands" to fight on the side of the
French-Carib alliance. Their children, by Island Carib women who may themselves have had some mixed ancestry, might have developed different personality traits transmitted and/or inculcated by their fathers. Several writers have
assumed that the distinctive personality traits of the Africans made a difference
in the way in which the Black Caribs managed their internal and external
affairs (e.g., Beauçage 1966; Coehlo 1955; Taylor 1951).

In any case, as I suggest in chapter 1, the political system headed by war
chiefs persisted until the middle of the eighteenth century, and many of its
elements may be seen to have remained among the succeeding Black Carib
polity, at least until the deportation in 1797. But at the same time, the increasingly important African component combined with push factors deriving
from the escalated conflict with the British for land in St. Vincent to change
the situation for the early Black Caribs. The African element probably infil-
trated the religious system at about the same time. Men who became religious
leaders, or *buwiyes,* were accorded status second only to that of war chiefs
among the Island Caribs (Dreyfus 1982:6–7, 13). The earliest blacks among
them may have achieved considerable prestige by introducing modifications to
the religious ritual that were comparable to, though different from, what the
Island Caribs had previously known. Mystical knowledge of the living world
could be achieved through successful communication with ancestral and other
spirits, and many African societies excelled in such endeavors. Even today
among the Garifuna the *buwiye* and related practitioners are looked up to,
whether in Central America or in New York City.

Although prior to deportation the Black Caribs were said to be slaveowners, and forty-one slaves were in their company when they surrendered in
the fall of 1796, slaving as a military and economic endeavor had disappeared.
In fact, there is no record of any Black Caribs ever having engaged in slave
trading per se. It is tempting to suggest that this was due to the fact that many
of their own ancestors had been enslaved and that they eschewed it for humani-
tarian or ideological reasons. Unfortunately, that explanation is not consistent
with the recorded enmity among the Caribs and other blacks on St. Vincent or
with the fact that they held slaves themselves. Rather, endeavors other than
slave trading occupied their attention and competed for their energy. Not only
were they increasingly required to defend their territory, attacked by land and
by sea, but they found a ready market for both their agricultural produce and
their labor among the French on Martinique and St. Lucia and among the
English on Trinidad (Anderson 1983:57).[8]

Thus, success as a chief would no longer have depended upon the number of captives taken but more upon a man's ability to negotiate with Europeans, including the ability to trick the latter and to organize forays against them. Polygyny for chiefs (or captains, as they were later called by the Spaniards) was still standard practice and is portrayed in the painting by Brunius entitled *Chatoyer and His Five Wives.*[9]

Women's Roles. There is a paucity of information about the domestic duties of the Island Carib women except to note that they tended the gardens and collected shellfish near the shores. Then, as now, they must have provided a certain amount of family stability when the men were absent. Uxorilocality would have produced a core of related women living and working together. Whatever the dangers to women of being captured or dying in childbirth, the frequent mention of polygyny suggests that any imbalance in the sex ratio favored women over men. But we have no clues as to the usual age of marriage for both sexes or what rules governed the remarriage of widows, so it is not possible to detail how the system might have adjusted to a higher level of male mortality.

As among the Island Caribs, the Black Carib women were primarily responsible for the gardens, in which the number of cultigens had increased considerably with European and African introductions, even though the staple remained cassava. The presence of Europeans on St. Vincent provided a local market for agricultural produce, and women seem to have been active in this. There is no mention of women having worked as domestics or in any other capacity for Europeans at this time, although Anderson (1983:65) related that young boys made good (i.e., quiet and docile) household servants if they were removed from their parents at an early age.

Black Carib women, like their immediate predecessors, wove cotton cloth[10] and sleeping mats and perhaps made pottery, but it was the men who hunted and fished, made canoes, basketry, and wooden household utensils, wove silk-grass hammocks and fishnets, constructed houses, and cleared the land for gardens. Industry, as well as bravery, must have been a highly prized personal characteristic in both sexes.

To the extent that the Black Caribs and Yellow Caribs on St. Vincent may have raided each other's settlements for wives, fear of capture may still have been a feature of life for the women. More important, however, must have been the risk of losing one's husband at sea or in warfare. Death from disease was no doubt a more common threat after greater contact with the outside world was established. A smallpox epidemic was specifically noted as having caused great depredations among the Vincentian Caribs in the mid-1780s (Morris 1787:181).

Death, though apparently a nearly daily occurrence, was nevertheless a major trauma and greatly feared. Proper burial was essential in order to honor the dead and protect the living. Island Caribs were said to take great risks to recover the bodies of their fallen comrades (Dreyfus 1982:13). Black Caribs also had such a custom, as noted during the Carib War (WO1/767, f.279).[11] The abandonment of corpses during the ensuing epidemic of 1796–97 (see chapter 1) was, therefore, exceedingly unusual, signaling extreme psychological stress, if not general societal disarray or breakdown.

The earliest descriptions of funerals mentioned women dancers (Baxter 1970:26, quoting Las Casas) and spirits speaking to the living through the mouths of women (presumably in trance), both of which suggest that some elements of the rituals seen today were already in place among the Island Caribs. But we know nothing of the planning for the ceremonies or of women's participation as shamans.

The nineteenth-century Methodist missionaries in Belize also mentioned women dancing and singing during what they called "devil dances," but as they were men themselves, they tended to approach the males for information — with the implication, at least, that men were in charge. This may have been merely an ethnocentric and gender-centric view. Still, the documentation of women as the dancers, singers, and trancers is strong for all three cultural phases. Whatever this implies for the personality of women, it seems likely that prestige and status accrued to those women who were most effective in achieving the trance state. As Kerns (1983) shows in marvelous detail, the strength of the present-day Garifuna woman in large part stems from her participation in the religious system. Female shamans, however, are only documented for Garifuna in the anthropological accounts, and it is my view that such roles are relatively new—the product of male migration, much as are the consanguineal household and matrifocality (see chapters 8 and 9).

Childcare is a subject for which we have virtually no information for either the Island or the early Black Caribs. Even Brunius's paintings show few babies and no young children. Only one of Chatoyer's five wives is shown with an infant, in this case in a sling about the mother's neck. Anderson (1983:67) said babies were carried like garden produce: in baskets supported by tumplines resting on the women's shoulders. Several pictures survive of nineteenth-century Black Caribs in Central America, showing children two or three years of age astride the hips of women who are presumably their mothers or grandmothers. This is more typically African than Amerindian and survives to the present time. It is one of the motor habits mentioned by Aguirre Beltrán (1958) in his pioneering work on African influences in Mexico.

The Garifuna Domestic Domain and Personality Formation

Domestic organization of the Garifuna has been of continuing interest to me since 1955, and I have had an opportunity to replicate family and household studies in Livingston with major studies in 1975 and again in 1985. Comparisons with Belizean Garifuna households were made in Punta Gorda and Dangriga in 1976, and data for Trujillo and two of its nearby villages were collected in 1985.

Thirty years ago I was primarily concerned with the relationship between ideal and actual family and household composition and the ways in which both of these were influenced by the economic structure, which in turn seemed increasingly oriented toward migratory wage labor (Gonzalez 1969; see also R. T. Smith 1956). I postulated that households in which women occupied decision-making and authoritative roles provided social and cultural continuity in a world dominated by a capitalist system over which the Garifuna had no control but with which they were inextricably entwined through male migratory labor. Although my investigation of the historical background at that time was minimal, I suggested that there was no going backward for the Garifuna—that their "original" culture, whatever it might have been, had been largely destroyed or eclipsed and that they were best seen as a product of acculturation, of the very processes to which they were now adapted (Gonzalez 1970a). In Ortner's (1984) terms, my theoretical tools included evolution, adaptation, cultural ecology, political economy, and cultural materialism. I believed that what I dubbed the "consanguineal household" was an adaptation to male wage migration. When I discovered that the frequency of this domestic unit had not diminished a generation later, I felt that I was surely on the right track, since the job market in and around Livingston, where I had done nearly all my work, remained depressed and men continued to leave the area in search of work.

The actual mechanisms by which the households persisted related to courtship and marriage, as well as the idea that women could maximize economic benefits for themselves and their children by keeping men at arms' length, so to speak, and by switching their loyalties and sexual partners when better opportunities arose.[12] Thus, a woman might have several men upon whom she could depend for cash resources, each of them having become attached to her by fathering a child—the mystic relationship to that child constituting the binding tie. Although not particularly concerned at that time with the content of the rituals themselves, I did suggest that the ancestor cult could be seen as a mechanism that fostered, promoted, and maintained the affective relationships among children, their fathers, and their fathers' kin (Gonzalez 1959b).

As mentioned at the beginning of this chapter, I administered the Goodenough Draw-a-Person test to schoolchildren in Livingston in 1974, hoping this might be a way to "get into their heads," to see how they might view males, females, and their own place in the scheme of things. I was then drawing upon social psychology, whose practitioners at that time were particularly interested in father-absence and its effect upon children. My results (reported in Gonzalez 1979) seemed consistent with the idea that Garifuna notions of masculinity and femininity were different from those in other populations previously studied and that females were salient in the minds of children—among both boys and girls, as it turned out. Matrifocality—previously postulated on the basis of household composition and impressons of "strong" female roles—could now be seen to have a measurable effect and some objective psychological reality.

In 1985 I repeated the tests in both Livingston and in the Trujillo area (Tables 7.1–7.3 compare the previously published Livingston data with the new data). Although consanguineal households remain as common as ever among the Garifuna in both areas (see Tables 7.4–7.6), there were some changes in the frequency of self-sex drawings, which may or may not indicate a basic change in the process and outcome of personality formation. The results for girls did not change much and are consistent with those reported for other societies (Heinrich and Triebe 1972). Although boys drew their own sex first more often than before, it is significant to note that Garifuna boys between the formative years of seven and eleven *still* draw their own sex less often than do Garifuna girls of the same ages; and furthermore, their percentage of self-sex preference during that period is still lower than those reported in the nineteen studies reviewed by Heinrich and Triebe.

What do these findings mean? Although I am hesitant to push any interpretation too far because of the relatively small sample size and the continuing lack of cross-cultural comparative materials, I believe that the results do show a bias in favor of females in this culture and that the Garifuna child's mind-set on this matter differs from that found in many others. But I now find it difficult to associate this effect exclusively with the consanguineal household. As I suggest elsewhere (Gonzalez 1984b), I am no longer so sure that a classification of existing households by "type" is meaningful in the sense in which I once thought it was. The notion that consanguineal households are superior to those containing a married couple because they maximize the number of males who may be called upon to contribute to the household economy does not hold up in the face of new evidence. In fact, I now believe that in their domestic behavior most Garifuna may be said to treat households as though they were largely interchangeable. In other words, a house is not a home, and it is difficult to find any unit among them that corresponds to the latter concept as we know it.

Starting in early childhood and continuing until they are themselves the owners of a house, most Garifuna shuttle among houses belonging to other people—their mothers, fathers, other relatives, marital partners, or children. Garifuna tend to live out their lives from earliest childhood as individuals who become attached to, then detached from, various other persons and/or households for varying periods of time. I have come to think of them as individualists of the first order for whom loyalties to their ethnic group, their community of

Table 7.1 Percentage of Garifuna Boys and Girls in Livingston, Guatemala, Who Drew Their Own Sex First

Age (years)	Boys 1975	Boys 1985	Girls 1975	Girls 1985	Significance Boys vs Girls 1975	1985
6	33	71	—	50		
7	50	64	45	69	n.s.	n.s.
8	11	64	79	74	.0005	n.s.
9	18	43	93	88	.0005	.001
10	45	63	79	95	.04	.04
11	67	64	82	90	n.s.	n.s.
12	70	70	76	65	n.s.	n.s.
13	67	75	81	55	n.s.	n.s.
14	92	64	65	50	n.s.	n.s.
15–17	52	89	71	81	n.s.	n.s.
Overall	52	63	74	74	$p < .0001$	

$N = 318$ in 1975; $N = 389$ in 1985.

Table 7.2 Comparisons of Boys in Five Garifuna Settings Who Drew Their Own Sex First

Age (years)	Livingston 1975 No.	%	1985 No.	%	Trujillo 1985 No.	%	Sante Fe 1985 No.	%	Guadalupe 1985 No.	%
6	3	33	5	71	3	75	7	58	8	89
7	10	50	21	64	8	80	4	67	3	60
8	18	11	9	64	10	71	4	40	4	80
9	11	18	10	43	8	50	8	67	3	60
10	20	45	12	63	10	71	9	69	5	63
11	18	67	8	64	24	83	12	92	7	70
12	20	70	19	70	14	66	6	50	5	45
13	12	67	9	75	25	89	6	75	6	75
14	13	92	9	64	7	88	10	91	2	40
15–17	21	52	16	89	3	75	2	67	1	100
	146		118		112		68		44	
Overall %		50.5		66.7		74.8		67.6		68.2

Note: Sample was 100 percent of children in school; average percentage = 65.5.

Table 7.3 Comparisons of Girls in Five Garifuna Settings Who Drew Their Own Sex First

Age (years)	Livingston 1975 No.	Livingston 1975 %	Livingston 1985 No.	Livingston 1985 %	Trujillo 1985 No.	Trujillo 1985 %	Sante Fe 1985 No.	Sante Fe 1985 %	Guadalupe 1985 No.	Guadalupe 1985 %
6	0	—	6	50	3	75	6	75	2	100
7	20	45	18	69	7	100	10	100	7	70
8	14	79	23	74	9	60	15	83	10	100
9	15	93	21	88	15	88	9	82	5	71
10	24	79	20	95	9	75	16	70	6	75
11	28	82	19	90	20	74	4	44	4	80
12	21	76	13	65	24	75	6	67	1	100
13	16	81	6	55	11	79	4	57	6	100
14	17	65	9	50	6	100	2	100	5	83
15–17	13	71	13	81	2	100	0	—	1	100
	168		148		106		72		47	
Overall %		74.5		71.7		82.6		75.3		86.5

Note: Sample was 100 percent of children in school; average percentage = 78.7.

Table 7.4 Types of Garifuna Households in Cristales (Trujillo), Honduras, 1982

	No.	%
Consanguineal		
1 parent and children	63	20.5
1 or more single parents and children and/or grandchildren and/or other consanguineal kin	100	32.5
Siblings or other kin, one generation only	1	0.3
	164	
Solitary	3	7.5
Affinal		
1 couple and children	69	22.4
1 couple and others, extended lineally or laterally	40	13.0
1 couple only	10	3.2
2 or more couples and others	2	0.6
	121	
Total	288	100

Source: Compiled from data collected by the local Catholic church in Trujillo, 1982.

Table 7.5 Types of Garifuna Households in Guadalupe, Honduras, 1985

	No.	%
Consanguineal		
1 parent and children	9	10.1
1 or more single parents and children and/or		
grandchildren and/or other consanguineal kin	27	30.3
Siblings or other kin, one generation only	2	2.2
	38	
Solitary	10	11.2
Affinal		
1 couple and children	17	19.1
1 couple and others, extended lineally or laterally	20	22.5
1 couple only	1	1.1
2 or more couples and others	3	3.4
	41	
Total	89	100

Table 7.6 Types of Garifuna Households in Livingston, Guatemala

	1956		1975	
	No.	%	No.	%
Consanguineal				
1 woman and children	84	23.2	23	18.3
2 or more women and children	40	11.1	17	13.5
1 or more women and children				
plus a consanguineally related				
male	40	11.1	16	12.7
	164		56	
Solitary	0	0	6	4.8
Affinal				
1 couple and children	149	41.0	52	41.3
1 couple only	49	13.5	12	9.5
	198		64	
Total	362	100	126	100

Note: Questionnaires for 1956 and 1975 were phrased differently than in 1982 and 1984–85, so the categories are not exactly comparable with those used in Tables 7.4 and 7.5.

birth, and their kin are often sacrificed by the necessity to make their way alone.

Individualism is fostered also by the methods of child-rearing. As noted earlier, Garifuna women today carry children in their arms when very young and on one hip when older, though they are inclined to leave children at home whenever possible to avoid having to carry them at all. When at home infants may be left in cloth hammocks, which are safer than flat surfaces since leverage is difficult to achieve until the child approaches a year of age. Although it cannot be said that the Garifuna mother is uncaring, her physical involvement with her baby is minimal in comparison with many other cultures. She may not breast-feed at all, and even when she does she is likely to wean the child by the age of one year or less.[13]

This tendency toward early weaning is also related to the facility with which the Garifuna mother is able to leave her young child with a caretaker for either short or long intervals (see Sanford 1971; Kerns 1983:51; Gonzalez 1984a). We have no information on this subject for earlier time periods, but based upon my observations in the middle 1950s, the newer out-migration of women merely exacerbates an already common occurrence. I suspect fosterage has been characteristic of Black Caribs in the larger towns at least from the beginning of this century, when women became more involved with the cash economy and simultaneously sought foster care as a means of improving the life opportunities for their children, especially sons. The practice also alleviated pressure on domestic resources as new children followed, especially if fathered by new partners. Anderson's (1983:65) note that young boys sometimes became servants in St. Vincent suggests an even earlier origin.

Sanford (1976), who concentrated upon fosterage in an earlier study, believes it has had a profound influence on the development of the adult personality. On the one hand, it promotes flexibility and adaptability—qualities that prepare children for the complex urban world into which many of them migrate in adulthood (1976:30–31). On the other hand, children are taught to manipulate personal relationships to their own benefit, thus creating adults who are prone to suspect each others' motives (1976:15).

Hadel (1972:23) also comments upon this lack of trust in one another and the inability to carry out cooperative work as a general character trait. Kerns (1983:75) appears to agree with this assessment, noting that women often admonish their children that they must "fight for themselves," which she claims refers at once to self-reliance, the nature of work, the structure of conflict, and the value of personal autonomy.

Men are not reticent about handling children—either in loving and caring ways or in taking disciplinary action when needed. The fact that they are not more involved with child-rearing is more related to their frequent absences from home than to any macho sense that children are the special province of women. Women can and do take strong verbal and physical action to correct children's behavior, but as boys get older and stronger, the women are more likely to call for adult male assistance in disciplining them. If the boy's father is not available, a woman may call upon the father's brother; if her relations with the father are not good, she may seek her own brother or another male relative, who will use whatever physical force is necessary to mete out punishment. Older women are more likely to use psychological stratagems, threatening supernatural intervention after their own death or trying to instill shame and/or guilt by reminding wayward offspring that their behavior has caused embarrassment or pain. In extreme cases a woman will announce her shame to the neighborhood by keening, as when a death in the family occurs.

Child-rearing is no longer left only to the family, however. Ever since St. Vincent days there have been attempts, usually by missionaries, to establish schools among the Caribs. The Vincentian and Belizean Black Caribs were known to favor the learning of European languages, and it is clear today from listening to children's songs and games that these were strongly influenced by nineteenth-century England. For several generations the Belizean Garifuna have enjoyed a reputation for scholarliness—many of their young men having found employment throughout the former colony as schoolteachers—and their abilities in language learning are legendary. In a visit to Punta Gorda in 1976 I listened with fascination to court proceedings in which a single Garifuna translator handled English, Creole, Maya, Kekchi, and Garifuna. This emphasis on formal education in Belize has clearly contributed to the relative ease with which Garifuna there are beginning to move into the national arena as leaders (see Part 3).

Data on school attendance in Livingston and Honduras indicate a different pattern, however. As shown in Tables 7.7–7.9, Garifuna children in those countries have higher drop-out rates than other ethnic groups among whom they live. Still, they do enroll in the lower grades, and it is possible that their notions about the shape of male-female roles in the world have been altered somewhat by their experiences there. This may account, at least in part, for the somewhat higher frequency with which boys now draw their own sex first in the Goodenough test administered. Since male children in the more isolated villages show a lower self-sex percentage than in the towns, it may be that the tests are also a measure of acculturation to the outside world.

Symbolic Representations of Society and Personality

The collections of songs and stories made by Hadel (1972) and Howland (unpublished notes) emphasize a few themes above all others. Probably the most common is the lament that describes the anguish of separation (Cayetano 1977). As I have discussed (see chapter 4), travel and death are often equated

Table 7.7 School Enrollment in Livingston, Guatemala, 1985

	Garifuna	Ladino	Other[a]	Total	% Garifuna
Kindergarten					
Female	21	4	6	31	67.7
Male	17	3	6	26	65.4
Public school grades 1–6					
Female	204	93	40	337	60.5
Male	211	61	65	337	62.6
Private school grades 1–6					
Female	16	25	0	41	39.0
Male	5	25	1	31	16.1
Junior high school					
Female	21	31	14	66	31.8
Male	41	20	11	72	56.9
Total	536	262	143	941	56.9

[a]Includes Indian, East Indian, mulatto, Chinese.

Table 7.8 Grade School Enrollment in Rural Honduras, 1985

	Garifuna	Ladino	Total	% Garifuna
Grade 1				
Female	23	6	29	79.3
Male	27	5	32	84.4
Grade 2				
Female	17	1	18	94.4
Male	14	3	17	82.4
Grade 3				
Female	23	2	25	92.0
Male	16	0	16	100.0
Grade 4				
Female	10	2	12	83.3
Male	17	2	19	89.5
Grade 5				
Female	18	2	20	90.0
Male	11	2	13	84.6
Grade 6				
Female	8	0	8	100.0
Male	14	1	15	93.3
Total	198	26	224	88.4

Table 7.9 School Enrollment in Trujillo, Honduras, 1985

	Garifuna	Ladino	Other[a]	Total	% Garifuna
Kindergarten					
Female	101	43	8	152	66.4
Male	81	33	9	123	65.8
Grades 1–6					
Female	140	70	6	216	64.8
Male	144	88	17	249	57.8
Junior high school					
Female	141	234	7	382	36.9
Male	77	108	6	191	40.3
Commercial school					
Female	14	28	0	42	33.3
Male	3	21	1	25	12.0
High school					
Female	70	303	8	381	18.3
Male	41	146	6	193	21.2
Total	812	1,074	68	1,954	41.6

[a] Includes Miskito and mulatto.

symbolically. In one sense, the Garifuna who travel may be socially dead, for one never knows if they will come back. And when spirits return to possess the bodies of the entranced, friends and relatives inquire about their health and that of other dead ones, almost as though they had traveled to New York City rather than the afterworld. Both death and travel are considered inevitable, necessary, and fearful, yet fascinatingly mysterious, and those who leave become more powerful than those who stay—the dead through their new supernatural powers and the travelers because of their increased economic resources and information networks. Such thoughts help assuage the grief felt at death or separation, remove some of the fear of one's own death, and motivate young people to seek migration. Most of those left in the villages have little idea of where and how their absent loved ones live or work; and sometimes they feel it is easier to communicate with the truly dead than with the merely migratory.

Thus, it is the pleasure and the responsibility of those who stay behind to inveigle both types of "travelers" to return. They do this in rituals of various sorts, as well as in prayers, secular songs, letters, phone calls, and messages sent with other travelers. Although the spirits of the dead are often invoked, it is also the case that when they do return, they are appreciated only in the context of ritual occasions, wherein they are magically controlled by the *buwiyes*. It is incumbent upon migrants to return in the event of illness or death of a parent, as well as for rituals in honor of their own ancestors. Holidays such as Christmas have long been important for home visits, and to the Christian ceremonies the Garifuna have added various ethnic rituals—most prominently, the *Wanaragua* or John Canoe dance complex. To complete the cycle, songs are sung bemoaning the absence and perhaps the disloyalty of those who did not return.

Another prominent motif in oral literature is the jealousy felt by spurned or abandoned lovers. Here again, however, the travel motif may appear, for as indicated earlier, one of the most common reasons for changing partners is the physical separation resulting from migratory wage labor. Over the years I have collected large amounts of data showing that only a small minority of people are monogamous, staying permanently with their first sexual partner. All children are aware from an early age that "love" is not the same as "marriage" and that most unions will be brittle and short-lived—in spite of a recurring fantasy, especially among women, of attracting and holding a desirable mate.

Filial devotion, especially of children toward their mother, is expected. Yet there are numerous songs in which mothers lament their absent children— especially sons—who not only do not return but do not write or send money to support them in their old age. As long ago as 1948 Taylor reported this motif in letters written by a Belizean Black Carib woman to her absent son. Other themes in songs and stories recount the treachery of those who through devious techniques bilk their relatives—most often siblings—of their rightful share of an inheritance. The division of property, especially of houses and house sites, is often a matter of bitter dispute, even before the death of the owner. The songs warn listeners to be ever on guard to protect their own best interests.

Individualism, then, may be seen as an ever-present theme in Garifuna culture. Another theme is the domestic power and general importance of women. I suggest elsewhere (Gonzalez 1984b:8) that women may have become central to the domestic situation by default, for there is no evidence from Island Carib or Vincentian Black Carib times that women held anything like the position they hold today. The powerful warlike "Amazon" of the European imagination was certainly not based on what they saw of Island Carib/Arawak women. Some feminist scholars once hoped they might find evidence to support an early matriarchal "stage" of society, as has been postulated by J. J. Bachofen (1931) and Louis Morgan (1877). Matrilineality was thought to have been a survival from such times. However, most scholars have now abandoned that notion, as they discover that even matrilineal societies are ruled by men.

Ironically, the closest thing we have to matriarchy in the world may be a product of modern, not primitive, times. Garifuna matrifocality may be observed in the way children think about adults, as well as in the running of a household, in community affairs, and especially in the rituals related to the ancestral cult. Women's dominance ceases only when the community faces outward, although in Belize one may even find Garifuna women in the national legislature and other public offices. In Honduras and Guatemala the women remain strong within the ethnic group but are nearly invisible in external contexts. How, then, did matrifocality evolve among the Garifuna and perhaps elsewhere? I suggest that it occurred by default as the roles in which only males could perform were either removed from the society altogether or opened to women as substitutes in the absence of men.

The role of warrior and soldier is one such example; Garifuna have not served in that capacity since 1832, after the Morazán fiasco in Omoa and Trujillo (see chapter 2). Hunting and fishing were also once male prerogatives, as were long-distance canoe travel, trading, and raiding. None of these is presently an integral part of Garifuna life, although fishing is still done by many of the men who remain in the villages and by the handful who see it as a profession. Long-distance canoe travel and its associated economic activities can no longer be undertaken because of political and legal restrictions on free border crossings, so such travel today is largely confined to public transportation systems—to which women have equal access. And women have no hesitation, in Honduras at least, in undertaking short-distance canoe trips alone or with a female companion, if there is no available male.

The wooden and basketry items that only men could make are rapidly becoming obsolete or are purchased from other indigenous peoples who market them in or near Garifuna towns. Also, the political roles of men were superceded by the European and, later the Central American governments under whose power they came to live following 1797. And, as shown in chapter 4, though a few men continue to serve as *buwiyes*, women are equally acceptable in this role today; in fact, when it comes to managing ritual life in general, women are clearly more important. In short, Garifuna men are more likely to gain prestige and honor through new and specialized roles outside their communities, especially in their work situations. When they perform well, they receive accolades from both their fellows and their employers. Women, by contrast, are still most likely to remain all their lives within the Garifuna system (even when they go to school, visit the United States, or make other temporary forays outside.) In this they build reputations by having children and managing their households well and, eventually, through their participation in various religious activities and rituals.

As I will further develop in chapter 9, the psychosocial adjustment of the Black Caribs in the face of change between 1797 and 1940 seems to have been generally positive. It is important to remember, however, that during that time they migrated within a fairly bounded and not too extensive territory, and they may be thought of as having dominated the wage-laboring niche within that area. As Barger (1977) has shown, and as the Carib data seem to confirm, there is no necessary relationship between culture change and the mental health of "traditional" peoples. Rather, following Leighton et al. (1963:238), pathological influences arise along with sociocultural distintegration, which may or may not be a product of change. In the case of the Vincentian Black Caribs, the deportation and its associated changes only enriched and strengthened both the culture and the people's sense of personhood and ethnic identification.

I will argue in the next chapter that migration, which once was the backbone of the economy, is today directly leading to sociocultural disintegration. For both men and women, this migration produces an inevitable psychological conflict. Much as they have come to value both the experience itself and the resources it opens to them, it has clearly taken a toll. The struggle to support two (or more) domestic establishments, to participate in two cultures, and to manage the necessary legal and traveling logistics for repeated journeys, is often more than an individual can bear. Chapter 8 will deal more with the permanent effects of the migratory process upon both the individual and the ethnic group, as well as upon the villages and the Garifuna culture.

NOTES

1. Dary Fuentes's (1981) account is the result of an undergraduate Guatemalan student ethnographic tour to Livingston. It is riddled with errors—many trivial, but others so serious that it should be read and used with considerable caution. For example, she has "Caribs" living in San Benito, Peten; the dark-skinned people there are actually descendants of escaped Belizean slaves and have no Garifuna heritage. The drawings show "Caribs" in rowboats rather than canoes, women with babies on their backs in Mayan Indian (not Garifuna) style, and men beating on tall, standing drums unlike anything ever used by Garifuna. Still, the stories are recorded in considerable detail (one hopes they were tape-recorded directly). For the most part, they appear to be complete and unedited, and as raw data they are probably trustworthy.

2. During my field stint, which lasted only four months, I was accompanied by a colleague, Dr. Charles Cheek, and a group of five students. Somehow the ambience did not lend itself to the uninterrupted search for ethnographic data and especially not to the collection of texts. I was constantly interrupted by the other demands of the project and by my stewardship of the household in which all of us lived. I did tape-record a number of songs, which I then asked local informants to translate into Spanish. Sometimes they were unable to do so, claiming that the words of the songs were so archaic that they were meaningless to them. Attempts to find informants whose hearing, patience, Garifuna, and Spanish were adequate to the job were unsuccessful in the short time available to me. I have drawn upon these materials to some extent, but they are not as rich as those of Hadel and Howland. In part this is because the old songs are finally disappearing, as Taylor predicted.

3. There is an interesting event documented in the U.S. Archives (RG 84, Jan. 29, 1918). A Scottish businessman, resident in Livingston in 1918, was said to have been shot to death by a Garifuna man, who then fled. He was found four days later with a "self-inflicted" wound in the chest. The true circumstances, of course, will never be known. However, one cannot help but wonder if (a) the Garifuna had been shot first and returned the fire in self-defense, or (b) the Garifuna had been so distraught by his action that he turned the pistol upon himself. It is also perhaps significant that the European may be presumed to have fathered at least one child by a local Garifuna woman. There is today a family of lighter-skinned Livingston Garifuna who bear this European's surname, although the pronunciation and spelling have been Hispanicized. Could it have been a case of sexual jealousy? Killing a rival in the heat of passion is not a typically Garifuna response. Suicide in the face of betrayal by a loved one is not unknown, although poison has been the favored means.

4. Mertz (1977) follows Witkin et al. (1962) in his reasoning and analysis, and the interested reader may wish to pursue the idea there. It should be noted that the entire concept has its critics, and in relation to non-Western cultures it might be postulated that a lower degree or slower achievement of psychological differentiation should be considered normal.

5. I do not presume to present any sophisticated psychological analysis of personality. Neither does my use of the term imply anything so technical as Basic Personality Structure or Modal Personality, although some of the data presented here could be useful to those attempting to establish or describe such. Rather, I define personality as that complex of distinguishing behavioral and attitudinal traits characteristic of a particular individual or generally characteristic of the members of a particular social group.

6. In an earlier publication (Gonzalez 1973) I define the supradomestic as that which is between the domestic and the jural domains in any given society. This covers "state" or community institutions related to schooling, health, nutrition, and any other areas affecting the well-being of individuals. In simpler societies these are all handled within the household and/or family, but with the advent of the state, new institutions are developed to deal with them on a broader level, thus taking full control away from the kinship and residential unit.

7. Dreyfus (1982) suggests precise locations and linguistic (ethnic?) names for several of the Carib- and Arawak-speaking groups in both the Caribbean and on the South American mainland at the time of the conquest. She is persuasive that it was the Kalinago who inhabited St. Vincent and the other islands with which I have been concerned here. See also Escardo (1978) and Figueredo (1978).

8. Given their skills in what we now term "guerrilla warfare" and their knowledge of the area, it is surprising that there are no references to the Caribs having been employed to hunt down escaped slaves or to put down slave rebellions on other islands. Atwood (1791:222), in fact, suggested that the Caribs of Dominica could be used against runaway blacks and in defense of that island, should it be invaded—this in spite of his observation that the Caribs at that time spoke their own language and French but no English.

9. This is perhaps the single most famous of Brunius's various paintings and has been reproduced often. The most recent to do so is Kerns (1983:74ff.), but see also the jacket of Kirby and Martin (1972). Brunius was in the West Indies from about 1770 to

1773, possibly until 1777. He lived for the most part on Dominica, probably as a houseguest of the governor, Sir William Young. During his stay there, he visited St. Vincent and perhaps some of the other islands, sketching and painting. He recorded the dress and activities of slaves, free blacks, and Caribs, though it is not always easy to decide which are portrayed in any particular work. The National Library of Jamaica has the most extensive collection of his original paintings and engravings.

10. The cotton cloth was used in loin coverings for both sexes, as well as for hammocks. The use of headcloths, as shown in Brunius's paintings, was probably adopted from Africans, and at first these may have been made of homespun cotton, though it is likely that European cloth was substituted for all of these uses at an early date. Anderson (1983:68) referred to the Caribs wearing homespun loincloths even in the late eighteenth century, but the list of supplies sent along to Roatan includes both cloth and clothing.

11. It should be noted, however, that the same comment was made about Dominican maroons during their revolt on that island in 1791. Atwood (1791:232–33) thought it was to prevent the enemy from knowing how many losses they had incurred and attributed it to French influence. Although it may have served that function for the Europeans, it seems safe to assume it had other meanings for the Africans and Caribs.

12. Susan Brown (1975) and Carolyn McCommon (1982) were able to demonstrate that women who mated in this fashion were more affluent than their monogamous neighbors and that their children prospered. Their research designs were different, but both showed ingenuity in overcoming the inherent difficulties in gathering sound quantifiable data on the subject. Many other researchers in the larger Caribbean area and among some American blacks came to essentially similar conclusions (Ashcraft 1973; Bender 1967; Otterbein 1966; Stack 1974; R. T. Smith 1956; Whitten 1965).

13. The custom of introducing supplementary pap made of cassava starch and sugar at the age of about two weeks or less may be related to early weaning in that a child's hunger is largely stilled by this food and thus he or she will not suck so hard, reducing the mother's milk supply to the point where it does not suffice.

Right: Central Arawak Amazonian women grating manioc, early twentieth century (University of Pennsylvania Museum). *Bottom:* Girl grating manioc, Livingston, 1956.

Top: Plaiting a *petaca* (carrying basket), late nineteenth century, Livingston (Brigham 1887). *Bottom:* Man plaiting a basket, Punta Gorda, Belize, 1956.

Top: Tailor at work, Livingston, 1985. *Bottom:* Innovative stove for baking cassava, Honduras, 1985.

Buying shrimp and fish at the Livingston beach.

Top: Loading freight at Livingston, 1984. *Bottom:* A couple off to work their inland garden, Honduran Mosquito Coast, 1985.

Top: Wattle and daub house with large canoe in progress, Honduras, 1985. *Bottom:* Woman breaking up fight between two boys.

Left: Soccer on the beach. *Bottom:* Walking on stilts.

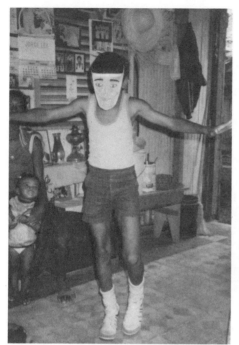

Left: Child practicing to be a traditional masked dancer. *Bottom:* Child practicing piano in an acculturated setting.

PART THREE

The Making of a Modern Ethnic Group

The main theme of an earlier book on the Garifuna (Gonzalez 1969) is that the migratory process has itself molded much of the way of life presently characteristic of the Garifuna and has been particularly effective as well in creating a domestic structure that is immune, so to speak, from any dangers to the family and community that might result from the absence of large numbers of men during the prime of their lives. Part 3 continues that discussion, showing how the migratory process originally developed among the Island Caribs, became more intense among the Black Caribs on St. Vincent, and finally reached its peak in nineteenth- and twentieth-century Central America. Chapters 8 and 9 describe how that process has now come to dominate both the sociocultural system and the lives of individual members of the society in ways many Garifuna, as well as observers of the Garifuna, believe to be harmful and ultimately destructive. These chapters also document the rise of a new sense of ethnic identity among the Garifuna—one that either heralds their final disappearance as a distinct people or their incorporation into the modern states within which they live today as an ethnically defined minority.

8

The Migratory Process

Migration as a Way of Life—Variant Patterns

The search for Garifuna roots in documents, folklore, and the remains of habitation sites has proven useful in many ways, but one of the most interesting conclusions to be drawn from the data is that even the Island Caribs were mobile, the men traveling regularly to trade with other indigenous groups throughout the Lesser Antilles and even to the mainland of South America. We can only speculate as to what resources the Kalinago might have controlled or what goods they might have manufactured that would have been of value to their neighbors.

Anna Roosevelt (1980), an archaeologist with considerable experience in the lowland South American area and most recently at the mouth of the Orinoco itself, suggests that the volcanic rock of the islands would have been a valuable export commodity for tool making—either in its raw form or as already finished axes, knives, and so on.[1] Unfortunately, there is as yet no solid evidence to back such speculation. Another thought is that cassava bread, or *areba,* might have been welcomed by those in the Orinoco delta area where manioc grew poorly or not at all. The famed watertight baskets of the Island Caribs would have been ideal for transporting such a product long distances over water. Indeed, it is hard to imagine any other native goods that would have needed such protection. The fact that the Caribs had such a lightweight, portable foodstuff must also be considered a contributing factor in the trade itself, since the paddlers would have needed to replenish their energy on long voyages during which they could neither stop nor cook.

In addition to whatever they might have carried of their own manufacture, most probably the Island Caribs acted as middle-men in this long-distance trade, transporting goods from one site to another for resale. It is becoming increasingly clear from analysis of early documents that they did make these journeys, and a few references suggest what some of the effects might have been on the home communities. Breton (1958) mentioned the frequent absence of a number of the men—some taking their wives and families with them, but others merely taking temporary wives on other islands. If there were regular trading routes, it is conceivable that many men might have had permanent family connections in several spots. This is a well-documented, familiar pattern among the Black Caribs of Central America until very recent times, and it has not completely disappeared even today. There are some men who have one family in New York City and another in their home village—the danger today being that such a life-style is generally frowned upon and may cause problems if and when either wife chooses to visit the other site. The increasing mobility of women has been a prime factor in the decline of polygyny.

After the French settlement in the Lesser Antilles during the seventeenth and eighteenth centuries, with primary colonies at Martinique, St. Lucia, Grenada, Guadalupe, and Dominica, and with a lesser presence on St. Vincent itself, the migration continued, though the patterns changed. Much of the indigenous population had disappeared by then—killed by disease, warfare, and disruption of their economies and social structures—so the Caribs sought new trading partners among the Europeans. We have a certain amount of reliable documentation for this trade which indicates that baskets, hammocks, tobacco, cotton, achiote, and various other products were traded for ironware, arms, ammunition, brandy, and wine. It may have been during this period that pottery making declined, as iron griddles and cookpots were increasingly available and probably considered superior because of their unbreakable nature. Also during these trading trips, some of the men found that their skills in maneuvering the difficult windward coasts of all of these islands were valuable to the Europeans, and loading ships must have become a part-time occupation. As late as the 1790s Alexander Anderson wrote that African slaves were useless in this endeavor until they had been taught by the Caribs (1983:60).

Although men traveled, we have no way of knowing how many did so and if this was a specialist's occupation or something young men engaged in before settling down to raise families and take on the duties of elders. Elsewhere I have published a typology of migratory activities that has proven useful for many scholars in considering the different effects each activity might have on the structure of the households left behind (Gonzalez 1961). Table 8.1 gives the different types I have postulated, together with suggestions as to which types were engaged in by the different Carib groups dealt with here. I have added a new category since my earlier publication—that of home retirement.

The Island Carib migrations were most likely either temporary or recurrent, or both. The same pattern seems to have been typical of the Vincentian Black

Table 8.1 Migration Patterns of Carib Groups

	Island Carib ?–1700	Black Carib		Garifuna 1960–present
		St. Vincent 1700–1797	Central America 1800–1940	
Temporary	?	?	×	
Seasonal			× (woodcutting)	
Recurrent	×	×	×	×
Permanent removal	×		×	×
Home retirement				×

Caribs, although the total size of the trading area was reduced, and, therefore, the length of time the men were away from home may have decreased. There is no evidence that either Island or Black Caribs willingly worked on planta- tions in the Antilles, so the seasonal category used earlier does not apply. Although a few men might have journeyed to France, never to return, or taken up permanent residence with French families as servants or retainers, this was apparently rare. Most Caribs, both Island and Black, were firmly tied to their home environments, seeking fulfillment as individuals through be- havior designed to realize Carib values. Since they controlled their own move- ments, there would have been no good reason to miss important occasions at home, whether they related to food producing, life-crisis rites, or the ritual cycle.

All the evidence suggests that when the Black Caribs were deported to Central America in 1797 the previously existing migratory patterns were in- tensified. Their dependence upon some foreign products and the cash needed to buy them had already been established. To the temporary and recurrent styles of migration was now added seasonal migration, especially as it related to woodcutting. In that industry, however, the "season" lasted for eight to ten months of the year, so absences would have been lengthy. Yet occasional visits home by canoe would have been possible, especially if the home settlements were not too distant. It now appears that the Black Caribs did establish their habitations near woodcutting operations all the way from Belize to Carataska Lagoon and the Patuca River (Gonzalez and Cheek 1986). Because of this tendency, it was not until after the start of World War II, when numbers of men joined the U.S. merchant marine or traveled to Scotland, did "permanent removal" become a significant migration category.

Case histories for men still living (or who were living at some time during my fieldwork, which has spanned a thirty-year period) show that even though several different patterns were adopted by different individuals, probably all men participated in the migratory process at one time or another after the Caribs' arrival in Central America. As has been shown in previous chapters, long-distance canoe travel persisted, with trade and/or the carrying of goods and persons up and down the Central American coastline, until the 1960s. A small amount of internal travel still occurs in Honduras, where transportation along the eastern coast depends to a great extent on local boatmen, some of whom have canoes equipped with outboard motors. Still, at least two legs of a journey I made in 1984 in that area were under paddle-power only.

Some of the men in my sample traveled off to work within Central America as young men to cut wood, to labor in sawmills, to load bananas, or to work at related activities. Once having acquired a certain amount of capital, many of these men returned home, built a house, acquired one or several canoes, and took up a more or less permanent residence in their village, fishing and selling hand-crafted items such as canoes, paddles, basketry, and wooden utensils to local villagers. This would come under the category "temporary migration" and was most prevalent among today's older men.

Other migrants returned from abroad with money they soon spent in various ways, only to be lured back by the need to provide more money, often because they had inherited and/or contracted responsibilities to several domestic establishments—those of their mother, one or more sisters, and one or more marital partners. They might continue their migrations in this fashion for most of their productive years, finally settling down in old age when they could count on being supported by their wives and children—through the gardening of the former and the wage labor of the latter. By this time they would either have built a house of their own, have inherited one from a parent, or have cemented a tie with a woman who owned a house. If a man had fathered several children by the same woman, had regularly (or even irregularly) provided for their maintenance, and proved himself still handy about the house and community, he would be assured a comfortable, if not affluent, old age. Before 1940 or 1950 most men, in fact, did manage their lives in this way. Repeatedly my household censuses turned up only one or two older men living alone, though there were always several women in such straits. Such a demographic picture, of course, is largely related to the fact that women live longer than men, and almost all of those in question were quite elderly and had recently lost their spouses. Informants agreed, however, that women would be more likely to be cared for by their children and that men had an easier time finding new (and younger) mates in the event of a partner's death.

Although the process originally started in the early 1900s with the building of the Panama Canal, it was not until the 1940s that large numbers of Black Carib men began to journey farther afield to find work. With the onset of World War II, a great many foreigners were required to man the merchant fleets of the United States and England, which supplied both the war vessels and fighting men abroad, since the ranks of American and British sailors had been depleted by the draft and by enlistments in the various armed services. Large numbers of West Indians were recruited, of whom Black Caribs made up a small percentage (Cameron 1944, 1946).

From the perspective of the towns and villages in Central America, these new opportunities led to a radical, systemic change. For the first time, men began to stay away, finding new lives, and often new wives, in America. Many of them, like the emigrant Chinese with lineage ties at home, sent money even after they stopped visiting regularly. Those who stayed on mostly affiliated themselves with the National Maritime Union, which helped them acquire U.S. citizenship, taught them how to bank their money, and gave them retirement benefits that freed them from the need to maintain close familial ties in Central America. Many traveled around the world, usually working first as deckhands or in the engine room or galley, then gradually moving up the ladder into more responsible positions, especially in food service. They acquired considerable knowledge of other cultures, some finding Garifuna-like traits in the Caribbean, in New Orleans, Africa, and/or South America.

These men saw their ethnicity in a different light than before—as a set of disparate symbols shared in vague ways by a large number of other people; it ceased to be a single, systematic set of values and prescribed behavior patterns. They began to think of themselves as citizens of the world, although at first most of them chose merely to live on the fringes of this new society. Often they married black American women who were not themselves particularly active politically, at least not yet.

Although the Black Caribs lost many men permanently in this fashion between 1940 and 1960, others continued the recurrent pattern of migration previously described. Occasionally a lost one will return to try to make amends —sometimes, it is believed, even after death. A recent case is that of Hipólito Ramírez, a naturalized citizen of the United States, who died in St. Petersburg, Florida, in 1982 at the age of eighty-five. He had purchased a house there, and his estate was worth about $40,000. Although he had carved out a new life, and at the time of his death had lost contact with most of his relatives except for a teenaged niece who lived with him, thousands of dollars from the proceeds of his estate were distributed among several of his heirs in Punta Gorda, Puerto Barrios, and Livingston, followed by an ancestral ceremony conducted in his honor. Garifuna with whom I spoke, including one who had been a U.S. citizen for twenty years, believed that he had either directed that all this be done in his will or that his spirit had appeared to his lawyer in a dream, giving her detailed instructions as to how to dispose of his property and how to arrange a ninth-night celebration in Livingston.

A columnist reporting on the case in a St. Petersburg newspaper provided a different view of the happening, one that, in checking with the principals themselves, I found to bridge the two cultures. A conscientious and adventuresome young court-appointed lawyer decided on her own to go to Central America to find the old man's heirs. While in Livingston, the lawyer and her companion, a writer, prevailed upon the heirs to hold a "memorial service" of the type they had heard about. They referred to it as a *punta,* but from the writer's descriptions it was a *chugu.* Everyone very much enjoyed the "party," which was apparently paid for by the old man's estate. Although the two American visitors had some idea of who the Garifuna were, their understanding of the culture was only superficial, and it is clear that there was neither will nor dream involved in the settlement of Ramírez's affairs.[2]

Permanent removal, then, is a tricky concept, for in the Garifuna worldview it is never too late to return. There remains some thought that a person should be buried in the natal or home village, and even now bodies will often be returned at considerable expense. But the idea that the *gubida* cannot travel long distances is being dispelled by stories such as that above, and I have been told that now many people are buried in the United States. Of course, there must be many hundreds for whom there are no records and who presumably have been so interred over the years.

A highlight of my most recent research was the discovery of a number of retired men — mostly sailors — living in Trujillo and also in some of the more isolated villages along the Mosquito Coast. In most cases these men had spent the best portions of their lives in the exterior. Many are U.S. citizens and members of the National Maritime Union; as such they receive both U.S. Social Security benefits and company retirement checks, which, especially when traded on the local black market, provide them with a good income. One man received more than $700 monthly, which netted him 1,750–2,100 lempiras per month. In an economy in which the daily unskilled wage is 6–9 lempiras, this makes him wealthy. With such incomes these men have built large, attractive, comfortable houses, furnished with goods purchased abroad and almost always containing at least one television set, a refrigerator, a gas stove, and a sewing machine. Indoor plumbing, including running water in both kitchen and bath, is always a feature and sets these people truly apart from others in the community, most of whom firmly adhere to the belief that the sea is the proper place to dispose of all wastes.[3] Table 8.2 illustrates the frequency of different types of housing and amenities in one barrio of Trujillo (cf. Table 8.3 for Livingston, Guatemala).

A few of these returned migrants use their cash to set up small stores or bars, often in the front of their houses. They help support many of their relatives, and they give elaborate and costly ceremonies for their ancestors. They are also generous with the local Catholic churches and are often considered pillars in the church lay organizations. They seemingly want for nothing and are the envy of their neighbors. Certainly, such role models are important for

Table 8.2 Garifuna Housing Components in Trujillo, Honduras, 1985

	Cement block	Wooden		*Bahareque*	Total
Walls	131	14		148	299

	Tile	Wood	Cement	Earth	Total
Floor	19	1	200	75	295

	Asbestos	Zinc		Thatch	Total
Roof	10	282		2	294

	Public system	Well		None	Total
Water	172	4		117	293

	Own generator	Public system		None	Total
Electricity	1	223		72	296

	Toilet	Septic tank	Latrine	None	Total
Human waste disposal	31	68	73	118	290

Note: The choice of wood versus mud (*bahareque*) walls seems more a question of taste and availability. Cement-block houses are usually preferred, providing the family can afford the construction. Similarly, I conclude that sanitary waste disposal is not merely a question of being able to afford a facility.

the younger men, a subject that will be explored later. For the present, however, keep in mind that home retirement has so far been noted only in Honduras. This may relate to the fact that Honduran Black Caribs left earlier and were more often employed in the Merchant Marine than were their brothers in Guatemala and Belize. They seem to have been recruited in the major ports of Cortes and La Ceiba, as well as in Trujillo, where the United States carried out training exercises at the beginning of the war.

The case histories I gathered suggest that migratory patterns after 1940 more and more fell into the category of permanent removal, with short visits home of a length that accommodated the vacation allowances provided by most American employers. Those without secure jobs tend to stay away, for to return is expensive and/or risky if one is without proper papers. In Livingston, I see no evidence that home retirement will become much of an option, nor does it yet appear as an important phenomenon in Belize, for reasons that I will detail in chapter 9.

Ideally, to deal effectively with the migratory process as a whole, we should know the number of Garifuna now living in the United States. Practically, as

Table 8.3 Garifuna Housing Components in Livingston, Guatemala, 1984

	Cement block	Wooden	*Bahareque*	Cane	Total
Walls	0	168	56	54	278

	Tile	Wood	Cement	Earth	Total
Floor	0	23	179	76	278

	Asbestos	Zinc		Thatch	Total
Roof	8	175		95	278

	Public system	Well	Rain	None	Total
Water	115	17	77	69	278

	Own generator	Public system		None	Total
Electricity		exact data unavailable			

	Toilet	Septic tank	Latrine	None	Total
Human waste disposal	45	0	104	129	278

Source: Data gathered by the Guatemalan Public Health Department.

has been recognized by both scholars and government officials, there is no way to do more than estimate how many illegal or undocumented immigrants have flooded U.S. cities (Morris and Mayio 1980). Because Garifuna are not the only ones from their respective countries who migrate, we cannot even estimate their number by counting those who come with their papers in order. Nevertheless, to provide some basis for the estimates that follow, Table 8.4 gives what data we have on total *legal* immigration from the three countries of concern here — Belize, Guatemala, and Honduras. Keep in mind that the totals are further swelled by the many children born in the United States to immigrants who are counted as U.S. citizens, even though they remain culturally and socially members of their parents' ethnic group.[4]

Looking at Garifuna migration patterns from the perspective of the villages of departure is equally difficult. Precisely because so many people leave without the proper papers, those who stay behind in the towns and villages are edgy about such inquiries. Hadel (1972) notes that it was impossible to count the number of people in any village because there was so much coming and going. The same problem plagued my work as early as 1956, which led me to construct a special household census form on which there was a place for "absent members of the household" and on which I tried to record the length of time these members had been away. Repeated journeying soon filled up

Table 8.4 Immigrants Admitted to the United States by Country of Origin

Year	Belize	Guatemala	Honduras
1973	528	1,759	1,330
1974	573	1,638	1,390
1975	534	1,859	1,357
1976	500	1,970	1,310
1977	930	3,599	1,626
1978	1,033	3,996	2,727
1979	1,063	2,583	2,545
1980	1,120	3,751	2,552
1981	1,289	3,928	2,358
1982	2,031	3,633	3,186
1984	1,492	3,937	3,405

Source: U.S. Immigration and Naturalization Service, *Statistical Yearbooks.*

more space than I had allocated. The same thing happened when I asked people in how many places they had themselves lived during their lifetimes.

How do Garifuna migrants manage their undocumented entry? They use all the same means that have been recorded for other Caribbean and Latin American groups. Some go first to Belize, then overland across Mexico, entering through California or Texas—by bus, on foot, or hidden in the trunk of a car or under a truck. Others stow away on ships out of any of the major ports in the area, Santo Tomás (Guatemala) being somewhat preferred because of the shorter run.[5] Those who earn their living as sailors are sometimes hired on as "gypsy" hands in local ports and jump ship when they reach the United States. There are always plenty of phone numbers to call for assistance once they arrive. Others obtain tourist visas and then simply overstay their allotted time, though this is said to be a more difficult route if one has documented relatives in the United States, since it is assumed they will assist in the defection and are the first people the immigration authorities contact.

Finally, of course, some people try several means to obtain a set of papers. Fake passports and other documents may be purchased for a fee, or the passport (and visa) of a previous migrant of similar age and build may be borrowed. Marriages to permanent residents or citizens may be arranged, or student visas may be sought by those who qualify for entrance to higher educational institutions—increasingly a viable maneuver; whether they ever attend school is unimportant, since the visa is merely a means of getting into the country. Few of these people have any intention of returning to their native country, and it is well recognized that the U.S. Immigration and Naturalization Service has no good way to prevent such entries. The literature on whether the United States stands to gain or lose by preventing illegal entry is enormous, but it is not my intent to review that question here, nor to take a strong stand one way or the other. What is clear is that there are both benefits and costs to this country, some of which will be discussed in chapter 9.

Immigrant Life in the United States

All things considered, then, I estimate that there are between 75,000 and 100,000 Garifuna in the United States as of this writing, most of them living in New York City, although a significant number reside in Los Angeles, New Orleans, Chicago, and Miami, and a few have chosen Boston, Washington D.C., and other cities. Within New York, where I have studied Garifuna settlement patterns and their way of life, some are to be found in every borough, with the largest number in the Bronx and Brooklyn. Belizean English speakers tend to reside more often in Brooklyn, while the Spanish speakers are more at home in the Bronx and Upper Manhattan, along with Hispanics from many other areas, including Puerto Rico. Indeed, it is possible to live a lifetime in the area without commanding the English language at all. Nevertheless, most Garifuna do learn English, linguistic ability being something they have come to accept as part of their cultural (and, some believe, genetic) heritage. In fact, Belizeans often are fluent in Spanish as well, at least in some cases having learned this language in New York rather than at home!

Occupations include those of medical doctor (with training at New York University), Roman Catholic nun, banker, insurance salesman, grade-school teacher, butcher, mariner, seamstress, dressmaker, domestic servant, security guard, factory worker, delivery man, midwife, cab driver, and store clerk. As has been shown for other migrants, most Garifuna find jobs through friends and relatives already known to their employers, and some even have jobs waiting for them when they arrive.

Not all Garifuna who settle in New York have equal success. There are those whose lives are a continual struggle: they find it difficult to keep a job, they drink too much, they experiment with drugs, and sometimes they fall into crime because the opportunities are there and they are desperate. A few Garifuna who have become U.S. citizens or permanent residents receive welfare assistance of various types—primarily Aid to Dependent Children but also food stamps, public health care, and unemployment compensation. Others live by petty crime, especially in relation to drug dealing but also including theft and various frauds, such as accepting money to marry a nonresident so that person can obtain a visa.

In all of this, the Garifuna behave as do thousands of other immigrants— indeed, there may exist an immigrant culture, on the order of the culture of poverty, that successful immigrants must adapt to if they are to survive in their new surroundings. This culture includes information on how to keep one's employer happy, where to live, how to manage the subway system, where to shop for the best bargains or for greatest convenience or on credit, how to keep warm in winter, and how to manage the free public services available in their new country. Coney Island, the Bronx Zoo, the Statue of Liberty, Rockefeller Center, and other "standard" entertainment sites are not part of their initial fare. Instead, most immigrants buy a television set as soon as they can and gather with their compatriots to drink beer and rum, watch TV, and exchange gossip from home and from the local Garifuna community. Some women open their homes on weekends as small "clubs," charging for drinks and food. In summer the immigrants play soccer in organized teams in the parks, and in winter they huddle indoors and dream of their tropical homelands.

Although they want their children to be born and educated in the United States, most Garifuna find preschool toddlers to be too much of a burden, and they are often sent home to live with an aunt or a grandmother. Tables 8.5–8.6 give the age structure of households in Livingston, Trujillo, Santa Fe, and Guadalupe; the large number of preschoolers is significant. When children are older and can be held responsible for their own daily care and activities, the desire for superior schooling may cause parents to bring them back to New York if at all possible.

For those young people who do attend school in the United States, a different set of experiences must be dealt with and learned from. Being black, they join others of that minority in the schools they attend, but the disadvantages of that status in America may be compounded by their also being perceived as foreigners. Belizeans are classified as West Indians, which generally confers somewhat higher status than that accorded to Hispanic blacks, in part because of the former's historic socioeconomic success in this country, especially in the arts and in scholarly circles.[6] But the enmity between Afroamericans of U.S. birth and those from the Caribbean and Latin America has often been noted, and Garifuna immigrants soon become aware of it. Yet there are not enough of them in any one neighborhood so that they can create their own society; nor do they really want to. Thus, as their ancestors so often did, they learn to accommodate themselves to what they find.

Frazier's (1957) study of middle-class black Americans once served me well as I struggled to understand some of the behavior patterns I observed in those Garifuna who returned to Livingston as visitors in 1956–57. Gone now are the rhinestones embedded in front teeth, the zoot suits and flashy jewelry; "in" are dashikis, cornrows, and whatever else young, fashionable blacks are wearing in New York. Middle-aged Garifuna who have had moderate economic success look much like their American counterparts: they dress formally and well, the women in high heels, hats, gloves, and long gowns when the occasion demands. They are reasonably satisfied with their lives, and although they

Table 8.5 Number of Persons in Different Types of Households, by Age and Sex, in Cristales (Trujillo), Honduras, 1985

Age (years)	Consanguineal		Affinal		Solitary		Total		Grand Total
	M	F	M	F	M	F	M	F	
less than 1	11	4	9	9	0	0	20	13	33
1–5	66	49	47	36	0	0	113	85	198
6–17	149	144	96	102	0	0	245	246	491
18–20	61	37	15	41	0	0	76	78	154
21–30	45	84	30	54	1	1	76	139	215
31–40	11	40	22	30	0	0	33	70	103
41–50	9	33	29	24	1	1	39	58	97
51–55	4	18	9	17	0	1	13	36	49
56–60	4	24	11	13	1	1	16	38	54
61–70	6	24	31	16	1	7	38	47	85
71–80	6	16	12	12	2	4	20	32	52
80+	0	10	2	5	0	2	2	17	19
unknown	4	7	4	8	0	0	8	15	23
Totals	376	490	317	367	6	17	699	874	1573

Table 8.6 Number of Persons in Different Types of Households, by Age and Sex, in Guadalupe, Honduras, 1985

Age (years)	Consanguineal		Affinal		Solitary		Total		Grand Total
	M	F	M	F	M	F	M	F	
less than 1	1	1	6	4	0	0	7	5	12
1–5	17	30	36	27	0	0	53	57	110
6–17	40	32	40	53	0	0	80	85	165
18–20	6	9	7	4	0	1	13	14	27
21–30	6	19	9	22	1	0	16	41	57
31–40	2	12	10	15	0	0	12	27	39
41–50	4	14	7	6	0	0	11	20	31
51–55	2	5	8	6	1	2	11	11	24
56–60	0	4	7	11	0	2	7	17	24
61–70	1	3	8	3	1	1	10	7	17
71–80	0	4	5	1	0	1	5	6	11
80+	2	5	1	0	0	2	3	7	10
unknown	0	0	0	0	0	0	0	0	0
Totals	81	138	144	152	3	9	228	299	527

may return home to visit, most of them will probably remain in the United States until they die. The women are often more insistent on remaining than are the men, possibly because they find the housework in the village onerous and the amenities primitive.

Both newcomers and seasoned immigrants participate in voluntary associations of different kinds, the lay brotherhoods of the Catholic church being popular. A few Garifuna turn to the fundamentalist Protestant sects, but more seek out the various Afroamerican and Latin spiritist or spiritualist groups, primarily for health reasons. Although there are several *buwiyes* in New York, they are not to be found in every neighborhood, and the people are completely comfortable with these other specialists, whose methods are not so different from what they knew back home.

There are a few societies formed ostensibly to send aid to the home communities, but these have gone out of fashion in recent years, perhaps because it was discovered that too often the money collected stayed in the pockets of the organizers. During the 1970s these societies flourished, their leaders organizing dances, beer parties, and even excursions home for special holidays. People from other Latin American countries have formed similar associations, which have been analyzed as being of primary importance to the migrants themselves in adjusting to their new environment.

Another club of importance is the United Garifuna Cultural Association of Greater New York. Headquartered in Brooklyn, this group, in spite of its name, draws mostly Belizeans. The aim of its leaders is to raise the consciousness of the Garifuna to the impact of the diaspora on their cultural heritage, on the one hand, and to the condition of those left at home, on the other. To this end, social events are organized in which the gathered members are exhorted to use their native language, and cultural artifacts or pictures of dances and cassava preparation are displayed. At one such gathering I was asked to talk about my recent research in Trujillo, but when I asked the assembled audience how many of them had ever visited that community, only one hand (out of an estimated 200) went up. I fear that many had only a vague idea where Trujillo is located, and my sense is that the majority of those present cared little about the origins of the Garifuna but were there primarily for the gossiping, dancing, and feasting.

In Los Angeles a group of younger Garifuna have formed what they call the Walagante Dance Group. Like similar organizations in the home countries, theirs has found that non-Garifuna greatly appreciate the rhythms and exotic dance steps of the *punta,* the John Canoe, and other traditional rituals and entertainments. In Nicaragua some years ago, Nietschmann (1979:239) reports, a group from the coast were preparing to "put on" one of the more sacred dances in Managua. Although I have not seen the Californian performances, the costuming and choreography in Central America are a far cry from "traditional," being geared to Western tastes by the addition of flashy "uniform" dress, which sometimes exposes more flesh than would have appeared seemly to their immediate ancestors (though it would not have offended the Island Caribs.) To the extent that these performances increase the awareness and appreciation of the Garifuna presence as a distinct cultural group, they have served their purpose. They undoubtedly also act as a magnet to keep members of the group together in the new environment. They tend to attract the better educated, more affluent, and more activist Garifuna, both at home and abroad, and it is by such persons that the future evolution of the Garifuna as an ethnic group will be directed. These Garifuna are aware, both by observation and through their reading, of how American minorities asserted themselves to acquire a greater degree of political power, or at least the attention of those in power. They are also, for the most part, young enough to have witnessed the worldwide adoption of ethnicity as a socially and ideologically respectable device for classifying people—it having largely replaced both "race" and "tribe." [7]

If it is from among the immigrants that we find the seeds of a new ethnicity, we should remember that not all migration today is to the United States. As the educational opportunities have expanded within the Central American countries themselves, more young people have taken advantage of them to become trained in stenography, bookkeeping, law, engineering, and medicine. Some of them now live in the capital cities of each country, and in Honduras they also live in quite large numbers in the coastal cities of Puerto Cortes, Tela, and La Ceiba. Many are government employees, clerking in the ministries and local agencies, and at least one of them in Belize and one in Honduras have achieved ministerial rank. There is a Belizean Garifuna bishop of the Roman Catholic church, and that country also has several Garifuna priests. In both Belize and Honduras it is my sense that, with a few exceptions, those who have migrated to cities within their own country are "permanent removals," even though they do return on occasion to visit kinfolk. As they become involved in the developing urban world of the larger country, they may or may not lose sight of their forebears. Many of the younger people living in such towns and cities hardly speak the Garifuna tongue today.[8] Nevertheless, leaders will arise from this group to join those returning from abroad, and together they will make ethnicity their rallying cry for the 1990s. As we shall see, the process has already begun, and it cannot be separated from the concept of development.

The Impact on the Individual Migrant

More and more anthropologists are paying attention to individuals, realizing that to a large extent ethnicity is defined by the way people feel about themselves and their relations with others. Not all people are conscious of ethnicity as a feature of their lives or as part of their definition of self, so it goes without saying that if we are to understand the ways in which ethnicity operates in the world today, we must examine the forces that bring individuals to think of themselves as "ethnic" beings.

Ever since the early work of Manners (1965) on the importance of remittances in the Caribbean, most anthropologists have been aware that the people of that area could not survive without emigration. Usually emigration has been discussed with regard to the welfare of the local community, but it is also often crucial to the self-realization of the individual. It has been argued that, after emancipation, external migration was virtually the only way in which blacks in the Caribbean might get ahead in the world. In part this was due to physical factors, such as the poverty of soils depleted by generations of sugar-cane and other monocrops, and in part to social factors. Such things as over-population, racial prejudice, and the nonexistence of a manufacturing sector contributed to the notion that it was better to leave. According to Pastor and Rogers (1983:1), it has been for some time the predominant view in the Caribbean that emigration is a personal right, at the same time that it serves the economic and social interests of the home countries.

The Atlantic littoral of Central America, even though its history has been different than that of the Caribbean proper, has nevertheless suffered from some of the same physical and social problems and has tried some of the same solutions. The decline of the large banana plantations on that coast began in the 1930s, 100 years after emancipation had finally signaled the end of the inefficient and wasteful sugar industry in places like Jamaica. But the local workers—some of them descendants of West Indians whose fathers and grand-fathers had come to Central America seeking work, and some of them Black Caribs—found themselves in dire straits. Now totally dependent upon wages, and faced with a worldwide depression, they got through the decade of the 1930s as best they could. The United Fruit Company did not actually pull out of Trujillo until 1937, and it continued some operations in Belize until the outbreak of World War II and in Puerto Barrios, Puerto Cortes, and Tela until well into the 1950s. But it and other companies drastically reduced their operations. The workers traveled up and down the coast, taking whatever jobs they could find on the railroads, the docks, or in other enterprises.

For the Black Caribs, this was simply another slump in what had always been an uncertain economic world. They had been raised in a tradition that taught them always to explore new horizons and to hone new skills so as to meet new challenges. They were still widely perceived by Europeans as being hard workers, willing to go the extra mile, and not likely to become involved in labor disputes. They were conservative politically and in general; they could be counted on as "company men."[9] Many of them sought and received letters of commendation from their employers when they were laid off, to be used when applying for new jobs and later for framing and display.

As mentioned in the preceding section, the onset of World War II marked a new phase in Black Carib labor history. Although there was a certain continuity from earlier centuries, I believe the effect of migration on the individual changed radically after this time. Men traveled farther away and returned home less often. At the same time, they became more independent in their thinking and in their beliefs about cultural values. For some, this led them to be less ethnocentric than before. Many questioned the truth of the old religion, doubting the power of the *gubida* and the *buwiye*. Those who had been fortunate enough to secure a better-than-average formal education (usually in Belize) read widely and discovered a myriad of alternative philosophies, ranging from various forms of spiritualism in vogue during the nineteenth century (Brandon 1983) to Masonism, Rosacrucianism, and even out-and-out atheism.

Intellectually, then, these men were less able to adjust to the home environment when they returned for a visit; they had become alienated as a result of their new experiences, and to the extent that they tried to discuss or act in accordance with their new beliefs, they were seen as no longer being "Carib." I suspect that many or most of these men were lost to the system, even though they may have continued to send money home, for they were dutiful still, with a strong sense of familial obligation. Yet, they seemed to welcome the idea that they could live well elsewhere, and the ethnic pride their ancestors once felt vis-à-vis Africans, Miskitos, Indios, or others began to dissolve in the melting pot of the larger world.

Meanwhile, as Kerns (1983), McCommon (1982), Sanford (1976), and I (Gonzalez 1969) have described in detail, the women carried on, seeking sexual liaisons out of loneliness, passion, and hope, then spending the rest of their lives pursuing resources and attention from the various men with whom they had created a new life. They planted cassava, rice, and plantains to feed their families; they baked and sold bread to buy pencils and school notebooks; they trained their daughters *and* sons to cope with two worlds, often with little help from any adult males; and they preserved and eventually reshaped the old rituals, both sacred and secular. As I now review the period between 1940 and 1970, I believe it presented a real spiritual crisis for both men and women, and it was largely the women and the sons they trained who kept the Garifuna culture alive and provided the impetus for the emergence of a new ethnic consciousness and pride—the redefinition of the Black Caribs as Garifuna (Gonzalez 1976).

What was the fate of those who found neither success abroad nor a respectable work situation nearer home? In spite of the fact that Mertz (1977) has found father-absence to have had little effect on men's personalities, there are signs that permanent removal has had negative repercussions for many. Excessive male drinking, for example, has been commented upon by casual observers over the years. However, this apparently was not seen as a serious problem by the Garifuna themselves until fairly recently. Now many men admit to being alcoholics, and a few have joined Alcoholics Anonymous in order to battle their disease. Some attribute the new excesses to bad habits learned as sailors,[10] but alcoholism seems to be far more widespread than among the group who fall into that category. Much of it relates to boredom, unemployment, and a sense that there is not much else to do. The men drink in groups at bars and on streetcorners or on the beach, which at least gives them the satisfaction of companionship; but they also drink alone. The system seemingly has no way to apply controls at this point, for too many men have too few daily responsibilities. They may continue to drink until they either collapse or cannot buy or beg more alcohol. The more affluent retired men do not seem to have drinking problems as often as those who are younger but unemployed.

Some women, especially older women, also indulge in alcohol to the point of inebriation. I found one woman drinking alone in her house at ten o'clock in the morning when I paid an unexpected visit. Drinking has always been an important part of the ancestor rites, the custom dating back to Island Carib times. But today many women bring empty pint or half-pint bottles to rituals, the idea being to fill them with rum when it is passed around and then take it home for consumption later. This practice infuriates many hostesses, some of whom fly into a rage and refuse rum to anyone with a bottle in her hand.

I am somewhat at a loss to explain the increased drinking among older women, unless it is somehow also related to the sense of frustration they have when they view what is happening to their homes and to their men—whether of their own or of the younger generation. To the extent that they have become dependent upon cash remittances, and as the amount of time they spend in gardening declines, there are fewer activities to keep them busy. When the remittances fail to arrive, they know real hardship. They may have been left to care for several younger children, who are growing up without ambition and nowadays increasingly without much concern for or knowledge of the Garifuna past. Many times they struggled to feed grandchildren or nieces and nephews when there was no check in the mail; and in later years the checks were often mailed directly to the children, which tended to add insult to injury and ultimately brought about new problems.

The use of marijuana has become fairly commonplace among younger Garifuna in the towns, especially men but including some women as well. Older informants have attributed its use to the influence of gringo tourists; to boredom, as these young people await the call to join a parent or relative in New York; to teenage affluence, as a result of money sent to them directly by their absent parents; and to a desire to be "cool," like the teenagers they have known or heard about in New York. Probably there is some truth in all of these observations, but a more satisfactory explanation should also include the general sense of apathy concerning the possibility of a rewarding life in Central America and the decline of interest in the traditional Garifuna life-style and value system. To understand this, I now turn to a consideration of the effect of migration on the home villages.

Impact on the Home Villages and on Garifuna Culture Patterns

It is my belief that what we today call matrifocality became commonplace only after the 1930s. Kalm (1980) has suggested that the crucial variable in tipping the scale toward domination by women in any society dependent upon migration is the proportion of *obligated* remaining residents to absent kin. In her study of the island of Utila, one of the Bay Islands off the coast of Honduras, she found that in spite of the fact that many men had joined the U.S. merchant marine and later took up residence in the United States, the dominant family and household form on Utila remained strongly patriarchal. She believes it was because those who migrated left behind numerous male relatives who took over the decision-making roles on their behalf.

Utila is different from what we find in most Garifuna villages in that "as many as 25% of the men" are absent at any given time, for several months to several years (Kalm 1980:8). Although I cannot offer exact numbers, I believe that among the Garifuna the percentage of absent men is more than 50 and often ranges up to 75. Tables 8.7–8.10 tell the story. Since about 1960 women have begun to join the migrant force in ever larger numbers (Gonzalez 1984b), which further exacerbates the situation. In effect, the home villages are places in which the older and younger generations take care of each other until the latter are old enough to leave.

In the case of the Caribs, I believe there were two extenuating factors that turned them toward matrifocality after 1940. The historic traveling patterns to which they were already accustomed, and which had frequently left women in temporary charge of the household, combined with the fact that women were also capable of generating some outside income. When times were difficult and their men were gone, they either sold their garden produce, worked for wages whenever they could find employers, took in laundry, or sold lottery tickets. The evidence also points to the probability that larger numbers of Carib men left their communities than was the case in Utila, and that many of these men, in effect, abandoned their culture, choosing to become something other than Black Caribs.

What of the argument, so often made for the Caribbean in general, that the villages were overpopulated anyway and could not have supported all the

Table 8.7 Births by Sex and Ethnic Group, Trujillo, Honduras

Year	Garifuna M	F	Ladino M	F	Other M	F	Total M	F
1883	9	10	19	17	0	2	28	29
1893	1	2	23	13	0	0	24	15
1903	11	7	33	34	0	0	44	41
1913	38	36	58	54	4	4	100	94
1923	20	22	39	45	14	15	73	82
1933	44	48	95	91	14	16	153	155
1943	41	42	112	102	7	11	160	155
1953	42	36	99	108	9	3	150	147
1963	55	33	140	142	5	5	200	180
1973	49	55	258	250	8	1	315	306
1983	65	41	645	540	8	7	718	588

Source: Information compiled by the author from records at the Trujillo registry office.

Table 8.8 Deaths by Sex and Ethnic Group, Trujillo, Honduras

Year	Garifuna M	F	Ladino M	F	Other M	F	Total M	F
1893	5	9	45	20	0	0	50	29
1903	10	11	21	17	2	0	33	28
1913	18	9	41	29	2	0	54	38
1923	17	11	133	55	21	6	171	72
1933	18	10	68	33	9	2	95	45
1943	18	16	50	56	3	0	71	72
1953	5	4	38	25	1	0	44	29
1963	8	5	29	21	0	0	37	26
1973	12	15	40	24	1	1	53	40

Source: Information compiled by the author from records in the Trujillo registry office.

Table 8.9 Births by Sex and Ethnic Group, Rural and Urban Livingston, Guatemala

Year	Garifuna M	F	Ladino M	F	Indian M	F	Total
1947	38	28	37	30	103	107	343
1957	50	43	39	50	141	145	468
1966	44	44	42	43	244	230	647
1976	34	40	275	232	322	319	1222
1983	40	41	375	365	434	362	1617

Source: Data compiled by the author from municipal records.

Table 8.10 Deaths by Ethnic Group, Livingston, Guatemala

Date	Garifuna	Indian	Ladino	Other	Total
1901	44	10	43	3	100
1911	54	10	46	0	110
1921	53	60	41	5	159
1931	65	69	117	6	257
1941	47	192	36	0	275
1951	32	128	23	0	183
1961	27	42	12	0	81
1971	15	na	na	na	na
1981	16	106	66	0	188

Source: Data compiled by the author from municipal records.

people who were born there? In such cases, it is suggested, emigration provided the income that allowed for the survival of the village and, presumably, of the rural values and folk culture of the past. Outside remittances not only support many people who could not themselves be productive, but they provide the economy with foreign exchange. However, as Pastor and Rogers (1983:7) point out, these same remittances can contribute to local inflation and to dependence on luxury goods more appropriate to the United States than to a developing country. The latter is certainly the case in Livingston, where the youngsters sport fashionable New York jewelry and clothing, sunglasses, Walkman radios, and marijuana. It is more difficult to argue against the television sets, refrigerators, and modern plumbing now found in many of the towns and villages (see chapter 9).

There is no doubt, however, that these consumer goods are not equally distributed among the population and that few improvements are being made in any of the Garifuna towns and villages that benefit the general public health and welfare. A few individual households stand out as oases of splendor amid an increasingly degraded general environment. Water supplies are polluted by bacteria and mud, and electrical outages are frequent and annoying if one has come to depend on electricity, as most people in the towns have (many of the villages are as yet without electrical service). The mosquito population breeds in stagnant water, and rats and cockroaches commonly share a household's foodstores. Streets are rutted, muddy, and may be overrun by stray dogs, which at least help keep down the accumulation of garbage. Refuse is, for the most part, merely thrown into the sea or into open gullies or streams, even in the heart of town; in fact, many people merely throw their household trash out their back doors, although a few take care to bury it. All of these conditions are as typical of the villages as of the towns, but they are more offensive and dangerous to the public health in the towns due to the greater number of people who live there.

Schools and health facilities are in somewhat better shape, in large measure due to multinational assistance efforts by both private and government agencies. Although one might expect that the prospect of emigrating to the United States would encourage school attendance, this seems not to hold true, at least in Livingston and Honduras. As noted in chapter 7, Garifuna children in those countries attend school while in the lower grades but gradually drop out. Their primary goals are to perfect a second language—be it Spanish, as in Honduras and Guatemala, or English, as in Belize. Beyond that they also value literacy, the ability to do simple arithmetic, and some knowledge of the world beyond their own borders. I was amazed in 1956 to find that nearly everyone had attended at least the first three years of school and counted themselves as literate. Of course, their literacy was of a low level, and many did not in fact read very much. Furthermore, many of the older women were only minimally fluent in a second language, having forgotten much of what they had learned in their youth. But the basic introduction to the outside world was there.

There are some contrasts with this picture today in that children often learn Spanish (or English) simultaneously with Garifuna, and not infrequently they prefer it. In Trujillo I regularly passed by a small private nursery school attended by some ten or twelve Garifuna youngsters between the ages of two and five. They continually chattered with each other in Spanish, even when playing in the yard with no adults in evidence. Because many households in the towns have television sets, most children have some opportunity at an early age to learn about other ways of doing things. What they learn about the world in school is often only a caricature of what they have seen on television. As for the teenagers, their parents were successful in New York City with only a minimum of education, so they see no reason why that should not be enough for them. And perhaps it is. But what they do not realize is that times are changing even in the United States and that it may be more difficult for their generation to gain admittance to the Promised Land and to find jobs there. And the skills they will need if they stay in their own country are simply not being learned.

Thus, I conclude that development, if it is to occur, must come from the outside, but via Garifuna leaders. Even though they willingly adapted themselves to change when it was clear that it suited their interest, the Black Caribs also were traditionally suspicious of those outsiders who would foist change upon them, which too often in the past has led to their near-destruction. They may also be jealous of those of their own who become educated and take on the roles associated with other cultures—particularly the dominant one. Many of the first Garifuna to obtain college degrees were shattered when they found neither jobs in their home countries nor respect in their home villages. The parents of two young people now studying medicine in Guatemala City swear their children will never return to Livingston to set up a medical practice.

Conditions are now so poor along the coastline in Garifuna territory that I believe things can and will change. Migration as a way of life has at least taught the Garifuna to keep their eyes open and adopt what they need and what seems to work elsewhere. What they must have now is local political power to improve their environment, their incomes, and their sense of respectability. Ethnicity may be an important key; some of those who have migrated are trying it out at various doors, both at home and abroad. Chapter 9 will further explore the relationships between ethnicity and development for the Island Caribs/Black Caribs/Garifuna over the past 200 years.

NOTES

1. Roosevelt (1980) is an invaluable general source, but this particular suggestion was made during discussion of the subject and based upon her recent work on Marajo Island.

2. An informant of mine, a non-Carib resident of Livingston with whom the two Americans stayed while in Livingston, noted that they had been entranced by the exotic nature of the ceremony and had entered into it wholeheartedly as a kind of rare touristic treat, even though they also appreciated its fundamentally religious nature. The fact that the American lawyer and her companion had actually caused the event to occur was either unknown or unrecognized by the Garifuna with whom I spoke, and few even mentioned the Americans' presence. The assumption was that Ramírez had continued to care enough about his family and native culture to have made his own arrangements, or else that his wandering spirit found it could not rest without a proper ceremony. This says a good deal about cultural persistence, and, of course, it confirms what Garifuna have always believed about the power of the *gubida:* in this case it was assumed that Ramírez had been influenced by those he encountered "on the other side" and that, as one of them, he was able to appear in dreams as he chose. This story makes it clear that the impetus is assumed to derive from the spirit, not the predisposition of the dreamer.

3. Studies of housing in Livingston and Trujillo in 1984 showed that most houses were still without any form of sanitary facility. Adults and older children go to the beaches at dusk or before dawn to relieve themselves. Most Garifuna households depend upon chamber pots for emergencies or for those who are unable to make the trek; these pots are emptied into streams or directly into the sea. In smaller populations the wave action has kept the beaches clean, and the house sites thus are free of human excrement. Today this practice presents a serious public health hazard in the larger towns. Parasites cycle between humans and the fish that feed close to shore. And it is offensive to tourists to be confronted with human feces as they take moonlight or early morning walks along the otherwise idylic tropical beachways.

4. There is often an intense desire to give birth in the United States so that the children will be an American citizens, that being recognized as a distinct advantage both to them and their primary relatives, who wrongly believe they may thus claim a "preference" in seeking permanent residence (see Gonzalez 1985). It remains to be seen whether these children later consider themselves to be primarily North Americans or Central Americans. In either case, being Garifuna may itself become increasingly meaningful to them.

5. A story—I do not know if it is true—was being circulated during my last stay in Livingston to the effect that some fourteen persons had frozen to death in the walk-in freezer of a ship on which they had been hidden and then abandoned by whomever had arranged the trip.

6. This is not the place to detail the story of West Indians in the United States. However, personalities such as Marcus Garvey, Paul Robeson, Harry Belafonte, Orlando Patterson, Katherine Dunbar, and Paule Marshall, to name only a few, show how pervasive has been their influence in the arts and letters.

7. In one sense it appears that ethnicity is now used as a euphemism for these other characteristics. Yet anthropologists have for seventy-five or more years been pushing the notion of cultural relativity, and to the extent that ethnicity incorporates the wholistic notion of "a culture" and/or "a people," it is a far preferable way of distinguishing subunits of the species. Ethnicity is no more immune to abuse, however, than the terms it replaces.

8. When I sought to hire four assistants for work in collecting data in Trujillo and its surrounds, I made intimate knowledge of their own language a prerequisite for application. I was surprised at the number of young people in their late teens and early twenties who admitted to an imperfect command of the language.

9. In 1937 there was a massacre in the village of San Juán, Honduras. An arms cache, presumably brought there by Black Caribs, was uncovered on the beach or in the nearby bush. Government forces, constantly fearing revolution, rounded up all the adult men in the village and shot them in cold blood as both punishment and warning. This incident is sometimes cited today to suggest that the Caribs themselves were intent upon revolution for social reasons. While in Trujillo in 1984 I was told by a Garifuna elder who had been in the area at the time that the arms had been smuggled in as a business deal by Caribs who were awaiting payment before turning them over to a revolutionary party. In the meantime, however, a Carib office worker, loyal to the government and the fruit company, reported the existence of the cache to the authorities, with the results just described. The story was told to me as an illustration of how internal disagreements sometimes had drastic results.

10. It is not clear whether heavy drinking and/or alcoholism are really typical of sailors, but this is certainly the popular perception and has been upheld by at least one sociological analysis (Sherar 1973).

9

The Meaning of Development

Units of Analysis

It is fitting that this book should conclude with some thoughts about the nature of the so-called development process and how it has affected and may be anticipated to affect the Garifuna people. When dealing with the international development complex, it might be asked whether it is appropriate or useful to think of development in relation to a transnational ethnic group at all, for the unit of reference in development planning and discussion has most often been territorially defined—as in nations, regions, or villages. In Africa, where "tribes" have been redefined as "ethnic groups," development projects have often been focused upon them, but in such cases there has been some sort of indigenous political system through which action can be coordinated, if not controlled.[1] The same has been true for those native American groups that have tribal councils through which development agents can work. I know of only one project, recently funded by the Swiss in Honduras, aimed at dispersed and unorganized ethnic groups with the object of helping them retain or re-establish their cultural identity and in the process improving the socioeconomic conditions under which their members live.

In most parts of the world, responsibility for administering development projects funded by foreign or international agencies has fallen upon national host governments and their delegated subordinates, the latter sometimes being heads of local units (such as governors of regions or mayors of towns or cities) and sometimes (probably more often) representatives of the central government, usually acting through a ministry. As anthropologists and political scientists have long warned, plural societies present a problem in that one sector of the population usually dominates the others, and minority groups command only limited, if any, power. Even when development projects are ostensibly aimed at the latter, members of the target group usually have little influence in their design and implementation, and failure of the project is often the result (Chambers 1983; Pitt 1978). Governmental and other elites are likely to argue that the minority groups are in such a plight because they are uneducated, unambitious, and incapable of managing their own affairs. Put so bluntly, most people today would demur, but the attitude is nevertheless deep-seated and common, even among highly placed international development experts (Harrison 1985).

The other side of that coin must also be examined, for I believe we can go too far in assuming that development "from the bottom up," as it is sometimes phrased, is necessarily a panacea for the previously described state of affairs. The case of the Island Caribs/Black Caribs/Garifuna is instructive, for we have here an example of a people who managed their affairs very well for several hundred years, even when confronted with what might have seemed insurmountable odds against them in the form of first French, then British, then Spanish, and finally several Central American (still culturally European) government forces. The lack of central authority was not, in earlier times, an obstacle to their economic advancement. Yet today, for the most part, the Garifuna seem not to be able to pinpoint their problems, nor to take effective action to save their culture, much less to improve living conditions in their Central American villages and towns. To the extent that their culture is dependent on rural or village life, they may face an impossible task, for the Garifuna are rapidly becoming an urban people, as I will further elaborate. And that too is part of the problem. It is the thesis of this book that the Garifuna are no longer in control of their own destiny because the world system to which they had made effective cultural and psychological adaptations over the past several hundred years has used up and destroyed the ecological niche they once dominated.

The Definition of Development

If we can agree that "development"[2] implies a process in which a society achieves the structural means of improving life for more of its people, including a measure of autonomy to determine what "better" means for them, then I would suggest that only the Black Caribs (of the three "groups" or phases dealt with in this book) can be said to have been in control of their own "development."[3] It is important to remember that the Caribs/Garifuna have never had a central organization. Unlike many modern ethnic groups elsewhere, they were never a chiefdom, a tribe, or a kingdom. Even the Miskitos had achieved, by the middle of the eighteenth century, a greater degree of "central" authority, although they had been assisted in this by the British, who encouraged them in establishing a "kingdom" (Denis and Olien 1984).[4]

The Black Caribs became an ethnic group at some point on St. Vincent when they were driven to recognize their common values and interests in the face of the threat of European domination. Thus, in that sense their ethnicity is related to other characteristics that I have suggested define a "neoteric society" (i.e., one that has become adapted to recent extraneous conditions; Gonzalez 1970a). The adaptation process requires the bending of older, traditional beliefs and practices to conform with the new setting, and it may also include the instant adoption of new traits, which must then be endowed with the symbols of tradition in order to make them sufficiently authoritative to command behavior (Gonzalez 1986a; Hobsbawm 1983).

The Island Caribs were virtually destroyed—consciously and purposely—by the European onslaught in the fifteenth and sixteenth centuries. The Black Caribs of St. Vincent constructed a new culture out of the ruins of the old by adding to it new technologies and ideologies borrowed in part from their African heritage and in part from the Europeans with whom they engaged in trade and war. They were doing very well—indeed, it could be said they enjoyed a developing economy—when their military defeat in 1797 almost sent them the way of their Island Carib ancestors. By sheer ingenuity, persistence, luck, and lack of competition in the new niche in which they found themselves in Central America, they recovered (then enormously increased) their population size and their cultural integrity, and they managed to preserve the latter and their relative autonomy as a distinct people until World War II. It is more than merely interesting from an anthropological point of view that the Black Caribs managed this in part because of their liberal attitudes toward the absorption of other people and of new ideas. A Garifuna writer recently opined that his people's "ability to emulate the dominant social group and to conceal their 'essence'" enabled them to achieve some margin of success (Arzú 1985:29), which is one way of interpreting much of what I have documented in this book; indeed, I would agree that the strategy served them well. But in another sense, it is also true that the Black Caribs have not been so bound by something we often call "tradition" that they could not progress. In fact, I maintain that they continually "progressed," or developed, between 1750 and 1940. Development in this sense can arguably be considered a subcategory of what has been called "specific evolution" (Sahlins and Service 1960), and it may apply to many historical as well as contemporary societies.

Development is most often defined—usually using macroeconomic criteria —as the incorporation of traditional societies into the global capitalist, mercantile, and industrial system that began in western Europe as early as the thirteenth century (Wallerstein 1974, 1980; Wolf 1982). Furthermore, the process is most often considered to derive its impetus from the most "developed" (i.e., high-energy capturing) segments of that world system (White 1943) rather than from the social segment undergoing development. This definition is more restrictive than the above in relation to both time and place. It also suffers from the implicit projection of a single, or unilinear, model of development, one that almost by definition makes development unachievable for those who do not accept the primacy of industrialization, consumerism, and the value of property in defining status and promoting personal happiness. Finally, development depends upon and defines capitalism as a system that inevitably advances at the expense of all others. Some feel that this logically precludes the possibility of "development" in the sense of betterment for the people "at the bottom"; in fact, it has worsened conditions for many over the past century, if not longer (Frank 1969). Using this definition, it is possible to argue either case; that is, that the Black Caribs, and the countries in which they have lived, have become "more developed" or, if using other criteria, "more underdeveloped" through time.

A still more restrictive definition would make development a modern (i.e., late twentieth century) phenomenon, one linked with conscious efforts to bring about fundamental changes in a society through capital loans and grants, technology transfer and technical assistance. This is related to what Wolfe (1977) has called the "supranational organization of production," and it is *demanded* if that organization is to succeed and persist. Development in this sense has become part of the foreign policy of most of the more highly industrialized nations. The ideological rhetoric that accompanies such efforts suggests an altruistic motive, but the reality is that the developed nations have as much or more to gain from the process than those they succeed in changing. I refer to this system as the "modern development complex," made up of actors known as *donors, target groups,* and *technical experts,* who carry on a variety of projects and programs involving "leadership training," "institution building," "technology transfer," "collaborative research support programs," and the like. There is an implicit value orientation in this that extols the increased consumption of goods, most of which are manufactured elsewhere using energy from fossil fuels and provide the individual user with greater control over the immediate environment. This implies better health, lower mortality, greater personal leisure, and increased physical comfort and psychological pleasure (Adelman 1986; Cernea 1984, 1985).

It is difficult to quarrel with these goals, just as it is impossible to deny the evidence that these benefits have resulted from the development process in many parts of the world. But the fact that they do not always result is usually ignored by the developers, in spite of good will, large expenditures of money, the efforts of scientific experts in many fields, and the criticisms of social scientists who have observed many local-level failures and have warned of the philosophical and practical traps that await administrators of the modern development complex (e.g., Bunker 1985; Lipton 1977; Spicer 1952). The Garifuna have hardly been touched by the modern development complex, but they are victims nonetheless of the economic system that forces people "to barter their souls for the destructive powers of commodities" (Taussig 1980:xii). The following sections suggest various ways of viewing "development" among the Garifuna during the past 200 years.

Migration and Development

I have argued in earlier chapters that as a direct result of their migration to the United States after World War II, Black Carib men began to lose their sense of ethnic identity; this was followed by a decline in the fortunes of the home villages, even though this was not at first apparent because money continued to flow from abroad and there was always the expectation and hope that the men would themselves return. But as there were fewer men to continue the religious ceremonies, discipline the children, fish, assist in horticultural activities, and maintain the houses and public places in the communities, all of these first became the responsibility of women and then, in time, either disappeared or deteriorated. As has been shown earlier and by other ethnographers, only the religious system and child care remain as important village endeavors, and both of these have suffered in comparison with earlier times. I do not mean to suggest that the women were incompetent in their management skills but that they lost animus as it became more apparent that continuity over the generations was unlikely.

Remittances from abroad have been most often hailed as a benefit to the home village, but lately other voices have suggested that remittances might do more harm than good, especially in relation to development (see Stinner, Albuquerque, and Bryce-Laporte [1982] for both sides of the question). Rubinstein (1983:299), in speaking of St. Vincent, notes that permanent removal and consequent investment overseas has reduced agricultural production at home. He also cites other writers who suggest that emigration leads to declines in fishing and agriculture as the funds that arrive in the village are turned first to subsistence needs and then to luxury items. When investment occurs, it is often in unproductive lands that are then left uncultivated or in tertiary business enterprises, many of which fail because of an already glutted market.

Reliance on remittances also has been noted to have the same kinds of impact on youth in the West Indies as I have suggested it had on Garifuna youth (see chapter 8). "The wish to leave is a preoccupation among the rural youth and produces a 'migration mentality' in which escape from the island is viewed as the only means of achieving anything in life" (Rubinstein 1983:298). However, Rubinstein also suggests that we should not treat migration as an independent variable but as a product of "overarching national and transnational political and economic forces deeply imbedded in history" (1983:304).

I would agree, even though I have in previous chapters described Carib migration primarily in terms of the individual and the local community.

In dealing with the Caribs I must emphasize that in 1834 things were different on the Central American coast than they were in the West Indies. It is instructive to compare the fate of those Caribs who remained on St. Vincent with those who were deported. Of course, there are too many variables to do this with much confidence, and it has been repeatedly noted that those remaining were supposedly Red or Yellow, not Black Caribs, a reflection of differences in outlook, culture, and perhaps even abilities. A more likely explanatory model, it seems to me, would emphasize that the opportunities open to those who remained did not differ much from those available to former slaves. St. Vincent Caribs tended to merge with the other black peasant populations on the island, losing most of everything that had once identified them as a distinct ethnic group. Efforts today to reestablish some semblance of that former status are laudable but probably doomed to a short life.

Those who were deported were able to maintain themselves and their culture, however, and migratory labor was the mechanism that saved them. It cannot be said that the companies and concerns for whom they worked were any more altruistic or public spirited than any others; they were, even in the nineteenth century, multinational concerns that would stop at nothing to make a profit. Archival accounts of the activities of the first woodcutters in Belize, Guatemala, and Honduras make for scandalous reading. Many a group of workers—from Europe, the United States, the West Indies, the interior of the Central American countries themselves—were brought to the coast to work, treated shamefully, and left in confusion and despair if they did not die first. Dozier (1985) has documented this for Nicaragua; I have data from Honduras and Guatemala that must await publication at a later date.

In this tropical lowland setting, the Black Caribs proved themselves more hardy and adept than many others, and they were rewarded with what were then considered good wages and considerable respect, as noted in chapter 6. The Miskitos, who as warriors had enjoyed great favor with the British in the seventeenth and eighteenth centuries, were not generally considered good wage laborers, for they had acquired a reputation for surliness, unreliability, and drunkenness. Constant gifts of rum and broken promises over two centuries had taken their toll, and even the stalwart Methodists gave up on them (MMS, box 225); it was the Moravian church that eventually led many of them out of their alcoholic despair. By the turn of the nineteenth century, when the multinationals were expanding in the area, the Miskitos had largely retreated to the hinterlands on either side of the Rio Coco, in what are now the countries of Honduras and Nicaragua, although some also lived along the coast, sometimes in settlements adjoining those of the Black Caribs.

The retreat of the Miskitos left the Black Caribs as the major "indigenous" laboring population on the Mosquito Coast between Belize and Bluefields, and the evidence suggests that they were able to fit into the new commercial system largely *on their own terms*—at least in the beginning. In the nineteenth century they had no ambitions to export wood themselves, to build canals or railroads, to seize control of the national government, or to dictate to other ethnic groups how they should live. Their needs for cash were not extensive, and their wages enabled them to buy what they did not produce themselves. As was repeatedly noted by observers of the time, if they felt they were treated poorly, they merely packed up and left the area, just as their ancestors had done and as some South American lowland groups still do (Adams 1982:3). Their economy depended upon the mobile labor of the men and the shifting horticulture of the women, supplemented by the ever-present protein resources of the sea and forest. In the latter, they were several steps ahead of the former slave or creole population of Belize and the West Indian immigrants—both groups largely eschewing horticulture and foraging in favor of wage labor. All of the black groups on the coast had health advantages over whites, Indians, and mestizos.

Consumption and Development

There are several ways in which we may link modern consumption patterns to the expanding global capitalistic system, not the least being an unceasing effort of the latter to increase the list of foreign goods wanted by indigenous populations. As early as the eighteenth century a British official commented that the problem with the Miskitos was that they still did not consume enough European products to make it worthwhile to trade with them and that more gifts should be made to introduce British goods and create a market (Long 1774:318). Thomas Young (1847:126–27) made extensive lists of items desired by the different native populations of the coast in 1840 to guide the merchants in selecting goods for sale there. The Black Caribs were said to constitute a particularly good market for dishes and cutlery, showing that they had already begun to adopt some European values about food service. Indeed, from the beginning of their employment on the coast in the 1800s, they were paid partly in goods and partly in cash. This was due to the fact that the woodcutters were also merchants—the two endeavors having been managed by the same entrepreneurs almost from the beginning of the British presence in Belize.

By the 1900s, when the United Fruit Company established its large plantation-railroad-commissary complexes in Central America, the Black Caribs were already hooked (if that is the right word) on European cloth for clothing and blankets, china, glassware, cutlery, machetes, knives, guns and ammunition, iron pots and griddles, kerosene lamps, jewelry, buttons and buckles, fishhooks, harpoons, and a myriad of other items, including some foods. Belize was a source of such specialty items as tea, refined sugar, white flour, soap, and rum. The company commissaries in Honduras and Guatemala took much of the business away from the Belizean merchants and probably established some new "needs." An old man in Trujillo told me recently that the corrugated "tin" roofing panels once available through the "company" were of better quality than anything found locally today.

From the perspective of the Black Caribs, however, their ability to acquire such items was a measure of their development. They considered themselves to be affluent when they could supply their homes and families not only with the necessities of life but with what they considered luxuries. Still, when I did fieldwork in Livingston in the mid-1950s, their list of wanted goods was not much different from that given above. I recall that most of the women still went barefoot and that I was responsible for introducing and creating a demand for rubber thongs (made in Japan) in the village. They were placed in stock by the local Chinese merchants, and by the time I returned in 1960 everyone was wearing them—long before they could be found in Guatemala City.

When electricity became available some four hours a day in the early 1950s, a few people acquired radios, which could be heard in unison at six in the morning, again at noon, and at five in the evening when the local generator was turned on. Soon thereafter battery-powered radios were invented, and they promptly flooded the town, for they were cheap (so were the batteries); they soon became a favorite gift or booty from trips abroad. As such trips increased in frequency—especially to the United States—other new imported goods were seen in the community, including life-sized (white) baby-dolls, no-iron clothing made of nylon (and later polyester), high heels, sunglasses, cameras, plastic flowers in plastic vases, plastic baby pants, plastic baby bottles, plastic dishes—the list of plastics was seemingly endless. Soon many of these items began to be manufactured in Guatemala and were locally available. Today, two or three of the more affluent Garifuna members of the community have purchased motorcycles (even though there are no roads, Livingston being reached only by sea or by private plane), and their homes boast refrigerators, electric fans, and televisions.

The major point I wish to make here is that so long as recurrent migration was the predominant pattern, the wants and needs of the Black Caribs seemed to keep pace with their local situation. They purchased what was locally in style and available, at prices they did not consider exhorbitant in relation to the amount of work it took to acquire them. Their health was certainly not perfect, but the population had grown steadily since 1797 (see Table 5.2) and they were considered relatively healthy by Central American standards. Their own beliefs and practices in relation to health and disease were reasonably effective and, before the introduction of antibiotics after World War II, not inferior to what was available to other peasant and many urban populations, even in the more developed nations (Gonzalez 1966). Development in this area should have come about "naturally," that is, in the same way other improvements had come to them over the years—through their observation that new medicines and practices would be in their own best interest.

Population and Development

The question of population increase is important and must be discussed in relation to what has happened to the Black Caribs/Garifuna since 1940. In fact, mortality decreased following the war, much as it did all over the world, as lives were saved by antibiotics and other medical innovations. And, as was true in so many other less developed societies, the birth rate did not decline proportionately. It is certainly not coincidental that the population explosion occurred at approximately the same time as did migration leading to permanent removal. At the macrolevel, the two can be seen as effects of the ever-expanding global system. Apologists for that system would call both the foreign job market and the medical advances "benefits" of development, and in a sense they were. From the perspective of individual Black Caribs and their families, coming as they had through a decade of relative poverty as the banana industry declined, the new opportunities seemed to promise recovery and advancement. They were not alone in failing to perceive that life for so many of their children foretold an era of poverty and eventual cultural and social decline.

For a people whose number had been reduced to a total of perhaps 1,700 less than 200 years before, reproduction was a primary societal goal and a personal achievement. "Family planning" meant having as many children as possible during one's prime. Sexual activity was glorified in song, story, and proverb, and children were the outward sign that one had been successful in making sexual conquests. This was as true for women as for men (McCauley 1981; McCommon 1982). Only in recent years have some women become concerned enough to take precautions lest they end up with too many children to raise alone. In the past, men could be cajoled, or pressure could be put upon their relatives, to see that they made at least some contribution to their children's upbringing. Today, with greater distances between them and the mothers, more children are utterly abandoned by their fathers. Yet, the prestige in having children remains. In Livingston in 1985, informants named several teenage boys who had already fathered two, three, and even four children but who had never held a job. Although some of the older people— especially women—have long foreseen and feared that outcome and rue their grandchildren's unchecked sexual activities, they are helpless to turn the tide.

Given the larger number of mouths to feed, both men and women were pleased with the job opportunities opening up to men during and following World War II. Whether they saw the new migration as a means of warding off poverty or merely a way to improve their lives through the acquisition of more consumer goods and comforts, the Black Caribs, like so many others, increasingly fell into this economic trap. The results of their "modernization" have parallels elsewhere (Kottak 1983; Lele 1975; Scott 1976), but the migratory element seems to have added a special dimension. The new life was not unlike what they and their ancestors had known, and it seemed, at first, even better than anything in the past. "Development" for the Black Caribs came to mean migration, and for the most part that notion has persisted, so that most young people today still see it as the only road to a better future. Unlike the Ecuadorian Jungle Quichua described by Whitten (1976, 1985), the Garifuna today have gone too far down the road toward Western civilization and urbanization ever to return.

Urbanization and Development

More Garifuna live in Trujillo today than on the entire Mosquito Coast, and more live in the cities of La Ceiba and Puerto Cortes (Honduras) than in the town of Trujillo; we can only guess at the number who live in Tegucigalpa and Guatemala City. Furthermore, there are signs that towns such as Livingston and Trujillo may be thriving but that the percentage of Garifuna who live there is declining (see Tables 8.7–8.10). In a very real sense, it may be said that Livingston is no longer a Garifuna town. Many of its current residents realize this, although they dislike admitting it. The concept of dual residence persists, so that even people who have been gone for years are thought of and listed as "residents." In 1975 I found a total of 129 empty houses in Livingston, their owners said to be "temporarily" away; by 1985 there were few such houses—nearly all had been sold or rented, many to non-Garifuna. Still, the former owners were often still referred to as town residents.

The urban trend is partly related to choices the people have made about horticulture, agriculture, and fishing. But more important, in my opinion, is the fact that these activities are not perceived as sufficient to provide a living and that migration today means urban living. Once they have experienced life in the city, they seem to prefer it.

A similar pattern may be seen in Punta Gorda and Dangriga in Belize. According to recent investigations by Palacio (1985), the percentage of Garifuna in these communities has dropped over the past decade, in spite of the fact that there has been considerable in-migration of Garifuna from Honduras over the same period. Palacio believes that most of the latter come to Belize as merely a stopover in their trek north, even though thousands of Central

Americans (especially Guatemalans and Salvadorans) come there to stay and carve out a new living through agriculture.[5]

Ethnic Consciousness and Development

Belize actually has more Garifuna who are highly educated and prepared for leadership in the modern world than either of the other countries. Many of these people are concerned, however, that fewer members than before appear interested in "bearing" their culture. Study and lobbying groups have been formed to record and perpetuate what they believe to be their traditions, and they have succeeded in having November 19 established as a national holiday commemorating their supposed arrival in the territory. In addition, the national legislature has renamed Stann Creek—it is now Dangriga, honoring the name by which the earliest Carib inhabitants of that town called it. Although there has been talk of having Garifuna made an official language, and of its being taught in the schools, that does not at this writing appear to be in the offing. As larger numbers of Garifuna emigrate, the pressure they are able to bring to bear decreases, even though some Garifuna now occupy important positions throughout the country. Garifuna leaders in Belize, as in Guatemala and Honduras, have not been able to consolidate the group so that they vote as a block in national elections. The reasons for this are complex, but to interpret it within the framework of the present analysis: the Garifuna have never been united politically; they have tended to see only the immediate and local problems; and many still do not identify with the larger nationality.

Richard Adams (1981) has analyzed how Miskito Indians in Nicaragua have been ignored or neglected by both previous and present governments for some of the same reasons, although the situation there is different in that the Miskitos, at least, are not as acculturated as are the Garifuna today. In fact, I would judge the current Miskito situation as being somewhat more akin to that of the Black Caribs in previous years when their solution to problems with the outside world was merely to retreat. The Miskitos are still subject to recruitment by outsiders (both Nicaraguans and Americans) as a military force, however, and as such they have become armed rebels, torn between wanting their autonomy, on the one hand, and demanding a meaningful role in the modern state, on the other.[6]

The fact that Miskitos live on both sides of the Rio Coco, and thus in both Honduras and Nicaragua, has been a continuing problem for them, since it leaves them vulnerable to differing national regimes, each with its own agenda. Efforts to unify them have not been successful, largely because of continuing hostilities between Sandinistas and Honduran-based Contras assisted by the Reagan administration. The Miskitos have been pawns in that conflict. In the past, the Black Caribs were able to exploit to their own benefit the fact that they were a transnational ethnic group, moving from country to country when things were difficult. The modern Miskito situation points up the fact that the most powerful elements of the world system transcend even national boundaries.

Honduras is the only country today to have a significant number of Garifuna, but even there they make up a small percentage of the total population. Nevertheless, due to increased world interest in the plight of indigenous peoples, ethnicity, and development, they are managing to make their presence known, if not felt, even in the capital city. There is a small group of activists, many of them well educated and some with residential experience in the United States, who are attempting to mobilize not only the Garifuna but blacks of other ethnic identities to overcome what they perceive as long-standing neglect due to racial prejudice and class bias. Although the active participants are almost exclusively Garifuna, the name of their group, Organización Fraternal Negra de Honduras, suggests both the racial and cultural directions they are taking. Unfortunately, OFRANEH has undergone several unpleasant upheavals in its leadership since it was founded in 1984. The factionalism which has been so often apparent ever since St. Vincent days continues, as does the ambivalence about their Indian/African origins. The majority of Honduran Garifuna have taken neither side; in fact, they do not seem to know of the organization's existence. Yet OFRANEH is becoming recognized in Honduras. Indeed, in December 1985 some of the group's leaders joined with others, who represented various Amerindian groups native to Central America before the coming of the Black Caribs, in the first national conclave of ethnic groups of Honduras.

Recent Efforts by the Modern Development Complex

Another Honduras organization, known as ASEPADE (Asesores para el Desarrollo), has worked with the Garifuna as well as with other Honduran communities in a variety of development projects, including attempts to improve crop and animal production, food processing, and marketing. They have introduced into some of the Garifuna villages machines for grating cassava and newly designed stoves for processing it, both of which reduce the backbreaking labor of the traditional methods. So far, however, agricultural production has not increased, and no new markets have been developed, so it is not clear whether incomes have been augmented for a significant number of women. Although I am not aware of any planned projects in cattle husbandry, some Garifuna on the coast east of Trujillo have acquired a few animals, and in some cases small herds. Some peddle milk as a sideline, but the main object is to raise beef for sale in the increasing export market for that product (De Walt 1983). Since there is some evidence that Black Caribs in that area, like their neighbors and erstwhile mentors, the Miskitos, raised cattle as early as 1800, this may be seen merely as an intensification of an old pattern in response to new market conditions.

Fishing cooperatives have been tried both in Belize and in Honduras. A European donor nation gave several large refrigerated boats to a cooperative in Trujillo, with the consequences described earlier (see note 7, chapter 6). The government in Belize has regulated the fishing industry there, and although some Garifuna have found employment in it, most fishing is done, if at all, for their own consumption. There have been few projects aimed at improving local opportunities for men. Palacio (1982) describes the settlement of Georgetown, which was intended to assist Garifuna survivors of Hurricane Hattie in 1961. Conceived as an agricultural community, it failed—in Palacio's opinion because it was located inland, away from the sea to which the Garifuna are emotionally and culturally tied.

A few Garifuna have found employment in the sugar, cocoa, and perhaps marijuana industries in northern Belize. And according to Richard Wilk (personal communication), a new community—Bomba—has been established by them on the coast some twenty-five miles north of Belize City. Belizean Garifuna tell me the people of Bomba have nearly abandoned their heritage, however.

Development projects have been neglected in Livingston. Some current non-Garifuna residents of that town have stated to me that the town is "rich" because of the remittances of emigrants and has no need of Peace Corps or other development assistance. Aside from some public health improvements, the distribution of basic foods to children and to pregnant and lactating mothers, and the building of some new public school buildings within the last decade, there have been no local projects and nothing to help the residents improve their economic productivity—no crafts, no agricultural demonstration efforts, no introduction of small industry. There has been some effort to develop a tourist industry, and several bars and restaurants have been opened to cater to tourists. Garifuna dancing has been touted as an exotic indigenous "show," and Livingston hosts very large crowds on holidays, such as the day of San Isidro (May 15) and the week between Christmas and New Year's Day. Most of the tourists are Guatemalans from the capital city, plus a number of gringos—the term locally applied to any white foreigner (some of whom are also labeled "hippies" because of their clothing styles, use of drugs, and generally casual behavior patterns). Most foreign tourists come from Europe, New Zealand, and Australia, as well as a few from the United States and Canada. They spend little money but enjoy interacting with the Garifuna. Some stay on for extended periods, and two or three have settled in the town permanently.

A small gay community has attracted local notice, including one rather flamboyant transvestite male who provides considerable amusement to tourists. The capital city of Guatemala has a sizeable gay community, some members of which vacation or weekend in Livingston, and they may have introduced the life-style there. Several Garifuna men have been found very attractive by visiting white women, and some have succeeded in achieving resident status in the United States through marriage or other arrangements. A few Garifuna women have taken up with casual tourists, generally on less permanent bases. Prostitution by both men and women is now quite common, whereas in 1956 it was rare in Livingston itself.

A Swiss concern has recently built a luxury hotel in Livingston, hoping to draw an affluent clientele. Few Garifuna have been employed there, however, either in the construction work or as part of the service contingent; instead, Ladino workers were imported from elsewhere in the country. If the hotel proves a success, a few Garifuna may be hired as entertainers, and those who own canoes with motors might earn a decent living taking visitors on tours of scenic nearby areas, especially the famed Río Dulce. However, unless the town itself is given a face-lift, with significant improvements in sanitary waste disposal and the introduction of more sophisticated entertainment possibilities, it is not likely that the class of tourism envisaged by the Swiss will be attracted. The hotel has been a controversial issue for the several years it has taken to build it. Some believe tourists will be drawn to the site by its spectacular natural beauty, thinking that so long as they stay inside the confines of the hotel they will never see the town itself. If casino gambling is introduced, as some believe the owners eventually intend, and so long as marijuana is liberally available—smuggled in from Belize—the enterprise may succeed. But it is doubtful that it will contribute much to the development of either the town of Livingston or of the Garifuna as an ethnic group.[7]

The Possibilities for Future Development among the Garifuna

As I have outlined in a recent popular book (Gonzalez 1986b), I do not think all is lost, in spite of the rather pessimistic tone of the above remarks. However, there are some rather serious problems that must be addressed by the Garifuna and the national governments under which they live. First, continued dependence upon migration as the only road to economic betterment must be abandoned. What was once a viable socioeconomic strategy, offering considerable security and predictability, plus the opportunity of maintaining what they chose of their unique culture, has become no more than a means of staying alive. The returns are poor and the risks and costs are now so great that they threaten the continued survival of all the Garifuna can call their own.

The future of the culture, if there is to be one, must not be severed from the past. To this end, ASEPADE and OFRANEH together have sponsored workshops, as well as theatrical and musical events, to educate the public about

Garifuna origins and culture (A. Gutiérrez 1984; Gonzalez 1986b). Indeed, even more of their past should be sought—in Central America but also in St. Vincent, in South America, and in Africa, since their forebears came from all of these places. The concept of a homeland is important to all transplanted ethnic groups, and for living Garifuna, Central America is their home. The old way of life, dependent upon fishing, horticulture, and locally available wage labor is now only a thing of distant memory or story, and few really want to return to it. But something akin to it might be revived within the context of the modern industrial-commercial world.

Although there is no new, unoccupied niche waiting for their exclusive exploitation, there are some underdeveloped or underrepresented professions and activities into which the Garifuna might move. The "higher" educational levels now tend to encourage young people to enter white-collar professions such as schoolteaching, bookkeeping, secretarial work, and the like. Obviously, the demand for these will grow in a developing nation, but there will be too much competition for too few jobs, and many Garifuna will find themselves over-qualified for local openings and forced to leave the home community, and perhaps the nation, to find work. It is significant, however, that at least there is training locally available in the larger towns for these positions. In Jamaica, where data processing by computer for United States companies has become one way to earn a good living, young people—especially women—have quickly learned the required skills. This type of employment could be developed in Central America in time.

Basic production also must be stimulated. Plant, animal, and manufactured products, to be sold locally, nationally, or worldwide, could be developed and marketed in order to buy the many items upon which the Garifuna's valued way of life depends. For example, a small cassava-drying plant in each village for processing that root into cattle feed would stimulate commercial farming, which hardly exists among Garifuna today. Carpentry and cabinetmaking would be logical professions for men whose ancestors long excelled in wood-working. Coastal peoples will continue to need small water crafts and to require maintenance services for them. Marketing services, including advertising, packing, transportation, bookkeeping, and banking, might be problematic in the smaller villages but already are available in the towns.

Following improvements in production, various new services, such as plumbing, electrical contracting, sanitary engineering, brick manufacture and laying, bicycle and small appliance repair, and photography will increase in demand. Some of these will require specialized training or apprenticeships, and support will be required while the Garifuna learn the relevant skills. This would be excellent development assistance, but it may be difficult at first to convince young men and women that these activities would lead to a better life than they can find or create in New York City. Another dampening factor may be the perception that some or all of the above skills are the special province of Ladinos or mestizos (as in the case of the Swiss hotel in Livingston, whose owners found it necessary to bring in the latter for construction and other jobs).

Grassroots rural/urban development of this sort would be of enormous benefit to the Central American nations. The major cities are already overcrowded, and the coastal areas are underinhabited (except in Belize, where the opposite situation obtains). Some of these new products would replace imports and balance foreign exchange. And if that happens, the prestige and position of the Garifuna within those nations would improve—both as individuals and as an ethnic group. Just as the Black Caribs in 1800 became a valued asset to Honduras for their produce and their labor, so could the Garifuna achieve a similar reputation in the modern world. But they must find ways to immerse themselves more fully in their nation's affairs, for the ethnic group itself is not, and never has been, a viable political and economic unit.

The route presently being pursued by OFRANEH, in which Garifuna link themselves with other blacks, on the one hand, and join with other ethnic (and nonblack) minorities, on the other, *seems* to offer possibilities for political advancement and economic development. But it is not clear how these two are related. Too often the first leads to improvement of the finances of the leaders, not to sustainable development of the community or other social unit. Certainly, recognition of wrongs and/or inequalities suffered by minority groups can sometimes lead to enlightened public opinion and changes in the law. For example, in Honduras, Indian minorities (including Garifuna) have suffered steady encroachment on their lands and diminished access to natural resources since the beginning of this century (Cruz Sandoval 1984). While OFRANEH and other ethnic coalitions do not yet have overwhelming support among their constituents at the grassroots level, perhaps that is not necessary as long as the message is carried to the larger Honduran polity. It remains to be seen whether publication of their plight by social scientists and ethnic pressure groups will make a difference. In Belize there were at least token concessions made to the Garifuna people through the actions of a few leaders, even when many or most of them were ignorant of what was happening. But sustained planned economic development for the Garifuna has not occurred.

Whether modern nations can tolerate extremes of ethnic allegiance is debatable (see Worsley 1984:246). Those that have tried to stamp it out during this century, such as the United States, China, and the Soviet Union, have failed, perhaps because the time has not been right or, more likely, because people cannot live as large, undifferentiated masses without suffering anomie and eventual loss of productivity, patriotism, and joie de vivre. Ethnicity provides an intimacy that gives meaning to life and can mobilize peoples' energies, sometimes even on behalf of larger entities within which the ethnic group itself is immersed. Recognition of the ethnic (or religious, neighborhood, professional, etc.) group as a whole can take the place of personal rewards in large societies.

The opposite is also true: failure to recognize and reward the existence and contributions of an ethnic group can turn its members into radical revolutionaries, especially when members of the group are excluded from the material benefits available to other members of the larger society (Adams 1981). And if they do not become revolutionaries, they may become an apathetic, vice-ridden, discouraged, permanent underclass. A few members of the group who cannot stand such a life may find some way to leave, abandoning their kinfolk and their ethnic allegiance—a loss to the individual, to the ethnic group, and to the society as a whole. The Miskitos fall into the first category; many United States urban blacks fall into the second. The Central American Garifuna, unfortunately, seem headed for the second "solution," even though, ironically, they avoid such a life in their homelands by coming to the United States, where they disdain the life of native-born blacks suffering from the same sort of ethnic-related malaise. Many Garifuna, like Dominicans, West Indians, Africans, and other immigrant blacks, have been able to succeed in spite of the color barrier in America, for their behavior has led to upward mobility for themselves and for their children. Whether this process is one that can be continued in the face of increased immigration and efforts to control it remains to be seen. In my view, the situation has already deteriorated, and the evidence is in the villages. For a while many Garifuna will continue to migrate, but increasing numbers will return home disillusioned; others will never have the opportunity to leave.

For those left behind, their relatives' earnings overseas, or even in the capitals of their own countries, will continue to be an important source of income. Clearly, some of the more successful emigrants, as has happened with the Honduran Garifuna, would like to return home when they retire, but they want the amenities of life to which they have become accustomed on the outside.[8] In order to make dollars earned abroad work for the benefit of the worker and his or her community, the concept of a remittance bank has been introduced by Pastor and Rogers (1983:33–34). These banks, they say, "would assure emigrants that their remittances would not be lost and, indeed, would be invested in ways that would offer them a good rate of return, a financial stake in enterprises, and at a certain point, guaranteed jobs for them or their families in such enterprises." Emigrants would deposit their dollars directly into the bank, which would pay them interest and, at the emigrant's request, transfer agreed portions of their remittances and/or earnings to their families. Working with the World Bank and other institutions, the remittance bank would identify promising projects in the local private sector. Using capital from both international financing institutions and the remittances, the banks would contribute to the development process by making loans to worthy projects. Adoption of this idea would increase the amount of foreign exchange available to the nation, foster the habit of saving and making local investments, and encourage the eventual return of emigrants to the home country.[9] It would also help make possible some of the local development projects I have suggested above.

In conclusion, it seems to me that the Garifuna can survive as a distinct people only by continuing to adopt new behavior patterns that maximize their age-old proclivity for managing two cultures at once. So long as they retain their language (now written, as well as spoken), their musical and dance styles, certain symbolic foodstuffs, and elements of their religious system, the memory of their past will remain alive. Increasingly, due to modern transportation and marketing facilities, as well as to an ideology that expects, seeks, and promotes ethnic differences, they will be able to retain all of these, even in cities such as New York and Los Angeles.

Like members of other ethnic categories everywhere, some of the Garifuna will continue to choose foreign, urban lives; others will stay home and struggle with rural or small-town problems. Class differences, hardly notable as yet in the home communities, will increase and become more divisive in the future as economic opportunities are differentially presented and seized upon. In the past, affluence itself was not a primary classification device; although even in St. Vincent it is probable that chiefs were more affluent than others, their leadership abilities seem to have come first in establishing their social positions.

As more and more Garifuna move to and/or are born in the United States, their futures must inevitably be tied in with the fate of blacks here. Yet, they already seem to recognize that it is often useful and wise to separate themselves, as have others, from the native black masses. They feel superior to black North Americans, in part because they possess a unique, non-Western culture and in part because they still see themselves as a people whose past is unsullied by slavery. At the same time, they feel superior to Africans because they see themselves as having adopted the more "civilized" customs of the industrial world at an earlier date. In fact, as has been the case for some hundreds of years, the Garifuna continue in their ethnocentricity, even as they adapt to whatever they find useful in the world around them. In this, they may have found the key to ethnic survival in the modern world. The costs may be high, but their heritage has given them the means to accept those costs and still find ultimate benefit in their investment.

NOTES

1. By "indigenous" I refer to systems existing today that are "traditional" only in the loosest sense of that word. Most have, of course, been altered during the long colonial experiences they have suffered.

2. The literature on "development" is simply overwhelming. Were I to cite all the materials I have read over the past twenty years, and especially those that have in-

fluenced my thinking, this book would be double its present size. Therefore, since I am not making a critique of any particular viewpoint, I will cite only those works that seem especially relevant to the points I wish to make here. For a more comprehensive, annotated bibliography, the reader might examine Brokensha (1984), which is useful, even though itself far too brief.

3. In a general sense, most readers will probably agree that no people has total autonomy or perfect freedom of choice. So long as there are "others" with competing interests, a certain amount of accommodation must take place. As the world's population increases and as resources diminish, more competition and conflict may be expected. Management of conflict then becomes increasingly necessary as a component of the development process. The use or the threat of force by the more developed and powerful nations has too often been in evidence in the recent past (see Azar and Burton 1986; Foster and Rubinstein 1986).

4. Actually, considerable controversy exists as to how autonomous and how indigenous this kingship really was. Denis and Olien (1984) seem to have accepted at face value the modern-day Miskito view that it was a truly Miskito development. Helms (1982) sees it as purely a product of British imagination and example. My own archival work seems to support the latter view, although I also agree with Bourgois (1986:5), who says, "Regardless of the real colonial power relations involved, today the former existence of a Miskitu King has become a symbol which mobilizes nationalist aspirations."

5. Joseph Palacio, himself a Garifuna, is presently resident tutor at the University of the West Indies in Belize. As the only Belizean with a Ph.D. in anthropology, he is conducting research on all population segments in his country. Belize has long been underpopulated, and this fact, plus the unrest in neighboring republics, has attracted large numbers of new settlers. Most of the latter are Spanish-speaking Latin Americans, a fact that would inevitably change the ethnic balance even if it were not the case that the emigrants are mostly black, English-speaking, and of Angloafrican culture — creoles, as well as Garifuna.

6. Bourgois (1986) is the best recent analysis of the situation, in my opinion. For an interesting comparison of the Miskito case with that of the Panamanian Kuna, see Howe (1986).

7. The Methodist missionaries in Belize never had anything good to say about Livingston. Repeatedly they noted that it was "the most godless town on the entire coast," beset by devils, and a place where gambling and drinking occurred on the streets, even on Sundays (MMS, box 226, Feb. 23, 1886; box 735, Mar. 20, 1902, Oct. 10, 1903). They would have been distressed, but not surprised, to hear about these recent developments.

8. In this they are no different from people all over the world. China has recognized the necessity of introducing modernity, including creature comforts, modern fashions, and entertainments, into the villages in order to keep the people "happy down on the farm."

9. Pastor and Rogers (1983) do not mention, but it should be said, that many of the villagers would see this as a means of depriving them of their rights. Some means should be incorporated into the system to ensure that needy relatives are indeed taken care of.

Epilogue

The Unmaking of an Ethnic Group

Lest the reader acuse me of being too optimistic, even a Pollyanna, in my predictions for the future, let me add a final cautionary note. I do not have a crystal ball, and the scientific predictive power of anthropology is still uncertain; yet it is necessary to point out that the Garifuna may be on the brink of cultural annihilation. Sanford (1974) has already suggested this, and I and my son Ian have warned of the possibility, saying that New York City may be their "last frontier" (Gonzalez and Gonzalez 1979). Certainly, some of the materials presented in this book could lead the reader to that conclusion.

To a great extent, I believe the fate of Garifuna ethnicity is now in their own hands. The forces of modernization are inexorable, but ethnic consciousness and pride are very much in fashion. Those who are comfortable in their world —whether in the urban United States or in coastal Central America—must think about and make an effort to convey to the children something of their ancestral culture and their social heritage. Many may prefer to simply merge into the black middle class in America or into the black creole populations of Central America, as seems to be happening in Nicaragua. The next generation, as a result, may not know where their roots are, and they may well abandon their Garifuna loyalties, much as happened to European immigrants in late-nineteenth-century North and Central America.

Increasingly, however, I see signs that this will not happen for everyone. In the United States the concept of ethnicity seems to be firmly entrenched and is getting stronger. For many, it is chic to be "ethnic," and some young Garifuna who were not reared to think of themselves as such are researching their past and reinventing ethnic secular and even religious rituals. The preservation of the cultural past in written documents, such as those provided by anthropology, as well as in photographs, films, and musical recordings, will assist in this recovery—although it should never be forgotten that all such history is selective.

I will not engage here in discussion over whether this truly constitutes cultural preservation. It is, in a way, comparable to the argument over ancient Greek or Roman culture. Although there are today modern states occupying territory once controlled and inhabited by Greeks and Romans, they are not congruent with the social units that lived there in ancient times. Yet much of the culture of those ancient peoples lives on all over the world.

If we identify "Garifuna" as a living *sociocultural* entity, with its own political structure, autonomous both ideologically and socially, then we cannot hold out any hope for its persistence in the future. The Garifuna situation is far different in this regard than that of the Miskitos, whose physical dispersal and cultural fragmentation were curtailed at the end of the nineteenth century as the Black Caribs expanded on the shore at the Miskitos' expense. It may be argued that the Caribs/Garifuna, unlike the Miskitos, never had any *political* structure above that of the kin-based local unit anyway. What made them distinctive and what held them together was the persistence of their language and their way of life, as well as their sense of common origin. Even in this they have been interdependent with Western civilization for 500 years; that is, both their economy and much of their ideological infrastructure are closely interwoven with threads deriving from Europe and from the Africa that Europe brought to America, there to become transformed into something we call Afroamerica (Wolf 1982).

For now, the new ethnicity may be an important political tool in the Garifuna struggle to gain a better foothold in either their home country or in the United States—or for some, in both. Armed struggle, such as that in which the Miskitos seem now to be engaged, with its concomitant hope for at least a certain amount of ethnic autonomy, is an unlikely alternative for the Garifuna. Yet this does not preclude a certain amount of politically militant rhetoric aimed at garnering attention and redress for discrimination suffered at the hands of fellow citizens. Success in such efforts is likely to be measured by how many individual Garifuna achieve political office, personal affluence, and prestige, as well as by the extent to which Garifuna cultural contributions become recognized in their countries. In other words, what the Garifuna now seek through ethnic consolidation is economic and political absorption into the larger society.

The Island Carib/Black Carib/Garifuna story may be almost over. But the Garifuna component—a truly modern development—may be able to hold its own if it turns to cultural rather than social or political preservation. Yet that very process signals the unmaking of the ethnic group as it becomes merely a category or an identity individuals may choose or ignore, as their life-styles and desires dictate.

"It seems a shame," the Walrus said,
    "To play them such a trick.
After we've brought them out so far,
    And made them trot so quick!"
The Carpenter said nothing but
    "The butter's spread too thick!"

Lewis Carroll

References

Adams, Frederick U.
1914   *Conquest of the Tropics.* New York: Doubleday.
Adams, Kathleen J.
1982   "The Premise of Equality in Carib Societies." Paper presented to the Forty-fourth ICA, Manchester, England.
Adams, Richard N.
1981   "The Dynamics of Societal Diversity: Notes from Nicaragua for a Sociology of Survival." *AE* 8:1–20.
Adelman, Irma
1986   "A Poverty-focused Approach to Development Policy." In John P. Lewis and Valeriana Kallab, eds., *Development Strategies Reconsidered.* New Brunswick: Transaction Books, pp. 49–65.
Aguirre Beltrán, Gonzalo
1958   *Cuijla.* México: Fondo de Cultura Económica.
Alexander, J. E.
1833   *Transatlantic Sketches,* vol. 1. London: Richard Bentley.
Allaire, Louis
1977   *Later Prehistory in Martinique and the Island Caribs: Problems in Ethnic Identification.* Ph.D. dissertation, Yale University.
1980   "On the Historicity of Carib Migrations in the Lesser Antilles." *American Antiquity* 45:238–45.
Alvarado, Casto
1905   "Visita a la Mosquitia, Trujillo, 6 de agosto, 1866." *Revista del Archivo y de la Biblioteca Nacional* 2(3): 98–100.
Anderson, Alexander
1983   *Alexander Anderson's Geography and History of St. Vincent, West Indies.* Ed. Richard A. and Elizabeth S. Howard. Cambridge: Harvard University and the Linnean Society. (Unpublished ms. from 1797.)

Anderson, Conwell A.
1970   "Anglo-Spanish Negotiations Involving Central America in 1783." In Eugene R. Huck and Edward H. Moseley, eds., *Militarists, Merchants, and Missionaries.* University: University of Alabama Press, pp. 23–37.

Andrews, Kenneth R.
1978   *The Spanish Caribbean: Trade and Plunder, 1530–1630.* New Haven: Yale University Press.

Anguiano, Ramón
1798   Notas de una visita a varios indios de Honduras, y a Trujillo. AGCA A1.37/17514/2335. Reprinted in *Boletín del AGCA,* 7(2): 74–80 (1942).
1813   "Informe." AGCA A.1/26357/2875.

Annual Register
1796   "Articles of Capitulation Granted to the French Government in St. Vincents 11 June 1796 by Lt. Gen'l. Sir Ralph Abercromby." PRO.

Anonymous
1797   *Gazeta de Guatemala* 21:164–68.

Arens, William
1979   *The Man-Eating Myth: Anthropology and Anthropophagy.* New York: Oxford University Press.

Armstrong, Douglas V.
1985   "An Afro-Jamaican Slave Settlement: Archaeological Investigations at Drax Hall." In Theresa A. Singleton, ed., *The Archaeology of Slavery and Plantation Life.* New York: Academic Press, pp. 261–87.

Arzú, W. M.
1985   "A Logical Chronology of Months' Names in Garifuna 'Carib'." *BS* 13:29–40.

Ashcraft, Norman
1973   *Colonialism and Underdevelopment: Processes of Political Economic Change in British Honduras.* New York: Teachers College Press.

Atwood, Thomas
1791   *The History of Dominica.* London: J. Johnson.

Authentic Papers
1773   *Expedition against the Charibbs, and the Sale of Lands in the Island of St. Vincent.* London: J. Almon.

Azar, Edward E., and John W. Burton
1986   *International Conflict Resolution: Theory and Practice.* Sussex: Wheatsheaf.

Bachofen, J. J.
1931   *Das Mutterecht.* New York: Modern Library.

Baraud, Simón
1947   "Datos sobre la Mosquitia Hondureña." *Revista del Archivo y de la Biblioteca Nacional de Honduras* 25:336–39.

Bard, Samuel A. (Ephrain George Squier)
1855   *Waikna: Adventures on the Mosquito Shore.* New York: Harper.

Barger, W. K.
1977   "Culture Change and Psychosocial Adjustment." *AE* 4:471–95.

Barth, Fredrik
1956   "Ecological Relationships of Ethnic Groups in Swat, North Pakistan." *AA* 58:1079–89.
Basso, Ellen B., ed.
1977   *Carib-speaking Indians: Culture, Society and Language.* Anthropological Papers No. 28. Tucson: University of Arizona Press.
Baxter, Ivy
1970   *The Arts of an Island.* Metuchen, N.J.: Scarecrow Press.
Beauçage, Pierre
1966   "Les Caraibes noirs: Trois siècles de changement social. *Anthropologica* 8:175–95.
1970   *Economic Anthropology of the Black Carib of Honduras.* Ph.D. dissertation, University of London.
1982   "Échanges, inégalités, guerre: Le cas des Caraibes insulaires," *Recherches Amérindiennes au Québec* 12:179–91.
————, and Marcel Samson
1964   *Historia del pueblo Garífuna y su llegada a Honduras en 1796.* Tegucigalpa: Editorial Paulino Valladores.
Becerra, Longino
1983   *Evolución histórica de Honduras.* Tegucigalpa: Editorial Baktún.
Beckwith, Martha Warren
1929   *Black Roadways.* Chapel Hill: University of North Carolina Press.
Behn, Aphra
1973   *Oroonoko: Or, the History of the Royal Slave.* New York: W. W. Norton. (First published in 1688.)
Bender, Donald R.
1967   "A Refinement of the Concept of Household: Families, Co-residence, and Domestic Functions." *AA* 69:493–504.
Bennett, John W.
1976   *The Ecological Transition.* New York: Pergamon.
Bernárdez, Jorge
1984   "The Garifuna Language in St. Vincent." *Luganute Garifuna (Garifuna News:* Los Angeles) 1(2): 1, 7.
Biesanz, John
1953   "Cultural and Economic Factors in Panamanian Race Relations." In Olen E. Leonard and Charles P. Loomis, eds., *Readings in Latin American Social Organization and Institutions.* East Lansing: Michigan State University Press, pp. 245–50.
Blair, Emma H., and James A. Robertson, eds.
1903–9 *The Philippine Islands, 1493–1803.* 55 vols. Cleveland: A. H. Clark.
Bloch, Maurice
1974   "Symbols, Song, Dance and Features of Articulation: Is Religion an Extreme Form of Traditional Authority?" *European Journal of Sociology* 15:55–81.
1975   "Property and the End of Affinity." In M. Bloch, ed., *Marxist Analyses and Social Anthropology.* New York: Halstedt Press/J. Wiley and Sons, pp. 203–28.

1977   "The Past and the Present in the Present." *Man* (n.s.) 12:278–92.
Blondeel Van Cuelebrouk, M.
1846   *Colonie de Santo-Tomas.* Brussels: Le Ministre des Affaires Étrangères.
Boles, John B.
1983   *Black Southerners, 1619–1869.* Lexington: University of Kentucky Press.
Bolland, Nigel, and Assad Shoman
1977   *Land in Belize, 1765–1871.* Mona, Jamaica: Institute of Social and Economic Research.
Boromé, Joseph
1966   "Spain and Dominica, 1493–1647." *Caribbean Quarterly* 12(4): 30–46.
Bourgois, Philippe
1986   "The Miskitu of Nicaragua: Politicized Ethnicity." *Anthropology Today* 2(2): 4–9.
Bowker, R. M., and S. A. Budd
1944   *Make Your Own Sails.* New York: St. Martin's Press.
Boyle, Frederick
1874   *Camp Notes: Stories of Sport and Adventure in Asia, Africa and America.* London: Chapman and Hall.
Brandon, Ruth
1983   *The Spiritualists: The Passion for the Occult in the Nineteenth and Twentieth Centuries.* New York: Knopf.
Breton, Père Raymond
1665   *Dictionnaire Caraibe-François.* Auxerre, France.
1958   "Observations of the Island Carib: A Compilation of Ethnographic Notes from Breton's Carib-French Dictionary (1665)." Trans. Marshall McKusick and Pierre Verin. Human Relations Area Files, ST 13. New Haven, Conn.
Brokensha, David
1984   "Development Anthropology: Annotated Select Bibliography." In William L. Partridge, ed., *Training Manual in Development Anthropology.* Washington, D.C.: American Anthropological Association, pp. 95–117.
Bromley, Yulian
1983   *Ethnic Process.* Moscow: USSR Academy of Sciences.
Brown, Michael F.
1984   "The Role of Words in Aguaruna Hunting Magic." *AE* 11:545–58.
Brown, Paula, and Donald Tuzin
1983   *The Ethnography of Cannibalism.* Washington, D.C.: Society for Psychological Anthropology.
Brown, Susan E.
1975   "Low Economic Sector Female Mating Patterns in the Dominican Republic." In R. Rohrich-Leavitt, ed., *Women Cross Culturally: Change and Challenge.* The Hague: Mouton, pp. 149–52.
Buckley, Roger Norman
1979   *Slaves in Redcoats.* New Haven: Yale University Press.
Bullen, Adelaide K., and Ripley Bullen
1970   "The Lavoutle Site, St. Lucia: A Carib Ceremonial Center." *PLA* 3:61–76.
Bullen, Ripley P.
1976   "Culture Areas and Climaxes in Antillean Prehistory." *PLA* 6:1–10.

————, and Adelaide K. Bullen
1972   *Archaeological Investigations on St. Vincent and the Grenadines, West Indies.* Orlando, Fla.: William L. Bryant Foundation.
Bunker, Stephen G.
1985   *Underdeveloping the Amazon.* Urbana: University of Illinois Press.
Burdon, J. A., ed.
1933–35 *Archives of British Honduras,* vols. 1–3. London: Sifton Praed and Co.
Burke, John G.
1972–73 "The Wild Man's Pedigree: Scientific Method and Racial Anthropology." In Edward J. Dudley and Maxmillian E. Novak, eds., *The Wild Man Within: An Image in Western Thought from the Renaissance to Romanticism.* Pittsburgh: University of Pittsburgh Press, pp. 259–80.
Burton, R.
1685   *The English Empire in America.* London: Nathaniel Crouch.
Cáceres, Francisco
1958   "Informe rendido por el primer governador político de Colón." *Revista de la Sociedad de Geografía e Historia de Honduras* 37(1–3): 4–11.
Cameron, Frank T.
1944   "Personnel at Sea." *The Grace Log* (May, June, July): 13–16.
1946   "Caribbean Commandos." *The Grace Log* (Jan., Feb.): 25–27.
Carmichael, Mrs. A. C.
1833   *Domestic Manners and Social Condition of the White, Coloured, and Negro Population of the West Indies.* 2 vols. London: Whittaker, Treacher, and Co.
Carneiro, Robert L.
1961   "Slash-and-Burn Cultivation among the Kiukuru and Its Implications for Cultural Development in the Amazon Basin." In J. Wilbert, ed., *The Evolution of Horticultural Systems in Native South America: Causes and Consequences.* Caracas: Sociedad de Ciéncias Naturales La Salle, pp. 47–67.
1970   "The Transition from Hunting to Horticulture in the Amazon Basin." Proceedings of the Eighth ICAES, 3:244–48.
Carr, Archie
1953   *High Jungles and Low.* Gainesville: University of Florida Press.
Carter, Anthony T.
1982   "Hierarchy and the Concept of the Person in Western India." In Ostor, Fruzzetti, and Barnett, pp. 118–42.
Cassidy, F. G.
1961   *Jamaica Talk.* Basingstoke and London: Macmillan Education.
————, and Robert B. Le Page
1967   *Dictionary of Jamaican English.* Cambridge: Cambridge University Press.
Cayetano, Eldrid Roy
1977   "Garifuna Songs of Mourning." *BS* 5(2): 17–26.
Cernea, Michael M.
1984   "Putting People First: The Position of Sociological Knowledge in Planned Rural Development." Keynote address, Sixth World Congress for Rural Sociology, Manila.

————, ed.

1985   *Putting People First: Sociological Variables in Rural Development.* Washington, D.C.: World Bank.

Chagnon, Napoleon A.

1968   *Yanomamo: The Fierce People.* New York: Holt, Rinehart and Winston.

Chamberlain, Robert S.

1980   *Francisco Morazán, Champion of Central American Federation.* Coral Gables: University of Miami Press.

Chambers, J. D., and G. E. Mingay

1984   *The Agricultural Revolution, 1750-1880.* London: B. T. Batsford.

Chambers, Robert

1983   *Rural Development: Putting the Last First.* London: Longmans.

Chandler, David Lee

1972   *Health and Slavery: A Study of Health Conditions among Negro Slaves in the Viceroyalty of New Granada and Its Associated Slave Trade, 1600-1810.* Ph.D. dissertation, Tulane University.

Charles, Cecil

1890   *Honduras: The Land of Great Depths.* New York: Rand McNally.

Checchi, Vincent, et al.

1959   *Honduras, a Problem in Economic Development.* New York: Twentieth Century Fund.

Cheek, Charles D., and Amy Friedlander

1986   "Pottery and Pigs' Feet: Space, Ethnicity and Neighborhood in Washington, D.C., 1880-1940." Ms. in possession of the author.

Chisholm, Colin

1801   *Essay on the Malignant Pestilential Fever, Introduced into the West India Islands.* London: Mawman.

1809   *A Letter to John Haygarth Exhibiting Further of the Infectious Nature of the Fatal Distemper in Granada during 1793, 94, 95, and 96.* London: Joseph Mawman.

CIAT

1983   *CIAT Report 83.* Cali: Centro Internacional de Agricultura Tropical.

Civrieux, Marc de

1976   "Los Caribes y la conquista de la Guayana Española." *Montalbán* 5:875-1021.

Clark, James

1797   *A Treatise on the Yellow Fever as It Appeared in the Island of Dominica in the Years 1793-96.* London: Murray and Highley.

Clyde, David F.

1980   *Two Centuries of Health Care in Dominica.* New Delhi: Prem.

Coehlo, Ruy

1949   "The Significance of the Couvade." *Man* (n.s.) 49:51-53.

1955   *The Black Carib of Honduras: A Study in Acculturation.* Ph.D. dissertation, Northwestern University.

Cohen, Milton

1984   "The Ethnomedicine of the Garifuna (Black Caribs) of Rio Tinto, Honduras." *Anthropological Quarterly* 57(1): 16-27.

Cohen, Ronald
1978 "Ethnicity: Problem and Focus in Anthropology." *Annual Review of Anthropology* 7:379–404.

Coke, Thomas
1793 *Extracts of the Journals of the Rev. Dr. Coke's Five Visits to America.* London: G. Paramore.
1808–11 *A History of the West Indies.* 3 vols. London: A. Paris.

Colledge, J. J.
1969 *Ships of the Royal Navy: An Historical Index.* Vol. 1: *Major Ships.* Trowbridge, England: David and Charles.

Colson, Audrey Butt
1977 "The Akawaio Shaman." In Basso, ed., pp. 43–65.

La Compagnie Belge de Colonisation
1844 *Amérique Centrale.* Paris: Rignoux.

Conzemius, Edward
1928 "Ethnographic Notes on the Black Carib (Garif)." *AA* 30:183–205.
1932 *Ethnographical Survey of the Miskito and Sumu Indians of Honduras and Nicaragua.* BAE Bulletin No. 106. Washington, D.C.: Government Printing Office.

Cosminsky, Sheila
1976 "Carib-Creole Relations in a Belizean Community." In Helms and Loveland, eds., pp. 95–114.

Courlander, Harold
1960 *The Drum and the Hoe: Life and Lore of the Haitian People.* Berkeley: University of California Press.

Cox, Edward L.
1984 *Free Coloreds in the Slave Societies of St. Kitts and Grenada, 1763–1833.* Knoxville: University of Tennessee Press.

Craig, Alan K.
1966 *Geography of Fishing in British Honduras and Adjacent Coastal Waters.* Baton Rouge: Louisiana State University Press.

Crapanzano, Vincent, and Virginia Garrison, eds.
1977 *Case Studies in Spirit Possession.* New York: Wiley.

Craton, Michael
1982 *Testing the Chains: Resistance to Slavery in the British West Indies.* Ithaca: Cornell University Press.

Crawford, Michael H., ed.
1984 *Current Developments in Anthropological Genetics.* Vol. 3: *Black Caribs: A Case Study in Biocultural Adaptation.* New York: Plenum Press.

Crouse, Nellis M.
1940 *French Pioneers in the West Indies, 1624–1664.* New York: Columbia University Press.

Crowe, Frederick
1850 *The Gospel in Central America.* London: Charles Gilpin.

Cruz Reyes, Victor C.
1986 "Apuntes históricas sobre las epidemias del siglo XIX en Honduras." Ms. in possession of the author.

Cruz Sandoval, Fernando
1984 "Los Indios de Honduras y la situación de sus recursos naturales." *América Indígena* 44:423–46.

Dalrymple, Campbell
1763 *Report on the State of the Island of Dominica, 1763.* Official Transcripts of Reports on the State of the British Colonies in North America and the West Indies, 1721–66. British Museum, Manuscripts, King's 205.

Dambrine, Manuel Fernando
1797 "Padrón de los Caribes que se hallan . . . (Trujillo)." AGCA A3.16/2025/ 194. (4) Honduras.

Da Prato-Perelli, Antoinette
1981 "Relations existent au début de la colonisation Espagnole entre les populations Caribes des Petites Antilles et celles du Venezuela." *PLA* 9:459–83.

Dary Fuentes, Claudia
1981 "Literatura popular de los Caribes Negros de Guatemala." *La Tradición Popular* (Boletín del Centro de Estudios Folklóricos, No. 34.) Guatemala: Universidad de San Carlos.

Davidson, George
1787 "The Case of the Caribbs in St. Vincent." In Thomas Coke, ed., *Coke's Missions in the West Indies—1787-89.* London: J. Paramore, pp. 2–19.

Davidson, William V.
1976 "Black Carib (Garifuna) Habitats in Central America." In Helms and Loveland, eds., pp. 85–94.
1979 "Dispersal of the Garifuna in the Western Caribbean." *Actes* of the Forty-second ICA, 6:467–74.
1983 "Etnohistoria Hondureña: La llegada de los Garífunas a Honduras, 1797." *Yaxkín* 6(1–2): 88–105.
1984 "The Garifuna in Central America: Ethnohistorical and Geographical Foundations." In Crawford, ed., pp. 13–36.

Davis, Richard H.
1896 *Three Gringos in Venezuela and Central America.* New York: Harper.

Day, Charles William
1852 *Five Years' Residence in the West Indies.* 2 vols. London: Colburn and Co.

Dennis, Philip A., and Michael D. Olien
1984 "Kingship among the Miskito." *AE* 11:718–30.

De Silva Ferro, D. Ramón
1875 *Historical Account of the Mischances in Regard to the Construction of a Railway across the Republic of Honduras.* London: C. F. Hodgson and Son.

Despres, Leo A.
1969 "Differential Adaptations and Micro-Cultural Evolution in Guyana." *SWJA* 25:14–44.
1984 "Ethnicity: What Data and Theory Portend for Plural Societies." In Maybury-Lewis, ed., pp. 7–29.
———, ed.
1975 *Ethnicity and Resource Competition in Plural Societies.* The Hague: Mouton.

De Vries, David Peterson

1857   *Voyages from Holland to America, 1632 to 1644.* New-York Historical Society Collections, 2d ser., vol. 3, pt. 1. New York.

De Walt, Billie R.

1983   "Microcosmic and Macrocosmic Processes of Agrarian Change in Southern Honduras: The Cattle Are Eating the Forest." In Billie R. DeWalt and Pertti J. Pelto, eds., *Micro and Macro Levels of Analysis in Anthropology: Issues in Theory and Research.* Boulder: Westview Press, pp. 165–86.

————, and Kathleen M. De Walt

1984   *Sistemas de cultivo en Pespire, sur de Honduras: Un enfoque de agroecosistemas.* Tegucigalpa: Instituto Hondureño de Antropología e Historia.

Díaz Chávez, Filander

1981   *La revolución Morazanista.* 2d ed. Tegucigalpa: Editorial Guaymuras.

Dick, K. C.

1977   "Aboriginal and Early Spanish Names of Some Caribbean, Circum-Caribbean Islands and Cays." *Journal of the Virgin Islands Archaeological Society* 4:17–41.

Dickinson, N.

1797   "History of the Causes of a Malignant Pestilential Disease Introduced into the Island of Baliseau by the Black Charaibs from Saint Vincent." WO 1/82, f.661.

Dirección General de Estadística y Censos

1980   *Honduras: Histórica-geográfica.* Tegucigalpa: Talleres Nacionales.

Diskin, Martin, Thomas Bossert, Salomón Nahmad S., and Stéfano Varese

1986   "Peace and Autonomy on the Atlantic Coast of Nicaragua: A Report of the LASA Task Force on Human Rights and Academic Freedom." *LASA Forum* 16(4): 1–19.

Dobbin, Jay D.

1983   *Do'en Dee Dance: Description and Analysis of the Jombee Dance of Montserrat.* Ph.D. dissertation, Ohio State University.

Dobson, Narda

1973   *A History of Belize.* Port-of-Spain: Longman Caribbean.

Dole, Gertrude

1978   "The Use of Manioc among the Kiukuru: Some Interpretations." In Richard L. Ford, ed., *The Nature and Status of Ethnobotany.* Ann Arbor, Mich.: Museum of Anthropology, pp. 217–48.

Douglas, James

1868–69   "Account of the Attempt to Form a Settlement on the Mosquito Shore, in 1823." In *Transactions of the Literary and Historical Society of Quebec,* pp. 25–39.

Dozier, Craig L.

1985   *Nicaragua's Mosquito Shore: The Years of British and American Presence.* University: University of Alabama Press.

Dreyfus, Simone

1977   "Territoire et residence chez les Caraibes insulaires au XVIIeme siecle." *Actes* of the Forty-second ICA, 2:35–46.

1982   "The Relationship between Political Systems, History, Linguistic Affiliation, and Ethnic Identity, as Exemplified by XVIth to XVIIIth Centuries Social Organization of the So-Called 'Island Caribs' (Arawak-Speaking) and 'True-Speaking Caribs' of the Mainland Coast." Paper presented at the Forty-fourth ICA, Manchester, England.

1983–84 "Historical and Political Anthropological Interconnections: The Multilinguistic Indigenous Policy of the Carib Islands and Mainland Coast from the Sixteenth to the Eighteenth Century." In Audrey Butt Colson, and H. Dieter Heinen, eds., *Themes in Political Organization: The Caribs and Their Neighbors. Anthropologica* 59–62:39–55.

Drummond, Lee
1977   "On Being Carib." In Basso, ed., pp. 76–88.

Dudek, Martin
1985   "Canoes, Fish and Fishing". Term paper for field course, Trujillo, Honduras. Department of Anthropology, University of Maryland.

Dundas, Henry
1796   "Observations Relating to Measures of Defense Allowances for the Navy." Correspondence, Ms. 60/024, Melville Papers. Greenwich: National Maritime Museum Library.

Durón, Rómulo E.
1965   *Don Joaquín Rivera y su tiempo,* vol 1., no. 3. Tegucigalpa: Ministerio de Educación Pública.

Du Tertre, Jean-Baptiste
1667–71 *Histoire générale des Antilles habitées par les François,* vol. 2. Paris: T. Jolly.

Edwards, Bryan
1819   *The History Civil and Commercial of the British West Indies.* 5 vols., 5th ed. London: G. and W. B. Whittaker.

Eighmy, Jeffry L., and R. Brooke Jacobsen
1980   "Extension of Niche Theory in Human Ecology: Three Patterns of Niche Occupation." *AE* 7:286–99.

Elington, Claudina
1985   "Presión arterial en pacientes de raza negra (protocolo de investigación)." Guatemala: Facultad de Medicina, Universidad de San Carlos.

Ellis, A. B.
1985   *The History of the First West India Regiment.* London: Chapman and Hall.

Escardo, Mauricio
1978   "Who Were the Inhabitants of the Virgin Islands at the Time of Columbus' Arrival?" *PLA* 7:245–57.

Escure, Genevieve J.
1978   "Linguistic Variation and Ethnic Interaction in Belize: Creole/Carib." Paper presented to the Ninth Congress of Sociology, Upsala, Sweden.

Farabee, W. C.
1967a   *The Central Arawaks.* Philadelphia: University of Pennsylvania, The University Museum. (First published in 1924.)

1967b   *The Central Caribs.* Philadelphia: University of Pennsylvania, The University Museum. (First published in 1924.)

Fewkes, J. Walter

1922   "A Prehistoric Island Culture Area of America." *Annual Report* of the BAE (1912–13), 34:10–12, 35–281.

Figueredo, Alfred E.

1978   "The Virgin Islands as an Historical Frontier between the Tainos and the Caribs." *Revista/Review Interamericana* 8:393–99.

Floyd, Troy

1967   *The Anglo-Spanish Struggle for Mosquitia.* Albuquerque: University of New Mexico Press.

Forde, C. Daryll

1934   *Habitat, Economy and Society.* New York: Dutton.

Foster, Byron

1981   "Body, Soul and Social Structure at the Garifuna Dugu." *BS* 9(4): 1–11.

1982   "An Interpretation of Spirit Possession in Southern Coastal Belize." *BS* 10(2): 18–23.

Foster, Mary LeCron, and Robert A. Rubinstein, eds.

1986   *Peace and War: Cross-Cultural Perspectives.* New Brunswick, N.J.: Transaction Books.

Fowler, Henry

1879   *A Narrative of a Journey across the Unexplored Portion of British Honduras.* Belize: Government Press.

Frank, Andre Gunder

1967   *Capitalism and Underdevelopment in Latin America.* New York: Monthly Review Press.

Frazier, E. F.

1957   *Black Bourgeoisie.* Glencoe, Ill.: Free Press.

Fruzzetti, Lina, Akos Ostor, and Steve Barnett

1982   "The Cultural Construction of the Person in Bengal and Tamilnadu." In Ostor, Fruzzetti, and Barnett, eds., pp. 8–30.

Furnivall, J. S.

1977   "The Plural Society." In John Stone, ed., *Race, Ethnicity, and Social Change.* North Scituate, Mass.: Duxbury, pp. 206–12.

Galindo, Juán

1833   "Notice of the Caribs in Central America." *Journal of the Royal Geographical Society of London* 3:290–91.

García Granados, Miguel

1952   *Memorias.* 4 vols. Guatemala: Editorial del Ministerio de Educación Pública. (First published in 1877.)

García Peláez, Francisco de Paula

1852   *Memorias para la historia del Antiguo Reyno de Guatemala.* 3 vols. Guatemala: L. Luna.

Garrido, P. Santiago

1964   *El santo misionero, Manuel de Jesús Subirana.* San Salvador: Editorial LEA.

Garrison, Vivian
1982   "Folk Healing Systems as Elements in the Community." In Uri Rueveni
        et al., eds. *Therapeutic Intervention: Healing Strategies for Human Sys-
        tems.* New York: Human Sciences Press, pp. 58–95.
Geertz, Clifford
1973   *The Interpretation of Cultures.* New York: Basic Books.
Geggus, David P.
1982   *Slavery, War and Revolution: The British Occupation of St. Domingue,
        1793–98.* Oxford: Clarendon.
Gibbs, Archibald Robertson
1883   *British Honduras: An Historical and Descriptive Account of the Colony
        from Its Settlement, 1670.* London: Sampson Low, Marston, Searle and
        Rivington.
Gillin, John P.
1936   *The Barama River Caribs of British Guiana.* Peabody Museum Papers
        No. 14. Cambridge, Mass.
Glazier, Stephen D.
1980   "A Note on Shamanism in the Lesser Antilles." *PLA* 8:447–55.
Gomberville, Sieur de
1682   "Relation de la Guyane, et du commerce qu'on y peut faire." In d'Acuna,
        ed., *Relation de la Riviere des Amazonas.* Paris.
Gonzalez, Nancie L.
1959a   "West Indian Characteristics of the Black Caribs." *SWJA* 15:300–307.
1959b   "The Nonunilineal Descent Group in the Caribbean and Central America."
        AA 61:578–83.
1960   "Changes in Black Carib Kinship Terminology." *SWJA* 16(2): 144–59.
1961   "Family Organization in Five Types of Migratory Wage Labor." *AA*
        63:1264–80.
1963   "Patterns of Diet, Health and Sickness in a Black Carib Community."
        Tropical and Geographical Medicine 15:422–30.
1966   "Health Behavior in Cross-Cultural Perspective." *Human Organization*
        25(2): 122–25.
1969   *Black Carib Household Organization.* Seattle: University of Washington
        Press.
1970a   "The Neoteric Society." *Comparative Studies in Society and History* 12(1):
        1–13.
1970b   "Towards a Definition of Matrifocality." In Norman Whitten, Jr., and John
        Szwed, eds., *Afro-American Anthropology: Problems in Theory and
        Method.* New York: Free Press, pp. 231–43.
1973   "Women and the Jural Domain: An Evolutionary Perspective." In Dorothy
        G. McGuigan, ed., *A Sampler of Women's Studies.* Ann Arbor: University
        of Michigan Press, pp. 47–57.
1976   "From Black Carib to Garifuna: The Coming of Age of an Ethnic Group."
        Actes of the Forty-second ICA, 6:577–88.
1979   "Sex Preference in Human Figure Drawings by Garifuna (Black Carib)
        Children." *Ethnology* 18:355–64.

1984a   "The Anthropologist as Female Head of Household." *Feminist Studies*
         10(1): 97–114. (Reprinted in Tony Larry Whitehead and Mary Ellen Con-
         away, eds., *Self, Sex, and Gender in Cross-Cultural Fieldwork.* Urbana:
         University of Illinois Press, 1986, pp. 84–100.)
1984b   "Rethinking the Consanguineal Household." *Ethnology* 23:1–12.
1985   "Giving Birth in America." In Rita J. Simon and Caroline B. Brettell, eds.,
         International Immigration: The Female Experience. Totowa, N.J.: Little-
         field Adams and Co., pp. 241–53.
1986a   "Garifuna Traditions in Historical Perspective." *BS* 14(2): 11–24.
1986b   *The Garifuna Story.* Tegucigalpa: Instituto Hondureño de Antropología e
         Historia.
————, and Charles D. Cheek
1986   "Black Carib Settlement Patterns in Early Nineteenth-Century Honduras:
         The Search for a Livelihood." Paper presented at the annual meeting of the
         American Anthropological Association, Washington, D.C.
————, and Ian Gonzalez
1979   "Five Generations of Garifuna Migration." *Migration Today* 7(5): 18–20.
Goodman, Felicitas D., Jeannette H. Henney, and Esther Pressel
1974   *Trance, Healing and Hallucination.* New York: Wiley and Sons.
Goodwin, R. Christopher
1980   "Demographic Change and the Crab-Shell Dichotomy." *PLA* 8:45–68.
Great Britain
1860   *Calendar of State Papers, Colonial Series, America and West Indies, 1574–*
         1660. London: Her Majesty's Stationery Office.
1880   *Calendar of State Papers, Colonial Series, America and West Indies, 1661–*
         1668. London: Her Majesty's Stationery Office.
1920   *Peace Handbooks.* Vol. 21: *North, Central and South America: Atlantic*
         Islands. London: Her Majesty's Stationery Office.
Griffith, William Joyce
1965   *Empires in the Wilderness: Foreign colonization and Development in*
         Guatemala, 1834–1844. Chapel Hill: University of North Carolina Press.
1972   "Attitudes Toward Foreign Colonization: The Evolution of Nineteenth-
         Century Guatemalan Immigration Policy." In *Applied Enlightenment:*
         Nineteenth-Century Liberalism, pt. 4. Middle American Research Institute
         Publications, No. 23. New Orleans: Tulane University Press.
1977   "The Personal Archive of Francisco Morazán." *Philological and Documen-*
         tary Studies 2(6): 201–86.
Grime, William E.
1979   *Ethno-botany of the Black Americans.* Algonac, Mich.: Reference Publi-
         cations.
Gullick, C. J. M. R.
1976a   "Carib Ethnicity in a Semi-Plural Society." *New Community* (Journal of
         the Community Relations Commission) 5(3): 250–58.
1976b   *Exiled from St. Vincent: The Development of Black Carib Culture in Cen-*
         tral America Up to 1945. Malta: Progress Press.
1978   "Changing Carib Agricultural Systems." Paper presented at the Tenth
         ICAES, Paris.

1979 "Ethnic Interaction and Carib Language." *Journal of Belizean Affairs* 9:3–20.

Gullick, Mary I.
1980 "Changing Carib Cookery." *PLA* 8:481–87.

Gutierres, Pedro
1905 "Diario de lo ocurrido al Batallón de Olancho, Caribes, Companía del Jícaro y Esquadrón de Segovia de Tegucigalpa el día 30 de marzo y llegaron a Maqsaya el 18 de abril, 1812." *Revista del Archivo y de la Biblioteca Nacional* 2(1): 3–8.

Gutiérrez, Alfredo
1984 *Manual educativo cultural Garífuna.* Tegucigalpa: ASEPADE.

Gutiérrez, Simón
1822 "Reporte al Ayuntamiento de Tegucigalpa." In Alvarado, p. 100.

Haag, William C.
1968 "The Identification of Archaeological Remains with Ethnic Groups." *PLA* 2:121–24.

Hadel, Richard E.
1972 *Carib Folk Songs and Carib Culture.* Ph.D. dissertation, University of Texas, Austin.
1975 "Male and Female Speech in Carib." *National Studies* 3(4): 32–36.

Haefkens, Jacobo
1969 *Viaje a Guatemala y Centroamérica.* Guatemala: Editorial Universitaria.

Hames, Raymond B., and William T. Vickers, eds.
1983 *Adaptive Responses of Native Amazonians.* New York: Academic Press.

Handler, Richard, and Jocelyn Linnekin
1984 "Tradition, Genuine or Spurious." *Journal of American Folklore* 97(385): 273–90.

Harrison, Lawrence E.
1985 *Underdevelopment Is a State of Mind—The Latin American Case.* Lanham, Md.: University Press of America.

Hasbrouck, G.
1927 "Gregor McGregor and the Colonization of Poyais." *Hispanic American Historical Review* 7:438–59.

Hawtayne, G. H.
1886 "Remarks on the Caribs." *Journal of the Anthropological Institute of Great Britain and Ireland* 16:196–98.

Hay, Samuel A.
1985 "Mr. Brown of the African Company in New York, 1816–1823." Paper presented to National Conference on Black American Protest Drama and Theatre, Morgan State University, Baltimore.

Heinrich, P., and J. K. Triebe
1972 "Sex Preferences in Children's Human Figure Drawings." *Journal of Personality Assessment* 36:263–67.

Helms, Mary W.
1969a "The Cultural Ecology of a Colonial Tribe." *Ethnology* 8:76–84.

1969b   "The Purchase Society: Adaptation to Economic Frontiers." *Anthropological Quarterly* 42:325-42.
1971   *Asang*. Gainesville: University of Florida Press.
1976   "Domestic Organization in Eastern Central America: The San Blas Cuna, Miskito, and Black Carib Compared." *Western Canadian Journal of Anthropology* 6(3): 133-63.
1981   "Black Carib Domestic Organization in Historical Perspective: Traditional Origins of Contemporary Patterns." *Ethnology* 20:77-86.
1982   "Miskito Slaving in the Seventeenth and Eighteenth Centuries: Culture Contact and Ethnicity in an Expanding Population." Paper presented at the Forty-fourth ICA, Manchester, England.

Henderson, George
1809   *Account of the British Settlement of Honduras*. London: C. R. Baldwin.

Henige, David P.
1974   *The Chronology of Oral Tradition: Quest for a Chimera*. Oxford: Clarendon Press.

Herrera, Guillermo
1911   "La Mosquitia en 1840." *Revista de la Universidad* (Tegucigalpa) 3(3): 174-77.

Hobsbawm, Eric J., ed.
1983   *The Invention of Tradition*. Cambridge: Cambridge University Press.

Hodder, Ian
1977   "The Distribution of Material Culture Items in the Baringo District, Western Kenya." *Man* (n.s.) 12:239-69.
1979   "Economic and Social Stress and Material Culture Patterning." *American Antiquity* 44:446-54.

Hodge, Walter H.
1942   "Plants Used by the Dominica Caribs." *Journal of the New York Botanical Garden* 43(512): 189-201.

Hodgson, Robert
1822   *Some Account of the Mosquito Territory*. 2d ed. Edinburgh: William Blackwood. (First published in 1757.)

Holm, John
1978a   *The Creole English of Nicaragua's Miskito Coast: Its Sociolinguistic History and Comparative Study of Its Lexicon and Syntax*. Ph.D. dissertation, University of London.
1978b   "Caribs in Central America." *BS* 6(6): 23-32.

Houdaille, Jacques
1954   "Negros Franceses en América Central a fines del siglo XVIII." *Antropología e Historia de Guatemala* 6(1): 65-67.

Howard, Thomas
1796-98   *Journal of a Voyage to the West Indies*. Ms., Boston Public Library.

Howe, James
1986   "Native Rebellion and U.S. Intervention in Central America." *Cultural Survival Quarterly* 10(1): 59-65.

Howland, Lillian G.
   1981   "Communicational Integration of Reality and Fiction." *Language and Communication* 1(2): 89–148.
   1984   "Spirit Communication at the Carib Dugu." *Language and Communication* 4(2): 89–103.
Humphreys, Robert A.
   1961   *Diplomatic History of British Honduras 1638–1901.* London: Oxford University Press.
Jenkins, Carol L.
   1980   *Patterns of Protein-Energy Malnutrition among Preschoolers in Belize.* Ph.D. dissertation, University of Tennessee, Knoxville.
   1983   "Ritual and Resource Flow: The Garifuna *Dugu.*" *AE* 10:429–42.
   1984   "Nutrition and Growth in Early Childhood among the Garifuna and Creole of Belize." In Crawford, ed., pp. 135–47.
Jesse, Charles
   1968   "Pierre Verin's Carib Culture in Colonial Times." *PLA* 2:115–20.
Jones, Alick R.
   1980   "Animal Food and Human Population at Indian Creek, Antigua." *PLA* 8:264–73.
Joyce, T. A.
   1916   *Central American and West Indian Archaeology.* New York: G. P. Putnam's Sons.
Kalm, Florence
   1980   "Seamen and Surrogates: A Test for Matrifocal Development in the Western Caribbean." Ms. in possession of the author.
Karnes, Thomas L.
   1978   *Tropical Enterprise: The Standard Fruit and Steamship Company in Latin America.* Baton Rouge: Louisiana State University Press.
Kepner, C. D., and J. H. Soothill
   1935   *The Banana Empire.* New York: Russell and Russell.
Kerns, Virginia
   1976   "Black Carib Paternity Rituals." *Actes* of the Forty-second ICA, 6:513–23.
   1977   "Third-Generation Research on the Black Carib: Bridging the Generation Gap." Paper presented at the annual meeting of the American Anthropological Association, Houston, Texas.
   1983   *Women and the Ancestors: Black Carib Kinship and Ritual.* Urbana: University of Illinois Press.
   1984   "Past and Present Evidence of Interethnic Mating." In Crawford, pp. 95–114.
Kirby, I. E., and C. I. Martin
   1972   *The Rise and Fall of the Black Caribs.* St. Vincent.
Kloos, Peter
   1971   *The Maroni River Caribs of Surinam.* Assen: Van Gorcum.
Kopytoff, Igor
   1986   "The Internal African Frontier: The Making of an African Political Culture." In Igor Kopytoff, ed., *The African Frontier: The Reproduction of Traditional African Societies.* Ms. in possession of the author.

Kottak, Conrad
1983   *Assault on Paradise.* New York: Random House.
Kroeber, A. L.
1939   *Cultural and Natural Areas of Native North America.* Berkeley: University of California Press.
———, and C. Kluckhohn
1963   *Culture: A Critical Review of Concepts and Definitions.* New York: Vintage (Random House).
La Barge, Richard Allen
1962   *Impact of the United Fruit Company on the Economic Development of Guatemala, 1846-54.* Middle American Research Institute Publications No. 29. New Orleans: Tulane University, pp. 1-72.
Labat, J.
1970   *The Memoirs of Pere Labat, 1693-1705.* Trans. and abridged by John Eaden. London: Frank Cass.
La Borde, R. P. de
1674   *Voyage qui continent une relation exacte de l'origine, moeurs, coutumes, religion, guerres et voyages des Caraibes, sauvages des Isles Antilles de l'Amérique.* A. Liège, Belgium: Chez P. van de Aa.
Lainez, Vilma, and Victor Meza
1973   "El enclave bananero en la historia de Honduras." *Estudios Sociales Centroamericanos* 2(5): 115-56.
Lamorthe, José
1958   "Informe . . . al ministro de relaciones de la República de Honduras . . . Black River, dic. 29, 1862." *Revista de la Sociedad de Geografía e Historia de Honduras* 36(10-12): 267-68.
Lasker, G. W.
1985   *Surnames and Genetic Structure.* Cambridge: Cambridge University Press.
Layng, Anthony
1983   *The Carib Reserve: Identity and Security in the West Indies.* Washington, D.C.: University Press of America.
Leighton, Alexander M., et al.
1963   *Psychiatric Disorder among the Yoruba.* Ithaca: Cornell University Press.
Lekis, Lisa
1960   *Dancing Gods.* New York: Scarecrow Press.
Lele, Uma
1975   *The Design of Rural Development: Lessons from Africa.* Baltimore: Johns Hopkins University Press.
Levin, Suzanne
1983   "Food Production and Population Size in the Lesser Antilles." *Human Ecology* 11:321-38.
Lévi-Strauss, Claude
1966   *The Savage Mind.* Chicago: University of Chicago Press.
Lewis, M. A.
1960   *Social History of the Royal Navy, 1793-1815.* London: Allen and Unwin.
Lewis, Marva
1975   "Carib Recipes." *National Studies* 3(6): 26-38.

Libro de Bautizos
    1832   Trujillo, Honduras: Parochial Records.
Lipton, Michael
    1977   *Why Poor People Stay Poor.* Cambridge: Harvard University Press.
Liverpool Papers
    1778–79   "Thoughts on the Importance of Our Colonies in the West Indies with
                Hints for Their Extension and Improvement." British Museum, Liverpool
                Papers, 38387, ff.1–14.
Lloyd, Christopher
    1954   *The Nation and the Navy: A History of Naval Life and Policy.* London:
                Cresset Press.
———, ed.
    1965   *The Health of Seamen,* vol. 107. London: Navy Records Society.
———, and Jack L. S. Coulter
    1961   *Medicine and the Navy, 1200–1900.* Vol. 3: *1714–1815.* Edinburgh and
                London: E. and S. Livingstone.
Long, Edward
    1774   *The History of Jamaica.* London: T. Loundes.
Love, Thomas F.
    1977   "Ecological Niche Theory in Sociocultural Anthropology: A Conceptual
                Framework and an Application." *AE* 4:27–41.
Loven, Sven
    1935   *Origins of the Tainan Culture, West Indies.* Gothenburg: Elanders Bak-
                fryckeri Akfiebolag.
McCauley, Ellen
    1981   *No me hables de muerte . . . sino de parranda.* Tegucigalpa: ASEPADE.
McCommon, Carolyn S.
    1982   *Mating as a Reproductive Strategy: A Black Carib Example.* Ph.D. dis-
                sertation, Pennsylvania State University.
Macfarlane, Alan
    1978   *The Origins of English Individualism.* Cambridge: Cambridge University
                Press.
McGuire, Randall H.
    1982   "The Study of Ethnicity in Historical Archaeology." *Journal of Anthropo-
                logical Archaeology* 1:159–78.
McKinnen, Daniel
    1804   *A Tour through the British West Indies.* London: J. White.
Macklin, Catherine L.
    1976   "The Garifuna Thanksgiving." *BS* 4(6): 1–6.
McKusick, Marshall
    1960   *Aboriginal Canoes in the West Indies.* Yale University Publications in An-
                thropology, No. 63. New Haven.
Manners, Robert A.
    1965   "Remittances and the Unit of Analysis in Anthropological Research."
                SWJA 21:179–95.
Mariñas Otero, Luís
    1983   *Honduras.* Tegucigalpa: Editorial Universitaria.

Martin, R. Montgomery
1836-37   *History of the West Indies*, vol. 2. London: Whittaker and Co.
Martínez López, E.
1931   *Biografía del General Francisco Morazán*. 2d ed. Tegucigalpa: Tipografía Nacional.
May, Stacy, and Galo Plaza
1958   *The United Fruit Company in Latin America*. National Planning Association Series on U.S. Business Performance Abroad. Washington, D.C.
Maybury-Lewis, David, ed.
1984   *The Prospects for Plural Societies*. Washington, D.C.: American Ethnological Society.
Mayer, Enrique
1982   *The Carib Reserve in Dominica*. Washington, D.C.: Organization of American States.
Mazier, L.
1906   "Región de Carataska." *Revista del Archivo y de la Biblioteca Nacional* 2(5): 129-31.
Mead, Margaret
1961   *New Lives for Old*. New York: New American Library.
Mejía, Medardo
1983   *Historia de Honduras*, vol. 1. Tegucigalpa: Editorial Universitaria.
Mertz, Ronald
1977   "Psychological Differentiation among Garifuna Male Students." *BS* 5(4): 17-22.
Messenger, John C., Jr.
1973   "African Retentions in Montserrat." *African Arts* 6:54-57.
Metraux, Alfred
1959   *Voodoo in Haiti*. Trans. Hugo Charteris. London: Oxford University Press.
Miller, David L.
1979   *The European Impact on St. Vincent, 1600-1763: Suppression and Displacement of the Native Population and Landscape*. M.A. thesis, University of Wisconsin, Milwaukee.
Mintz, Sidney M.
1984   *Sweetness and Power*. New York: Viking.
Montufar, Lorenzo
1970   *Francisco Morazán*. San José: Editorial Universitaria Centroamericana.
Morales, F., and Nelly Arévalo-Jiménez
1981   "Hacia un modelo de estructura social Caribe." *América Indígena* 41:603-26.
Morgan, Louis H.
1877   *Ancient Society*. New York: Henry Holt.
Morgan, Prys
1983   "From a Death to a View: The Hunt for the Welsh Past in the Romantic Period." In Hobsbawm, ed., pp. 43-100.
Morlan, Albert
1897   *A Hoosier in Honduras*. Indianapolis: El Dorado Publishing Company.

Morris, Milton, and Albert Mayio
1980 *Illegal Migration and United States Foreign Policy.* Washington, D.C.: Brookings Institution.

Morris, Valentine
1787 *A Narrative of the Official Conduct of Valentine Morris, Esq.* London: Logographic Press.

Munroe, R. L., and R. H. Munroe
1971 "Male Pregnancy Symptoms and Cross-Sex Identity in Three Societies." *Journal of Social Psychology* 84:11–25.

Murdock, G. P.
1949 *Social Structure.* New York: Macmillan.

Myers, Robert A.
1984 "Island Carib Cannibalism." *New West Indian Guide* 58(3–4): 147–84.

Narrative
1795 "Insurrection in the Island of St. Vincent." *St. Vincent Gazette,* Mar. 30. CO 260/9 (PRO).

Newson, Linda
1976 *Aboriginal and Spanish Colonial Trinidad.* London: Academic Press.
1984 "Silver Mining in Colonial Honduras." *Revista de Historia de América* (Instituto Panamericano de Geografía e Historia) 97:45–76.

Nicholaides, J., et al.
1983 "Crop Production Systems in the Amazon Basin." In Emilio Moran, ed., *The Dilemma of Amazonian Development.* Boulder: Westview Press, pp. 101–54.

Nicholson, Desmond V.
1976 "Precolumbian Seafaring Capabilities in the Lesser Antilles." *PLA* 6:98–105.

Niddrie, D. L.
1966 "Eighteenth-Century Settlement in the British Caribbean." *Transactions of the Institute of British Geographers,* no. 40, pp. 67–79.

Nietschmann, Bernard
1979 *Caribbean Edge.* Indianapolis: Bobbs-Merrill.

Ober, Frederick A.
1895 "Aborigines of the West Indies." *Proceedings of the American Antiguarian Society* 9:270–313.

Olien, Michael D.
1983 "The Miskito Kings and the Line of Succession." *Journal of Anthropological Research* 39(2): 198–241.

Oliver, Vere Langford
1894–99 *The History of the Island of Antigua.* 3 vols. London: Mitchell and Hughes.

Ortner, Sherry
1984 "Theory in Anthropology since the Sixties." *Comparative Studies in Society and History* 26(1): 126–66.

Ostor, Akos, Lina Fruzzetti, and Steve Barnett, eds.
1982 *Concepts of Person: Kinship, Caste, and Marriage in India.* Cambridge: Harvard University Press.

Otterbein, Keith
1966   *The Andros Islanders.* Lawrence: University of Kansas Press.
Owen, Nancy H.
1975   "Land, Politics and Ethnicity in a Carib Indian Community." *Ethnology* 14(4): 385–93.
Palacio, Joseph O.
1974   "Problems in the Maintenance of the Garifuna (Black Carib) Culture in Belize." Ms. in possession of the author.
1982   "Post-hurricane Resettlement in Belize." In Art Hansen and Anthony Oliver-Smith, eds., *The Problems and Responses of Dislocated People.* Boulder: Westview Press, pp. 121–35.
1983   "Food and body in Garifuna Belief Systems." *Cajanus* 16(3): 149–60.
1984   "Food and Social Relations in a Belizean Garifuna Village." *BS* 12(3): 1–35.
1985   "A Survey of Central American Immigrants in Four Urban Communities in Belize." Ms. in possession of the author.
Pares, Richard
1956   *Yankees and Creoles.* Cambridge: Harvard University Press.
Pastor, Robert A., and Rosemarie Rogers
1983   "The Impact of Migration on Development in the Caribbean: An Analysis and a Proposal." Paper presented at the annual meeting of the American Political Science Association, Chicago. (Published in 1985 as "Using Migration to Enhance Economic Development in the Caribbean: Three Sets of Proposals," in Robert A. Pastor, ed., *Migration and Development in the Caribbean: The Unexplored Connection.* Boulder: Westview Press, pp. 321–47.)
Peralta, D. Manuel M. de
1898   *Costa Rica y Costa de Mosquitos.* Paris: D. M. M. de Peralta.
Pérez Brito, Francisco
1797   Letter to Manuel Dambrine, Commandante de Trujillo. AGCA A3.16/2025/194, (4) Honduras.
Périgny, Maurice de
1911   *Les Cinq Républiques de l'Amérique Centrale.* Paris: Librairie P. Roger and Co.
Pim, Bedford
1863   *The Gate of the Pacific.* London: Lovell Reeve.
———, and Berthold Seemann
1869   *Dottings on the Roadside.* London: Chapman and Hall.
Pinckard, George
1806   *Notes on the West Indies.* 3 vols. London: Longman, Hurst, Rees and Orme.
Pitt, David C., ed.
1978   *Development from Below.* Chicago: Aldine.
Posnansky, Merrick
1983   "Towards an Archaeology of the Black Diaspora." *PLA* 9:443–50.

Price, Richard, and Sally Price
 1984   *First Time*. Baltimore: Johns Hopkins University Press.
Procuraduría General de la República
 1979   *Trujillo Con X*. Tegucigalpa.
Ragatz, Lowell
 1928   *The Fall of the Planter Class in the British Caribbean, 1763–1833*. New York: Century.
Raynal, Guillame Thomas Françoise
 1783   *A Philosophical and Political History of the Settlements and Trade of the Europeans in the East and West Indies*. 8 vols. Trans. J. D. Justamond. London: W. Strahan.
Report of the Committee
 1831   "Inquiry into the Financial, Commercial and Political State of the Island of St. Vincent." *West Indian Tracts* (London) 9:1–22.
Riggs, Fred W., ed.
 1985   *Ethnicity. Intercocta Glossary: Concepts and Terms Used in Ethnicity Research*. Honolulu: International Social Science Council.
Riviére, P. G.
 1974   "The Couvade: A Problem Reborn." *Man* (n.s.) 9:423–35.
 1977   "Some Problems in the Comparative Study of Carib Societies." In Basso, ed., pp. 153–56.
 1984   *Individual and Society in Guiana*. Cambridge: Cambridge University Press.
Roberts, Orlando
 1827   *Narrative of Voyages on the East and in the Interior of Central America*. Edinburgh: Constable.
Rochefort, Charles C.
 1666   *History of the Caribby Islands*. Trans. and abridged by John Davies. Rotterdam.
Roosevelt, Anna
 1980   *Parmana*. New York: Academic Press.
Rose, Richard H.
 1904   *Utila: Past and Present*. Dansville, N.Y.: F. A. Owen.
Ross, Charlesworth
 1970   "Caribs and Arawaks." *Caribbean Quarterly* 16(3): 52–59.
Rossi y Rubí, José
 1797   "Diario." *Gazeta de Guatemala* 1(21): 164–68.
Rouse, Irving
 1948   "The Carib." In J. H. Steward, ed., *Handbook of South American Indians*. Vol. 4: *The Circum-Caribbean Tribes*. Washington, D.C.: U.S. Government Printing Office, pp. 547–65.
 1956   "Settlement Patterns in the Caribbean Area." In Gordon Willey, ed., *Prehistoric Settlement Patterns in the New World*. Viking Fund Publications in Anthropology, No. 23. New York, pp. 165–72.
 1983   "Diffusion and Interaction in the Orinoco Valley and the Coast." *PLA* 9:3–14.

Royce, Anya Peterson
1982   *Ethnic Identity: Strategies of Diversity.* Bloomington: Indiana University Press.

Rubinstein, Hymie
1983   "Remittances and Rural Underdevelopment in the English-Speaking Caribbean." *Human Organization* 42(4): 295–306.

Rúbio Sánchez, Manuel
1975   *Historia de Trujillo.* 3 vols. Tegucigalpa: Banco Central de Honduras.

Russell, William
1778   *The History of America.* 2 vols. London: Fielding and Walker.

Sáenz, Pedro
1797   "Informe." *Gazeta de Guatemala* 16:127–28.

Saint-Louis, Loretta
1977   "Occupational Segregation in Dangriga." Term paper for a course at Boston University.

Sahlins, Marshall D., and Elman R. Service
1960   *Evolution and Culture.* Ann Arbor: University of Michigan Press.

Samayoa Guevara, Hector Humberto
1965   *La presencia de Luís Aury en Centro América.* Guatemala: Centro Editorial José de Pineda Ibarra.

Sanday, Peggy R.
1986   *Divine Hunger.* Cambridge: Cambridge University Press.

Sanford, Margaret S.
1971   *Disruption of the Mother-Child Relationship in Conjunction with Matrifocality: A Study of Child-keeping among the Carib and Creole of British Honduras.* Ph.D. dissertation, Catholic University of America.
1974   "Revitalization Movements as Indicators of Completed Acculturation." *Comparative Studies in Society and History* 16:504–18.
1975   "A Socialization in Ambiguity: Child-lending in a British West Indian Society." *Ethnology* 8:393–400.
1976   "Antagonists and Friends: Role Expectations between Men and Women in Belize." Paper presented at the annual meeting of the American Anthropological Association, Washington, D.C.

Sauer, Carl O.
1966   *The Early Spanish Main.* Berkeley: University of California Press.

Schwerin, Karl H.
1966   *Oil and Steel.* Berkeley: University of California Press.
1982   "The Kin Integration System among Caribs." Paper presented at the Forty-fourth ICA, Manchester, England.

Scott, James C.
1976   *The Moral Economy of the Peasant: Rebellion and Subsistence in Southeast Asia.* New Haven: Yale University Press.

Seeger, Anthony
1979   "What Can We Learn When they Sing? Vocal Genres of the Suya Indians of Central Brazil." *Ethnomusicology* 23:373–94.

1981   *Nature and Society in Central Brazil.* Cambridge: Harvard University Press.

Segal, Jerome

1986   "What Is Development?" Center for Philosophy and Public Policy, Working Paper DN-1. College Park, Md.

Sellers, Stephen G.

1969   *Religion and Social Change in a Black Carib Community.* B.A. honors thesis, Wesleyan University.

Selva R., Mário

1984   "Diagnóstico de salud del distrito de Lívingston, Izabal." Ms. in possession of the author.

Shepherd, Charles

1831   *An Historical Account of the Island of St. Vincent.* London: Ridgeway and Sons.

Sherar, Mariam G.

1973   *Shipping Out.* Cambridge, Md.: Cornell Maritime Press.

Shils, E.

1981   *Tradition.* Chicago: University of Chicago Press.

Sloane, Sir Hans

1707   *A Voyage to the Islands of Madera, Barbados, Nieves, St. Christopher and Jamaica.* London.

Smith, M. Estellie

1982   "The Process of Sociocultural Continuity." *Current Anthropology* 23:127–41.

Smith, Michael G.

1965   *The Plural Society in the British West Indies.* Berkeley: University of California Press.

1983   "The Role of Basic Needs and Provisions in Planning and Development." *Canadian Journal of Native Studies* 2:341–60.

Smith, Raymond T.

1956   *The Negro Family in British Guiana.* London: Routledge and Kegan Paul.

Smole, William J.

1976   *The Yanoama Indians: A Cultural Geography.* Austin: University of Texas Press.

Sorenson, A. P., Jr.

1971   "Multilingualism in the Northwest Amazon." *AA* 69:670–84.

Sorsby, William S.

1972   "Spanish Colonization of the Mosquito Coast, 1787–1800." *Revista de Historia de América* 73–74:145–53.

Southey, Thomas

1827   *Chronological History of the West Indies,* vol. 3. London: Longman, Rees, Orme, Brown and Green.

Spicer, Edward H., ed.

1952   *Human Problems in Technological Change.* New York: Russell Sage Foundation.

Squier, Ephraim George
1855   *Notes on Central America.* New York: Harper.
1858   *The States of Central America.* New York: Hurst.
1870   *Honduras: Descriptive, Historical and Statistical.* London: Trubner.
Stack, Carol
1974   *All Our Kin.* New York: Harper and Row.
Staiano, Katherine V.
1981   "Alternative Therapeutic Systems in Belize: A Semiotic Framework." *Social Science and Medicine* 15:317–32.
Stein, Robert L.
1979   *The French Slave Trade in the Eighteenth Century: An Old Regime Business.* Madison: University of Wisconsin Press.
Steward, Julian H.
1977   *Evolution and Ecology.* Urbana: University of Illinois Press.
Stewart, Col. David
1978   *Sketches of the Character, Manners, and Present State of the Highlands of Scotland, with Details of the Military Service in the Highland Regiments,* vol. 1. London. (First published in 1822.)
Stinner, William F., K. de Albuquerque, and Roy S. Bryce-Laporte, eds.
1982   *Return Migration and Remittances: Developing a Caribbean Perspective.* Washington, D.C.: Smithsonian Institution Press.
Sturtevant, William C.
1961   "Taino Agriculture." In Johannes Wilbert, ed., *Evolution of Horticultural Systems in Native South America.* Caracas: Antropológica, pp. 69–82.
Taussig, Michael
1980   *The Devil and Commodity Fetishism in South America.* Chapel Hill: University of North Carolina Press.
Taylor, Douglas M.
1935   "The Island Caribs of Dominica, British West Indies." *AA* 37:265–72.
1936   "Additional Notes on the Island Carib of Dominica, British West Indies." *AA* 38:462–68.
1945   "Carib Folk Beliefs and Customs from Dominica, British West Indies." *SWJA* 1:507–30.
1946a "Notes on the Star Lore of the Caribbees." *AA* 8:215–22.
1946b "Carib-Creole Tales from Dominica, British West Indies." *Journal of American Folklore*
1946c "Kinship and Social Structure of the Island Carib." *SWJA* 2:180–212.
1948   "Conversations and Letters from the Black Caribs of British Honduras." *International Journal of American Linguistics* 14:99–100.
1949   "The Interpretation of Some Documentary Evidence on Carib Culture." *SWJA* 5:379–92.
1950   "The Meaning of Dietary and Occupational Restrictions among the Island Carib." *AA* 52:343–49.
1951   *The Black Caribs of British Honduras.* Viking Fund Publications in Anthropology, No. 17. New York.

1952 "Tales and Legends of the Dominica Caribs." *Journal of American Folklore* 65(257): 267–79.

1958 "Carib, Caliban, Cannibal." *International Journal of American Linguistics* 24:156–57.

————, and Berend J. Hoff

1980 "The Linguistic Repertory of the Island Carib in the Seventeenth Century: The Men's Language—a Carib Pidgin?" *International Journal of American Linguistics* 46(4): 301–12.

————, and Irving Rouse

1955 "Linguistic and Archaeological Time Depth in the West Indies." *International Journal of American Linguistics* 21:105–15.

Teuscher, Philip Thorneycroft

1985 *Last of the Karaphuna.* Film. Teuscher/Pettys Productions.

Townsend, Thomas

1772 "Two Points against an Expedition against the Black Caribs on St. Vincent." Sydney Family Papers, William L. Clements Library, University of Michigan, Ann Arbor.

Tuan, Yi-Fu

1982 *Segmented Worlds and Self.* Minneapolis: University of Minnesota Press.

Turnbull, Gordon

1795 *A Narrative of the Revolt and Insurrection of the French Inhabitants in the Island of Grenada, by an Eye Witness.* Edinburgh: Archibald Constable.

Turner, Terence S.

1969 "Tchikrin: A Central Brazilian Tribe and Its Symbolic Language of Bodily Adornment." *Natural History* 78:50–59.

Turner, Victor W.

1967 *The Forest of Symbols.* Ithaca: Cornell University Press.

Uring, Nathaniel

1726 *A History of the Voyages and Travels of Capt. Nathaniel Uring.* London: W. Wilkins for J. Peele.

Vallejo, Antonio R.

1884 *Indice alfabético y cronológico de los títulos, escrituras de amparo y demás documentos relativos a los terrenos de la República de Honduras.* Tegucigalpa: Tipografía del Gobierno.

1889 *Primer anuario estadístico.* Tegucigalpa: Tipografía Nacional.

1893 *Primer anuario estadístico correspondiente al año de 1889.* Tegucigalpa: Tipografía Nacional.

Valois, Alfred de

1861 *Mexique, Havane et Guatemala; Notes de voyage.* Paris: E. Dentu.

Vansina, Jan

1985 *Oral Tradition as History.* Madison: University of Wisconsin Press.

Von Hagen, Victor Wolfgang

1940 "The Mosquito Coast of Honduras and Its Inhabitants." *Geographical Review* 30(2): 238–58.

Wagley, Charles
1940   "The Effects of Depopulation upon Social Organization as Illustrated by the Tapirape Indians." *Transactions of the New York Academy of Sciences* (Series 2) 3:12-16.
Wallerstein, Immanuel
1974   *The Modern World-System.* New York: Academic Press.
1980   *The Modern World-System, II: Mercantilism and the Consolidation of the European World-Economy, 1600-1750.* New York: Academic Press.
Washburn, Wilcomb E.
1959   "The Moral and Legal Justifications for Dispossessing the Indians." In James Morton Smith, ed., *Seventeenth-Century America.* Chapel Hill: University of North Carolina Press, pp. 15-32.
Waters, Ivor
1964   *The Unfortunate Valentine Morris.* Chepstow, Wales: Chepstow Society.
Watts, David
1985   "Development and Cultural Influences on Environmental Change in the Caribbean." Paper presented at the Forty-fifth ICA, Bogotá, Colombia.
Wells, Marilyn McKillop
1982a   "Dugu Visibility: The Role of a Religious Ceremony in Status Politics." *Tennessee Anthropologist* 7(1): 75-88.
1982b   "Garif Sporting Associations: A Symbol for Stratum Affiliation." Paper presented at the Forty-fourth ICA, Manchester, England.
1982c   "Spirits See Red: The Symbolic Use of Gusueue among the Garif (Black Caribs) of Central America." *BS* 10(3-4): 10-16.
Whipple, Emory
1971   *The Music of the Black Caribs of British Honduras.* M.A. thesis, University of Texas, Austin.
1979   "Carib Music, Dance and Folklore." Paper presented at the Forty-second ICA, Paris.
White, Leslie A.
1943   "Energy and the Evolution of Culture." *AA* 45:335-56.
Whitney, John Randolph
1902   *True Story of the Martinique and St. Vincent Calamities.* Washington, D.C.: U.S. Government Printing Office.
Whitten, Norman E., Jr.
1965   *Class, Kinship, and Power in an Ecuadorian Town.* Stanford: Stanford University Press.
1974   *Black Frontiersmen.* New York: Wiley.
1976   *Sacha Runa: Ethnicity and Adaptation of Ecuadorian Jungle Quichua.* Urbana: University of Illinois Press.
1985   *Sicuanga Runa: The Other Side of Development in Amazonian Ecuador.* Urbana: University of Illinois Press.
————, ed.
1981   *Cultural Transformations and Ethnicity in Modern Ecuador.* Urbana: University of Illinois Press.

Wilk, Richard A.
1984   "Households in Process: Agricultural Change and Domestic Transformation among the Kekchi Maya of Belize." In Robert McC. Netting, R. A. Wilk and Eric J. Arnould, eds., *Households, Comparative and Historical Studies of the Domestic Group.* Berkeley: University of California Press, pp. 217–44.

Wing, Elizabeth
1968   "Aboriginal Fishing in the Windward Islands." *PLA* 2:103–7.
———, and Sylvia Scudder
1980   "Use of Animals by the Prehistoric Inhabitants on St. Kitts, West Indies." *PLA* 8:237–45.

Winterbotham, William
1796   *An Historical, Geographical, Commercial, and Philosophical View of the United States of America, and of the European Settlements in America and the West Indies.* 4 vols. New York: Tiebout and O'Brien for J. Reid.

Witkin, Herman, et al.
1962   *Psychological Differentiation.* New York: John Wiley and Sons.
———, and John W. Berry
1975   "Psychological Differentiation in Cross-Cultural Perspective." *Journal of Cross-Cultural Psychology* 6:4–87.

Wolf, Eric R.
1982   *Europe and the People without History.* Berkeley: University of California Press.

Wolfe, Alvin W.
1977   "The Supranational Organization of Production: An Evolutionary Perspective." *Current Anthropology* 19:615–35.

Worsley, Peter
1984   *The Three Worlds: Culture and World Development.* Chicago: University of Chicago Press.

Wright, Pamela
1986   "Ethnic Names and Black Carib Identity." Afro-Indian Studies No. 5, Working Papers in Anthropology. Durham, England: University of Durham.

Young, Thomas
1847   *Narrative of a Residence on the Mosquito Shore.* London: Smith, Elder, and Co.

Young, William
1764   *Considerations Which May Tend to Promote the Settlement of Our New West-India Colonies by Encouraging Individuals to Embark in the Undertaking.* London: James Robson.
1971   *An Account of the Black Charaibs in the Island of St. Vincent.* London: Frank Cass. (First published in 1795.)

Index

Note on the Author

Nancie L. Gonzalez has studied the Garifuna since 1955, doing ethnographic fieldwork in Guatemala, Honduras, Belize, and New York City, as well as archival searches in England, Central America, the Caribbean, and the United States. She has also published on Indians and Ladinos in Central America, as well as on the Hispanos of New Mexico and on the Dominican Republic. The mother of three grown children, she teaches at the University of Maryland and lives in Washington, D.C.